A Common Heritage

A Common Heritage

Noah Webster's Blue-Back Speller

E. JENNIFER MONAGHAN

Archon Books
1983

Printed in the United States of America
    Set in Garamond and Garamond Italic type
Composition by:
    Four Quarters Publishing Co.
    Guilford, Connecticut 06437

Library of Congress Cataloging in Publication Data

Monaghan, E. Jennifer, 1933–
    A common heritage

    Revision of: Noah Webster's speller, 1783–1843.
Thesis (Ed. D.)—Yeshiva University, 1980.
    Bibliography: p.
    Includes index.
    1. Webster, Noah, 1758–1843.   2. Text-books—United
States—History.   3. English language—Study and
teaching (Primary)—United States.   4. English language—
United States—Orthography and spelling.   5. Education,
Primary—United States—History.   6. Publishers and
publishing—United States—History.   7. Educators—
United States—Biography.   I. Title
PE2813.A2M6   1982   428.1   82-11526
ISBN 0-208-01908-1

To my mother
Margery Alys Eveline Walker
and to the memory of
my father
Clement Willoughby ("Johnnie") Walker

"I wish to enjoy life, but books & business will ever be my principal pleasure."

Noah Webster to George Washington
December 18, 1785

CONTENTS

Acknowledgments

There are many persons I would like to thank for their insights, criticisms and comments. Two scholars in particular were invaluable: Richard L. Venezky of the University of Delaware, and Douglas Sloan of Teachers College, Columbia University. Dick Venezky's explication of the structure of English orthography (in a book by that title) lies at the base of many of the technical aspects of this book. It is, however, to his fine historical sense as well as to his specialized knowledge of reading theory and methodology that I owe so much. He critiqued this study at crucial stages and was immeasurably helpful to me in clarifying what I was about.

To Douglas Sloan, educational historian par excellence, I am also deeply indebted. He provided bibliographical assistance at the beginning of my research that proved to be the foundation for all that followed. He encouraged and supported my efforts throughout, and was most generous with his time and historical insights. His unfaltering grasp of the early American Republic has led me to reevaluate Webster's role as the spokesman for education within that Republic.

This book evolved from a doctoral thesis I wrote at Yeshiva University. I would like to thank Larry Kasdon, chairman of my committee, for encouraging me to undertake a historical dissertation. His extensive knowledge of the history of American reading instruction was extremely important to my work. I also wish to thank the other committee members, Susan Sardy and Nate Stillman, for their sound advice and cogent criticism.

The usual place to thank members of one's family is at the end of one's professional acknowledgments, but the help of my husband, Charles Monaghan, has been so material and of such high quality that I would like to note it here. His fine sense of proportion, his own remarkable grasp of American history, and his exceptional feeling for style have contributed more to this book than I can adequately acknowledge.

It is a pleasure to offer my appreciation and thanks to those librarians whose selfless efforts form the backdrop of any pursuit of the past. I would like to thank in particular the staff of the manuscript division of The New York Public Library who toiled up and down stairs with boxes of Webster's letters for me: Paul Rugen (then keeper of manuscripts), Jean McNiece and John Stinson; and the staff of The New York Public Library's rare book room who were on hand during my research, Lawrence Murphy, Francis Mattson, Dan Traister, Sheila Curl and Paul Guerrette.

My thanks are also due to other librarians throughout the eastern United States, in particular to the staffs of The New-York Historical Society, The Pierpont Morgan Library, the Sterling Memorial Library of Yale University, The Jones Library, Inc., The Historical Society of Pennsylvania and the American Antiquarian Society.

I would like to thank, too, those who assisted me in the physical production of the text. My friend, artist Virginia Hoyt Cantarella, drew the graphs for the appendixes of this book. Adrian Taylor, art editor of *Travel & Leisure* magazine, designed the book jacket. Tom Bechtle—known in our family as "that dashing young man with the typing machine"—typed the vast bulk of the manuscript with an accuracy worthy of Noah Webster himself, while Martha Cameron graciously chipped in at key moments.

Last, but by no means least, I wish to pay tribute to my children, Leila, Anthony and Claire, who endured my maternal mental and temporal absences with extraordinary good grace.

Introduction

Noah Webster's spelling book is a phenomenon by any standards. Perhaps only two books can lay claim to surpassing it in the total number of copies sold in the United States: the Bible, and the various editions of the famous *McGuffey Readers*. Estimates of the total sales of Webster's speller have ranged from 60 to 100 million. Back in 1950 the publishers of the "Old Blue-back," as Webster's 1829 edition came to be called, claimed a figure of 70 million.[1] There are even two editions of it in print today—a copy of the first edition of 1783, and a copy of an 1831 edition of *The American Spelling Book*.[2] While it is true that the overall sales of the *McGuffey Readers* are calculated to have reached 122 million,[3] William Holmes McGuffey's involvement with the series ceased only a few years after the first two readers were published in 1836. Later editions were essentially composites constructed by a number of people.[4] In contrast, *The Elementary Spelling Book* (the version of the speller that Webster published in 1829) retained its integrity as Webster's work through all post-Webster editions, which differed from his in only minor ways.

My book traces the history of the blue-back speller during Webster's lifetime. One of my major purposes is to attempt to discover why Webster's speller was so popular. The circumstances of the book during his lifetime should provide the answer. For already by the 1820s, the book was enjoying a popularity unprecedented in the history of American textbook publishing, save perhaps for the enduring *New England Primer*.[5] Webster's own account books reveal that he licensed over 3 million copies of *The American Spelling Book* between 1804 and 1818 alone. There is plenty of evidence to suggest that Webster was not far off the mark when he estimated that almost 10 million copies had been printed by 1829. His accounts disclose that another 3.75 million copies of the speller were licensed for printing between 1829, when it was published as *The Elementary Spelling Book*, and his death in 1843.[6] These are best selling figures even by today's "bestseller" standards. In the early American Republic they were astronomical.

Webster's speller, then, is highly significant because of its tremendous popularity during Webster's lifetime. It is also significant because of its origins. Until the American Revolution, the young American publishing industry had relied heavily on reprinting imported British works. In the absence of any national copyright legislation, let alone any international restrictions, British textbooks were reproduced en masse on the presses of colonial America without costing their American publishers a penny. Webster's first part of *A Grammatical Institute of the English Language* (his original title for the speller), when published in 1783, was one of the earliest efforts by any American after 1776 to capture the American textbook market. (A little book put out by the saintly Anthony Benezet of Philadelphia was the only post-revolutionary speller to precede it.)[7] Webster himself saw his little book as a contribution to the welfare of the country: he held that cultural independence went hand in hand with political independence, and saw himself as tossing his "mite into the common treasure of patriotic exertions."[8] With these aspirations, he had initially planned to call the book *The American Instructor* but had been dissuaded; in 1787 he retitled it *The American Spelling Book*. The book retained that title for another forty years.[9]

Every student of the early American Republic has noted Webster's contribution to its culture. For Webster was one of the first to suggest that the health and safety of the new nation depended upon an enlightened citizenry, which in turn depended upon (as the phrase went) "a general diffusion of knowledge." In a 1787 article published in his own *American Magazine*, Webster articulated the view of the role of education that would be shared by many leaders of the new American Republic.[10] His article appeared a year after Benjamin Rush, destined to become Webster's good friend, had advocated new forms of schooling as a force for converting men into "republican machines."[11] As Webster put it, "the Education of youth is, in all governments, an object of the first consequence. The impressions received in early life, usually form the characters of individuals, a union of which forms the general character of a nation."[12]

The American national character was not yet formed, wrote

Webster, and went on to argue that current methods of instruction could be improved. He advocated not merely a general "diffusion of knowledge," but an education which would "implant, in the minds of the American youth, the principles of virtue and liberty; and inspire them with just and liberal ideas of government, and with an inviolable attachment to their own country."[13] Public schools were to be the vehicle for this task. As for the spelling book, the textbook par excellence of the common school, Webster set it within the broader context of his plans for American education.

> When I speak of a diffusion of knowledge, I do not mean merely a knowledge of spelling-books, and the New-Testament. An acquaintance with ethics, and with the general principles of law, commerce, money and government, is necessary for the yeomanry of a republican State."[14]

For Webster, then, the spelling book was but the first text in a series of textbooks designed to mold the "national character."[15] He eventually abandoned the conviction that children's characters could be favorably molded by education alone, and instead looked to religion as the true bulwark of public morality. But he never forsook his ambition to provide American children with American textbooks: he wrote his last school text, *A Manual of Useful Studies*, only four years before he died.

Webster regarded his earliest text, the speller, as a nationalistic tool. He believed that it would create a standard American speech that would serve as a unifying force in the new Republic. How realistic an ambition this was is a question that will be postponed; but Webster's view that a spelling book taught children how to pronounce words was the common view not only of his own times, but of earlier years.

Almost every previous modern discussion has assumed that the purpose of a spelling book in Webster's time was the same as that of a spelling book today: namely, to teach children to spell. None of Webster's biographers has attempted to explain why a book with such an aim could have become so popular. Modern spelling books have a most modest sale when compared with that of beginning reading textbooks. Yet if one looks at textbooks of the early American Republic, there is not another work of any kind that remotely approaches the popularity of Webster's spelling book until the early 1820s. Nor, search as one may, can one find any examples of the kind of beginning reading textbooks with which we are familiar today—works with a controlled vocabulary and short, easy stories for children.

The explanation is very simple, if a little surprising: the spelling book was the book that taught children to read. It was called a "spelling" book because spelling was the method the child used in order to learn to read. The approach is perhaps better known to us as the "alphabet method," and was the standard reading method used on both sides of the Atlantic. A reader—a type of textbook that did not even exist until Webster wrote the first one in 1785—was for children who could already read. Not until William Holmes McGuffey published his first two volumes of the *Eclectic Reader* in 1836 would American children start learning how to read from a "reader" instead of a "speller."

This sets Webster's spelling book in an altogether different light. It was not just a book that taught children how to spell (although of course it did that as well); it was the book that taught them to read. Although they may well have seen a primer at home, the speller was the first school text to instruct them in the art of reading.

So the Webster spelling book, in its various forms, is of more importance to the history of American education than has formerly been appreciated. It deserves to be examined as the most popular reading instructional text of its day. A second purpose of this book, then, is to examine the spelling book on its own terms and in its own context. For Webster, of course, did not write his textbook in a vacuum. He had, it turns out, a useful model: a spelling book written by an Englishman, Thomas Dilworth, who titled his work *A New Guide to the English Tongue*. (Benjamin Franklin had been the first to produce an American edition, publishing it in 1747.) Webster himself learned to read from "Dilworth," as the work was affectionately known, and he would appropriate Dilworth's book for his own work.

If we had no other reliquaries than his spelling book, Webster would have deserved a niche in the history of American education. But, as we have already seen, his aims were far more ambitious. In the course of his long life, he devised a program of education that provided textbooks in every aspect of instruction. In the area of language alone, his works include the different editions of the spelling book, several grammars, and the first collection of pieces for reading specifically designed for children ever published in America.

Nor was this all: Webster extended the range of books on language at both ends. With considerable effrontery, he produced a new version of colonial America's most famous and popular text, *The New England Primer*. At the other end of the scale, he published, of course, his monumental *An American Dictionary of the English Language* of 1828, upon which he labored for a quarter of a century. This extraordinary effort was itself translated into a work suitable for children, the school dictionary that Webster issued two years later.

In addition, Webster produced works that the child could use in his school career sometime between the speller and the dictionary: he collaborated with Jedediah Morse on two geographies, wrote a biography of famous men, world and American histories, and a textbook of biology. He thus fulfilled a vision voiced in 1807, but conceived with his first spelling book: "My views comprehend a *whole system* of Education—from a Spelling Book through Geography & various other subjects—to a complete Dictionary—beginning with *children* & ending with *men*."[16]

Yet Webster's interest in education was just one facet of his intellectual life. He engaged himself politically from the first. As a young man, he was a leading propagandist for the American Revolution. He was one of the first to articulate the need for a strong central government (James Madison acknowledged his contribution). At the request of a member of the Constitutional Convention of 1787, Webster wrote a pamphlet in defense of the new Constitution. He numbered among his friends some of the idols of the early American Republic: he played whist with General George Washington and swapped ideas on phonetic alphabets with Benjamin Franklin. (Franklin even gave Webster his precious typefaces for a reformed alphabet.) Thomas Jefferson he counted among his enemies.[17] Webster was the editor of the catchall *American Magazine* for one short, unsuccessful year in 1788. Five years later, he supported Washington's administration by editing the *American Minerva* in New York, the city's first daily newspaper. He filled the paper with his own observations on political affairs.

Even when, hurt and dismayed by the factions in national

politics, Webster had long since retired to the sidelines of
national affairs, he retained his interest in them. "I feel all the
interest I ever felt in political affairs," he wrote at the age of
eighty, "but am continually pained to see the disorders and
corruptions which menace the ruin of our republic."[18]

Even this brief recital of some of Webster's involvement
with politics, language and education does not do justice to his
many other interests. As a son-in-law said of him, he had the
habit of "carrying on numerous and diversified employments at
the same time."[19] In 1801 Webster wrote a history of pestilential
diseases which is still admired today for its meticulous amassing
of statistics, even while its conclusions have long since been
discarded. He wrote on the financial effects of slavery while he
deplored its moral effects; he preserved Governor John Winthrop's 1630 journal for posterity by editing and publishing it
himself; he researched his own genealogy; he defended a strictly
literal interpretation of the Bible after he experienced conversion, and even produced a bowdlerized version of the Bible itself.

What is more, Webster involved himself in the community
in which he lived at every level. He eventually turned his back on
the national scene, but never on the local. He served in local
legislatures in New Haven, Connecticut and Amherst, Massachusetts. He was instrumental in opening educational institutions.
He helped to found a secondary school for his eldest daughter,
and he was a key member of the group that created the college at
Amherst, which he hoped his son would attend.

As we have noted, the sources on Webster's life are copious.
It is remarkable that there is any area left for disagreement on a
man whose life and works are so well documented. Yet he has
been differently interpreted by his biographers. Harry Warfel's
1936 portrait, written in the celebrationist context, shows
Webster as the "great man," courageously overcoming discour-
agement and even obloquy to seize his place as America's leading
lexicographer. Richard Rollins's recent study, in contrast, paints
a revisionist picture, particularly of Webster's later years. Rollins
sees a man who had abandoned virtually every patriotic and
social ideal of his youth, and who ended his "long journey" in
disillusionment, bitterness and despair.

Webster's spelling book, in its many revisions, was a
constant in Webster's life. So, although the focus of what follows
is primarily on this one work, the speller is of such longevity that

it also provides a valuable vantage point for observing the man himself. A final purpose of this book, then, is to see what can be learned about the man from his involvement with his own book. For, as I early discovered in the course of my researches, it is not possible to look at his spelling book without also encountering Webster himself at every turn.

I

Webster's Early Years
1758 to 1783

Noah Webster was born on October 16, 1758 in West Hartford, Connecticut. He was the fourth child, and second son, of Noah Webster senior, who owned and farmed ninety acres of land.[1] His early schooling took place at the district school. As Webster himself put it, he had, in those early years, "no other education than that which a common school afforded, when rarely a book was used in the schools, except a spelling book, a Psalter, testament or Bible." (The spelling book was Thomas Dilworth's).[2]

Like all farmers' sons, young Noah was expected to share in the everyday work of the farm. But his father found him, at the age of fourteen, taking a Latin grammar into the fields: "his rests under the apple trees were quite too long for a farmer's son."[3] Noah senior hesitated at first, nonetheless, when his namesake asked for a college education. Relenting, he arranged for Noah to go to the local Congregational parson, the Reverend Nathan Perkins, to learn classics. The next winter, Noah junior attended the Hopkins Grammar school, but finished his classical preparatory studies under Dr. Perkins. In order to pay for a college education for his son, Webster senior mortgaged his farm. (Noah was never able to repay this debt, and his father was ultimately forced to sell the farm.)[4] In September 1774, Noah Webster junior was admitted to Yale College.[5]

Young Webster must surely have found Yale a pleasurable, even a heady, experience. Certainly he made friends easily. He preserved the letters that his school friends sent him then, as well as after their ways had parted, letters from Zechariah Swift, "my

class mate & chum" Icabod Witmore, Wetmore Meigs, and Joel
Barlow.[6]

In later years Webster would condemn a classical education
for equipping youngsters so poorly for earning their living.[7] But
he received other benefits from his college experience: Yale
introduced Webster to the ideas and ideals of the Enlightenment.
He and his fellow students soaked up notions of the perfectibility
of man, the power of human reason, and the ever-present
possibility of change.[8]

Indeed, there was an anti-authoritarian spirit in the air:
events in the real world found an echo in college life. Two
months before the Declaration of Independence, Webster
delivered a sophomore Latin exercise. Titled "On Youth and
Old Age," it is a model of antiseptic pieties, asserting that a well-
spent youth is the proper preparation for a felicitous old age, and
that it is folly and madness to purchase the pleasures of youth at
the cost of grief in old age.[9] In his junior year, however, with the
revolutionary spirit abroad, Webster was one of twenty-six
students who looked for grief in their youth when they staged a
student protest: in order to register their disapproval of some
punishment which two of their fellows were about to receive, all
twenty-six marched out of the college chapel. (All subsequently
signed a recantation.)[10]

There were indeed topics more absorbing to the student
body than the prerequisites for a peaceful old age. Yale College
in those years was a hotbed of revolutionary sentiment. The
senior class of 1776—two years ahead of Webster's—would hear
the valedictory address given by Timothy Dwight:

> You should by no means consider yourselves as
> members of a small neighborhood, town or colony
> only, but as being concerned in laying the foundations
> of American greatness. Your wishes, your designs, your
> labors, are not to be confined by the narrow bounds of
> the present age, but are to comprehend succeeding
> generations, and be pointed to immortality . . . .
>
> Remember that you are to act for the empire of
> America, and for a long succession of ages.[11]

Revolutionary feeling was not confined to orations, however:
the students, although exempt from military service, formed
companies of volunteers and went through their military paces.

Their zeal was rewarded by a glimpse of General George Washington, who passed through New Haven in June 1775 to take command of the army at Charlestown. (Sixty-five years later, Noah Webster still recalled the occasion so vividly that he could name the owner of the house where Washington spent the night.) The following morning Washington, with General Lee, who had been a British officer and appreciated military precision when he saw it, "cried out with astonishment," reminisced Webster, "at their promptness." The student troop accompanied Washington out of town, marching to the music of Noah's flute.[12]

While young Noah was playing soldier on the New Haven streets, his eldest brother Abraham was seeing some real action. In the spring of 1776, he was in Canada with the American army.[13] He was captured by the British, but released—not surprisingly—when he came down with smallpox. A French woman nursed him back to health, and he made his way home to the Hartford farm. Noah, home for the summer vacation, accompanied his brother when Abraham rejoined the army. Noah passed an extremely uncomfortable night under canvas, where the greatest dangers that presented themselves were dysentery and the mosquitoes. (The latter were so virulent that the tents had to be filled with smoke all night.)[14]

During the following academic year, 1776–1777, the disruptions caused by the revolutionary war caused a food shortage for the students of Yale. It was decided that New Haven was no longer suitable for the conduct of college life, and the students were relocated to the interior of the state. The junior class, Webster among them, went with their tutor, Joseph Buckminster, to Glastonbury.[15]

By the autumn of 1777, the revolutionary war was reaching a climax. The great British commander, General Burgoyne, was starting his move south from Canada toward Albany, where he had hoped, by using the Hudson River as a barrier, to cut off all communication between New England and the western and southern colonies. In this crisis, all four male members of the Webster household—Noah Webster senior, Abraham, Noah himself and his younger brother Charles—voluntarily joined a regiment that was making its way up the east bank of the Hudson. Across the mighty river, the town of Kingston could be seen in flames; but before the regiment could reach Albany, they were met by a courier "waving his sword in triumph," as Webster remembered it years later, "and crying out as he passed, 'Burgoyne is taken. Burgoyne is taken.'" As the additional troops were no longer needed, they were disbanded, and the Websters returned home.[16]

These brushes with war, remote as they were, left an indelible impression on young Noah. Almost fifty years after the dash to the Hudson, Webster would evoke its memory to rebuff a critic who had made the grave error of dubbing him an "aristocrat." With a grandiloquence hardly warranted by the actual events, Webster penned an outraged letter to the newspaper:

> In the most critical period of the revolutionary war, when the British forces were attempting to cut off the communication between the Eastern & Southern states, when the companions of my youth were sinking into the grave by the sword or by a deadly pestilence, I offered to hazard my life to protect the liberties which *you*, Sir, now enjoy in common with others; I marched, a volunteer, to the bank of the Hudson, ill able to bear the fatigues of a soldier, & glad at times to find a bed of straw in a barn or a shed.[17]

In the winter of 1777–1778, Webster's class, now seniors, was ordered to return to New Haven, while the other classes remained in the country. Many seniors, Webster among them, refused to do so, and it was not until the next spring that classes started up normally in New Haven. After the final examination of the class in July, public exercises were held in the chapel, where Webster gave a "Cliosophic Oration" in English. The degree of Bachelor of Arts was conferred upon Webster and other graduating seniors that September in the college chapel. The seniors had to forego, temporarily at least, the normal public commencement celebrations because of the unsettled times.[18]

With Webster graduated many young men who would hold places of honor in the years ahead; some of them would remain Webster's friends for the rest of his life. Oliver Wolcott would become Secretary of the Treasury during the presidency of John Adams. Joel Barlow, a particular friend of Noah's, would become the quasi-official poet of the American Revolution.

After graduation, Webster returned home to the family farm in West Hartford. Now twenty, he had a degree, but no job. His plans were to become a lawyer, but he had yet to begin studying for the Bar examination. His father, moreover, had bad news for him. He informed Noah that he had done all he could for him financially—as indeed he had—and could do no more. Faced with this ultimatum, and aware that his brothers, too, felt that he had been favored long enough, Noah closeted himself in his room for three days to meditate on his future.

Thirty years later, Webster could still remember vividly the anxiety he experienced at this moment.

> Having neither property nor powerful friends to aid me, & being utterly unacquainted with the world—I knew not what business to attempt nor by what means to obtain subsistence. Being set afloat in the world at the inexperienced age of twenty, without a father's aid which had before supported me, my mind was embarrassed with solicitude, & overwhelmed with gloomy apprehensions.

While in this state of doubt, Webster read Johnson's *Rambler*, which affected him deeply: "for when I closed the last volume, I formed a firm resolution, to pursue a course of virtue thru life—& to perform all moral & social duties with scrupulous exactness—a resolution which I have endeavour'd to maintain, tho' doubtless not without many failures—"[19]

Determined to support himself financially, Webster opted for what countless other young men in his position had chosen before him, an interim teaching position. He went to Glastonbury, Connecticut—where, it will be recalled, he had been sent with his junior class two years earlier—and taught at the common school that same winter, the winter of 1778–1779. That summer, he returned nearer home, to teach in the brick school house at Hartford, where he boarded with Oliver Ellsworth,[20] who would later become Chief Justice of the United States. Out of school hours, Noah studied law in Ellsworth's extensive private library. In the fall, he returned to live with his family again, teaching school in West Hartford. The early months of 1780 were memorable for the intense cold and heavy snowfall. For three months Webster walked almost four miles a day to and from school, through snow so deep that it completely covered the rural fences.[21] This experience as a schoolmaster inspired him to write a series of essays on the defects of rural schools. They paint a dismal picture: school buildings so poorly built and so cold in winter that children pushed and jostled each other to get closer to the fire; a lack of desks; severe overcrowding, with seventy or eighty children in a class; and reading instruction in which the "pronunciation of words, as taught in our schools, is wretched."[22]

In the summer of that year Webster was able to forsake teaching to pursue his legal studies in Litchfield, Connecticut, where he was invited to live in the house of Jedediah Strong, a local Justice of the Quorum.[23] When Webster applied for admission to the Bar the following March, 1781, at Litchfield he was—along with everyone else applying at the same time— unaccountably refused. Then he applied at Hartford, and was admitted to practice law on April 3, 1781. That September, he finally attended the first public commencement to be held in Yale for seven years and received his Master of Arts degree.[24]

Obtaining the qualifications for practicing law was one thing; actually finding legal briefs was another. The legal profession was at a low ebb, with too many lawyers chasing too few suits. Once again Webster turned to teaching, but this time the school was to be a private academy, which he hoped to open himself. He placed the following advertisement in the local newspaper for a school in Sharon, a small town in Connecticut on the border of New York state.

> The subscriber, desirous of promoting Education, so essential to the interest of a free people, proposes immediately to open a school at Sharon, in which young Gentlemen and Ladies may be instructed in Reading, Writing, Mathematicks, the English Language, and if desired, the Latin and Greek Languages—in Geography, Vocal Music, &c. at the moderate price of Six Dollars and two thirds per quarter per Scholar. The strictest attention will be paid to the studies, the manners and the morals of youth, by the public's very humble servant,
>
> NOAH WEBSTER, Jun . . . [25]
>
> Sharon, June 1, 1781

The school opened the following month, with the children of some of Sharon's leading citizens.[26]

It happens that we have a glimpse of Noah Webster at this time of his life, through the eyes of nineteen-year-old Juliana Smith, whose family was prominent in Sharon. The "Sharon Literary Club" had been founded the year before, meeting every Monday evening from October to May.[27] The literary presentations were followed by dancing—except when the club was held in the parsonage. According to Juliana, she and her sister "maintained a seemly silence while the slower half of creation was laying down the law."[28] The club was the social center of Sharon, attracting over a hundred young people to each meeting, and Webster of course joined it. He contributed to the handwritten literary magazine which Juliana edited and produced bimonthly. His contribution took the form of a moral lesson in the guise of a dream.[29]

Another of Juliana's literary activities was keeping a journal for her brother Jack, who was at Yale. In it, she expressed her opinion of young Webster with alarming candor. "Mr. Webster has not the excuse of youth (I think he must be fully twenty-two or three), but his essays—don't be angry, Jack,—are as young as yours or brother Tommy's, while his reflections are as prosy as those of our horse." In fact, she added, the horse's might make the better reading. "At least they would be all *his own*, and that is more than can be said of N. W.'s . . . . In conversation he is even duller than in writing, if that be possible, but he is a painstaking man and a hard student. Papa says he will make his mark."[30]

Juliana's father would eventually prove to be right. Indeed, Webster was shortly to start on the venture which would profoundly alter his life. At this time, however, Sharon proved a disappointment, and Webster abandoned his little school only eight days after reopening it in October for its second semester.[31] It has been said that he was disappointed in love.[32] He spent that winter in Connecticut, wandering from village to village in an unsuccessful search for "mercantile employment."[33] In January, the first of his many manifestoes on behalf of his country, "Observations on the Revolution of America," appeared in a New York newspaper.[34] An attempt to reopen his Sharon school in the spring of 1782 apparently came to nothing.[35] Webster now crossed the Hudson and traveled to Goshen, New York, where he opened a "classical school." Some of his Sharon pupils followed him there.[36]

The intensity of emotion Webster felt at this time, and

which he recorded half a century later, has been noted by his
most recent biographer, Richard Rollins. Webster had only
seventy-five cents in his pocket, and was "without money and
without friends." For several months he experienced "extreme
depression and gloomy forebodings."[37] Rollins has seen this as a
crisis in Webster's life—a climax in Webster's adolescent search
for identity, after a series of failures or rejections.[38]

Webster emerged from this crisis successfully: he found
himself by identifying with the new nation's own search for
identity.[39] He turned again to writing, and to his experiences as a
school teacher. Now he conceived of a series of elementary
textbooks that would be worthy of the new republic. He began
with the first of the elementary texts, a spelling book. As he
himself put it in his memoir, he "began by compiling a Spelling
Book on a plan which he supposed to be better adapted to assist
the learner, than that of Dilworth."[40] He explicitly linked its
composition to the close of the Revolutionary War. "In the year
1782," he wrote on another occasion, "while the American army
was lying on the bank of the Hudson, I kept a classical school in
Goshen . . . I there compiled two small elementary books for
teaching the English language."[41]

During that spring and summer, Webster worked on his
speller. He wrote to his friends to tell them of his plan, and in the
fall of 1782 took off to Philadelphia, Trenton, Princeton, New
York and New Haven to solicit criticism of his manuscript,
obtain recommendations from prominent people, and to test
out the ground for copyright legislation.[42] At Princeton, Samuel
Stanhope Smith (then professor of theology and later president
of the college) gave him some suggestions on syllabic division,
and a good recommendation, which combined praise of the
spelling book with the opinion that authors were entitled to the
right of publishing and vending their own work.[43]

Webster's college friend Joel Barlow also proved helpful. He
liked Webster's plan about Dilworth, he told Webster, but
warned him that Dilworth was well entrenched in the schools.
"You know our country is prejudiced in favor of old Dilworth,
the nurse of us all, and it will be difficult to turn their attention
from it; you know, too, that the printers make large impressions
of it and afford it very cheap."[44]

It must have been precisely this example—the wholesale
reproduction of the British author Thomas Dilworth by American

publishers—that caused Webster to start that agitation for copyright protection, first for himself, and then for all American authors, which would one day earn him the title of "Father of Copyright." In retrospect, Webster's ability to appreciate the importance of such protection was remarkable. While copyright protection was an established feature of English law, only one American colony (Massachusetts) offered even the sketchiest of protection to its authors or publishers from literary piracy.[45] Publishers printed works previously published abroad or in America with impunity.[46] Webster, however, saw what number-less authors would later see: that there was money to be made by someone from a successful school text. His realization that he could only make a profit for himself from his own books if copyright legislation were passed to protect them from piracy, showed astonishing foresight in a young man of twenty-four. Had he not seen the need, or had he failed to obtain the necessary legislation, the *American Dictionary of the English Language* could never have been written. For, as we shall see, the income from his spelling book would support Webster and his family for twelve years while he worked on his dictionary.

As it was, Webster anticipated the need to protect his textbook before he had even completed it. In October 1782 he returned to Hartford to present a "memorial" to the General Assembly of Connecticut. In it, he asked the assembly to appoint a committee to examine his manuscript, and if the committee reported upon it favorably, to pass a law which would "vest in your memorialist & his assigns the exclusive right of printing, publishing & vending the said American Instructor in the State of Connecticut for & during the term of thirteen years from the passing of said act...." or for some other term that the assembly thought proper.[47] The memorial makes it clear that Webster originally planned a two-part work, to be called the *American Instructor*. The first part was to be a spelling book, the second a grammar; both volumes would serve as a replacement of Dilworth's book.

This memorial was too late to obtain a hearing at that particular session of the assembly.[48] Webster therefore left Hartford and returned to Goshen, where he labored through the winter to revise and complete his work. In the process he altered his plan, now envisaging a three-volume work, the last part of which was to be a "reader," or selection of pieces for reading and recitation, culled from other works. He incorporated into the revised edition of his speller some of the suggestions made by the college professors he had visited. One of the disadvantages of asking for advice from prominent people is that it is difficult to reject it when proffered: Webster succumbed to the unfortunate suggestion by Ezra Stiles, president of Yale, that he should discard the title *American Instructor*, with its suitably patriotic flavor, in favor of the pretentious *A Grammatical Institute of the English Language*.[49] The change would contribute to the ridicule and accusation of vanity that Webster would incur after the publication of his volumes.

In January 1783, Webster wrote to his friend and fellow lawyer, John Canfield, a Sharon resident whose daughter had attended Webster's school, to entrust him with a second memorial, again directed at the Connecticut General Assembly. Like many another who has tried to combine teaching with writing, Webster had found the going very rough and complained to Canfield that he was exhausted by his efforts. "I have been indefatigable this winter;" he wrote. "I have sacrificed ease, leisure, & health to the execution of it, & have nearly compleated [sic] it. But such close application is too much for my constitution. I must relinquish the school or writing Grammars . . . ." Then he remarked, striking a note that would become a constant refrain throughout his life, "The more I look into our language & the methods of instruction practised in this country, the more I am convinced of the necessity of improving one & correcting the other." He added another note that would also be a recurring theme in the decades to come—the theme of American cultural independence.

> Popular prejudice is in favor of Dilworth—& because he was universally esteemed in G[reat] B[ritai]n half a century ago, people are apt to slumber in the opinion that he is incapable of improvement. But he is not only out of date; but is really faulty & defective in every part of his work. America must be as independent in *literature* as she is in *politics*—as famous for *arts* as for *arms*—& it is not impossible, but a person of my youth may have some influence in exciting a spirit of literary industry.[50]

A few weeks later, Webster penned, but never presented, a

similar memorial to the New York legislature.[51]

As it turned out, the need for Canfield to urge an individual petition for copyright protection was rendered unnecessary, because the Connecticut legislature was in the process of passing a general law on the subject, which granted to an author the exclusive right to the earnings from his publication for a term of fourteen years. The law had been inspired not by Webster, but by author John Ledyard, seeking to protect his forthcoming book on Captain Cook's last voyage.[52] The statute is considered a milestone in the progress of the American law on intellectual property.[53]

Joel Barlow, Webster's college friend, who had already offered encouragement and advice to the budding author, further proved himself a good friend by being among those who presented a memorial to the United States Congress. At the time the United States Congress, under the Articles of Confederation, was limited in its power to legislate for all the states. It could, however, make recommendations to the states; and in May 1783, as a result of a report produced by a group that included James Madison, Congress passed a resolution that recommended that the several states secure to authors the fruits of their labor for a term of not less than fourteen years.[54]

In November, Webster had heard the good news from Enoch Perkins, a friend in Rhode Island, that Perkins had copied Connecticut's copyright statute, and had had it introduced to the Rhode Island upper house. This house had passed it, and Perkins was waiting confidently for the lower house to pass it at the next session.[55] The general move for copyright protection, aided by the Congressional recommendation, encouraged six states to pass copyright legislation by the close of 1783: Connecticut, Massachusetts, New Jersey, Maryland, New Hampshire and Rhode Island. Some fifty years later, Webster would recount his struggle for copyright legislation, casting himself in the stellar role as prime mover.[56]

In the spring of 1783, Webster went to Hartford, Connecticut (a state where copyright protection was assured) to get his work published. In a memoir of his life written half a century later, Webster looked back upon this time as one beset by difficulties. His book was regarded as "visionary," and the only friends to encourage him were John Trumbull and Joel Barlow. Webster himself was "destitute of the means of defraying the expenses of publication, & no printer or bookseller was found to undertake the publication at his own risk."[57] Barlow's and Trumbull's support was financial as well as moral: Barlow lent Webster $500, Trumbull a smaller amount. This enabled Webster to contract with Hudson & Goodwin of Hartford for the book. (Barzillai Hudson and George Goodwin published the *Connecticut Courant*.) The firm was to have sole right to the spelling book for "a term of years."[58] Hudson & Goodwin were more involved in the risk than Webster cared to admit, for they accepted what Webster delicately called his "obligation," even though they could only hope to be reimbursed if the speller were to sell well. "But it was not a time to shrink from the execution of his design," as Webster saw it, writing of himself in the third person; "he had confidence in its success, & took upon himself the risk."[59]

Now burdened with the unwieldy title of *A Grammatical Institute of the English Language, Part I*, Webster's replacement for Dilworth's spelling book was entered for Connecticut copyright in Hartford on August 14, 1783.[60] Webster spent a couple of months sending off copies of it to his friends.[61] Hovered over by its anxious parent, and better protected from being kidnapped than any previous spelling book, the Webster speller was born.[62] "The success was better than he had expected," reminisced Webster, "the edition of five thousand copies being exhausted by the following winter."[63]

Webster turned his attention immediately to finishing his grammar. At the beginning of March 1784, it was ready to go on sale.[64] Like its predecessor, this part, too, was published by Hudson & Goodwin.[65] Not until the following February was Webster able to complete and put to press the third and final part of his *Institute*, the reader.[66]

II

The First Speller
"To Inspire the Minds of Youth"

It was Webster's spelling book, the first part of his *Grammatical Institute*, that was destined to become a riproaring bestseller. Neither his grammar nor his reader—the second and third parts of the *Institute*—ever approached it in sales volume.[1] At a time when a lifetime sale of 25,000 copies could be considered the hallmark of a bestselling trade book, the speller would reach almost half that number a mere sixteen months after its first publication.[2] Hudson & Goodwin would publish two editions in 1784, and at least one edition every year after that, for decades. And, as we shall see, Webster would find other publishers, strategically sited all over the country. Only five years after its first appearance, the speller would have publishers in the states of Pennsylvania, New York, Connecticut, Vermont and Massachusetts.[3]

How a "spelling" book could attain such giddy heights of popularity is only explicable if we realize that the primary purpose of a spelling book in Webster's time was, and always had been, to teach children to read. Teaching them to spell was an important, but secondary, consideration. (We may differentiate these two purposes as "spelling-for-reading" and "spelling-for-spelling.") Spelling books were so called because spelling was inextricably tied up with reading. As far back as one can trace the history of reading methodology, children were taught to spell words out, in syllables, in order to pronounce them. It was a procedure better known to us as the "alphabet method," and it was the only method of "decoding" (as reading professionals term it today) that was in use. The central role played by spelling in learning to read is discussed in English works from at least 1588 on;[4] spelling was still being used to teach children to read, on both sides of the Atlantic, as late as the first decades of the nineteenth century. Not until the 1820s were alternative approaches to reading instruction broached: both the whole word method and a phonic approach would then be suggested as remedies for the defects of the alphabet method.[5]

A child of preschool age in the seventeenth or eighteenth century in the American colonies would probably have been introduced to a primer at home—most likely the perennially popular *New England Primer*, purchased partly for its inclusion of a catechism.[6] After about 1760, however, if not even earlier, a child who attended school would be presented with a spelling book as his or her first instructional text. Spelling books had, in fact, been a part of the American colonial scene from the first years of settlement. Indeed, in about 1643 an unidentified spelling book came off the first printing press established in colonial America, only a few years after the press was set up.[7] Other books followed elsewhere. A few were aimed at specifically American audiences,[8] but many more were reprinted in the colonies directly from their English originals, with no concessions whatever made to colonial circumstances. Spelling books by Nathaniel Strong, Henry Dixon, as well as by Thomas Dilworth, along with an anonymous speller, *A Child's New Plaything*, were English works, and had all been reproduced verbatim in the American colonies before 1750. Another English speller, written by Daniel Fenning, was available to Americans after 1769.[9]

Thomas Dilworth's *A New Guide to the English Tongue* became by far the most popular of all the spelling books in colonial America after the 1760s. When first printed in America by Benjamin Franklin in 1747, it was already in its eighth English edition.[10] Its popularity may be gauged by a spot check of its American editions between 1765 and 1771: it was issued nine times. (In contrast, rival spellers totaled eight editions altogether for the same period.)[11] By 1785, it was said to have gone through some forty editions.[12]

No matter who wrote it, every spelling book was based on the same presuppositions. As far as a psychology of learning was concerned, it assumed that children could only learn by rote, through memorization and repetition. Paired associate learning was the basis of the link between letters and their spoken counterparts. As for a theory of reading, a spelling book presupposed that reading involved pronouncing and that reading was therefore oral, not silent. The purpose of a speller was to teach children how to pronounce hundreds of words, most of which were not already in their oral vocabulary. The question of comprehension was deferred for other texts.[13] Basic to all of this was also an unstated conviction that to teach children to read was in some sense to teach them to speak. This explains titles of spellers on the lines of *A New Guide to the English Tongue* and *The Youth's Instructor in the English Tongue.*[14]

Mechanical in its view of how children learned and what reading was, the spelling book was also mechanical in its organization. (This was equally true, incidentally, of primers, which covered the same ground as spelling books in a smaller compass.) Spelling books had a set format. First, the child was introduced to all the letters of the alphabet, in both roman and italic letters. Then the child would meet the "syllabarium"—as old as the oldest hornbook—*ab eb ib ob ub* ("short" vowels) and *ba be bi bo bu* ("long" vowels).[15] Then came words of one syllable, followed by words of two, which preceded words of three syllables, and so forth. Syllables were divided for children by the simple device of a space.

In the standard spelling book, a "table" (which was a list of words organized alphabetically) was followed by a "lesson." A lesson was some kind of connected prose which used, for the most part, the words that had appeared in the preceding table, and which restricted itself to words which did not have more syllables than those reached up to that point. Children were expected to spell aloud all the words in a table before tackling the lesson. They would also, at least to start with, spell aloud each word in the actual reading lesson. Indeed, dropping the crutch of spelling was considered the hallmark of fluent reading. As a New York educator put it in 1765, "now when we can readily pronounce words off without Spelling, and go on without Hesitation, in a Manner intelligible to ourselves and others; we are said to *read.*"[16]

Heir to a long tradition of British spelling books,[17] Thomas Dilworth had made several improvements (at least as he saw it) over his predecessors. One of these was the refinement of subdividing the monosyllables into words of two, three and four letters, "with *six* short Lessons at the End of each Table, not exceeding the order of Syllables in the Foregoing tables." This eighteenth-century version of vocabulary control carried with it the usual drawbacks:

> It must be acknowledged, [admitted Dilworth in his 1740 preface,] that the first *Six Lessons* do but just make English, Yet, I hope, whoever considers the difficulty of composing *Sentences* to be read in *Lessons*, wherein each Word is confined to *three Letters*, will readily overlook the baseness of the *Language*.[18]

Dilworth's first lesson—and one which Webster, with minor modifications, would reproduce as his own first lesson—reads, in words indeed not more than three letters long:

> No man may put off the Law of God.
> The Way of God is no ill Way.
> My joy is in God all the Day.
> A bad man is a Foe to God.[19]

Dilworth's lessons were, without exception, adaptations from the scriptures. Among his tables he included a list of place names, which were, naturally enough, English.

The second part of Dilworth's book also followed in the footsteps of former spelling books. It contained the ever popular list of "Words, that are the same in *Sound*, but different in *Signification*"—that is, homophones. His third part billed itself as a grammar, and was the only portion of the book devoted to some kind of explication of letter-sound correspondences. The fourth part included twelve of Aesop's fables, "adorn'd with proper Sculptures" (that is, the crudest of wood cuts), and the final part presented prayers for children. Only in the fourth portion of the book, then, did the child meet anything that was not steeped in biblical material, while there was hardly a page in the book that did not preach at the child in some form. In this respect, it was no different, of course, from other spelling books of the same period.[20]

It is noteworthy that when Webster reworked Dilworth to make his own spelling book, he followed Dilworth in both form and content very closely. But it was not the similarities between his own book and Dilworth's that Webster stressed. Instead, he seized upon the occasion of this, his first appearance on the stage of book publishing, to draw sharp contrasts between his own work and its English model.

In a lengthy introduction to the first edition of his spelling book, Webster set his small work firmly in the mainstream of the American Revolution. "Greater changes have been wrought, in the minds of men, in the short compass of eight years past, than are commonly effected in a century," he wrote. The past attachment of Americans to Great Britain had undergone a total change. It might well be, he said, that English methods of education would be found to be as erroneous as their politics and their religion.[21]

Webster went on to assert that the grammatical study of the English language had been sadly neglected. The lack of some standard in orthography and prosody (which he defined as the spelling and pronunciation of words), had occasioned a great variety of dialects in both Great Britain and America. (In this statement, Webster made his first declaration of a position that he was to take all his life: notably, that the spelling book influenced the way children learned to speak.) The variety of dialects was not to be wondered at; for, he said:

> The sounds of our letters are more capricious and irregular than those of any alphabet with which we are acquainted. Several of our vowels have four or five different sounds; and the same sounds are often expressed by five, six or seven different characters. The case is much the same with our consonants: And these different sounds have no mark of distinction. How would a child or a foreigner learn the different sounds of *o* in these words, *rove, move, dove* or of *oo* in *poor, door?* Or that *a, ai, ei,* and *e* have precisely the same sound in these words, *bare, laid, vein, there?* Yet these and fifty other irregularities have passed unnoticed by authors of Spelling Books and Dictionaries. They study the language enough to find the difficulties of it—they tell us that it is impossible to reduce it to order—that it is to be learnt only by the ear—they lament the disorder and dismiss it without a remedy.[22]

The pronunciation of our language had been left to ignorance and caprice, Webster suggested. He had therefore tried to compile a system "designed to introduce uniformity and accuracy of pronunciation into common schools," and had taken pains to make it both simple and accurate.[23]

Webster then used his introduction to elaborate on the ways in which his own spelling book was an improvement over Dilworth's. In the first place, Webster had altered the usual method of dividing syllables. As had all spelling book authors before him, Dilworth had followed the precept that every syllable should begin with a consonant—preferably several consonants. This produced syllabic divisions like *ha bit* and *clu ster*. These in turn violated another cardinal principle, namely, that the vowel in an open syllable had to be "long." Dilworth's solution to this problem had been to add the marking (") after the offending vowel, producing *ha" bit* and *clu" ster*.[24] Remarking that "the only reason we divide syllables for children, is to lead them to the proper pronunciation of words," Webster had a few unpleasant words to say about Dilworth's markings and altered the method of syllabic division: from now on, such words would appear as *hab it* and *clus ter*.[25] Unknown to Webster, a Scottish spelling book author named William Perry had made the same reform.[26] It would become a permanent feature of the spelling book and dictionary landscape on both sides of the Atlantic Ocean.

Webster's second improvement over Dilworth was his alteration of the syllabic division of words ending with *-sion* or *-tion*. The conventional treatment had been to divide a word like *nation* into three syllables: *na ti on*. This use is still reflected in the prosody of some psalm singing today, but it had dropped out of conversational English speech well before Webster's time. Webster therefore divided such words into two syllables, such as *na tion*.[27] (This innovation, incidentally, had been suggested to him by Samuel Stanhope Smith of Princeton College, while Webster was touring colleges to obtain advice and recommendations.)[28]

Webster then took Dilworth to task for several other faults. Dilworth's third mistake, according to Webster, was to claim that a letter such as the *b* in *sub tle* was actually pronounced like a *t*. In fact, said Webster, these letters were mute. Fourthly, Webster criticized the lists of English towns and boroughs in Dilworth, which he pointed out were useless in America. Lastly, Webster excoriated Dilworth's grammar. In short, Webster remarked, "one half of the work is totally useless and the other half defective and erroneous."[29]

Having disposed of Dilworth, Webster devoted the remainder of his long introduction to his own plan. He had begun the work, he said, with easy monosyllables, and then proceeded to easy words of four syllables; for, as he rightly remarked, "some of our hardest words to pronounce are monosyllables." Webster went on to explain that he had put words of the same class into the same table, disregarding alphabetical order where necessary. He had also taken particular care to place together words whose pronunciation did not fall under his rules, especially those derived from the French or Greek, and list them in a separate table. In addition, said Webster, he had followed Johnson's dictionary for the spelling and accentuation of the words in his tables.[30]

One further change from Dilworth that Webster effected was to cut down on the use of the name of the Deity. He explained his reasons for this: "Nothing has a greater tendency to lessen the reverence which mankind ought to have for the Supreme Being, than a careless repetition of his name upon every trifling occasion." Instead, Webster employed easy dialogues and stories which were calculated "not only to entertain; but to inspire the minds of youth, with an abhorrence of vice, indolence and meanness; and with a love of virtue, industry and good manners."

The separate printing of the spelling book and the grammar book, another improvement, had obvious advantages in that children wore out a spelling book before they even had a chance to get as far as the grammar. Webster also noted that he regretted the custom of using the patronage of great names to introduce a book, and pointed out that he had used it only in part. If his work had merit, said Webster, with suspect artlessness, "it will make its own way into the world." The book was "a mite [thrown] into the common treasure of patriotic exertions," he said, and closed his introduction with a peroration:

> American glory begins to dawn at a favourable period, and under flattering circumstances. We have the experience of the whole world before our eyes . . . . It is the business of *Americans* to select the wisdom of all nations, as the basis of her constitutions—to avoid their

errours,—to prevent the introduction of foreign vices
and corruptions and check the career of her own,—to
promote virtue and patriotism,—to embellish and
improve the sciences,—to diffuse an uniformity and
purity of *language*,—to add superiour dignity to this
infant Empire and to human nature.[31]

Such, then, was Webster's conception of his spelling book in
1783. He saw it as a tool in America's struggle for cultural
independence from Great Britain. He envisioned the creation of
what he later called "a federal language," which would be
uniform throughout the United States and be distinctly different
from the tongue of the mother country.[32] These were grand
plans indeed for a young man who had just published his first
work.

In his belief that learning to read was somehow equivalent to
learning to speak—and that, therefore, the spelling book which
promoted the former also facilitated the latter—Webster's view
was identical to that of earlier spelling book authors. Thomas
Dilworth's title, *A New Guide to the English Tongue*, is indicative of
this widely held opinion, as we have seen. That a spelling book
could influence the spoken language was also taken for granted
by Webster's contemporaries. "All men are pleased with an
elegant pronunciation," wrote Colonel Timothy Pickering to his
wife from the American army camp in Newburgh in the fall of
1783. (He had just obtained a copy of Webster's speller, and had
sat up late into the night reading it.) "And this new Spelling-
Book shows children how to acquire it with ease and certainty."[33]
(Pickering's enthusiasm led him to write to Webster himself to
offer a few suggestions.[34] This letter led to their meeting in
Philadelphia in February 1786, and to a lifelong friendship.)[35]
Even before its publication, the spelling book had been hailed as
a leveler of spoken language: "the general use of it," wrote
Tapping Reeve, whose recommendation had been solicited by
Webster, "will go very far towards demolishing all those odious
distinctions occasioned by provincial dialects."[36]

Webster's claim, then, that his work would influence
pronunciation was not disputed by his contemporaries. Of all
that Webster set out to do, the "reformation of the language we
speak," as he described it, was the ambition he held most dear.[37]
Indeed, we find him writing, in his old age, in terms very similar

to those he used as a young man. "In the year 1783," he wrote in the preface to the first publication of his great *American Dictionary of the English Language* of 1828, "just at the close of the Revolution, I published an elementary book for facilitating the acquisition of our vernacular tongue, and for correcting a vicious pronunciation which prevailed extensively among the common people of this country."[38] Among the newspaper clippings to be found in the Webster papers is one from the New Haven *Daily Herald* of January 4, 1842. It was presumably written either by Webster himself or a member of his family. After lauding Webster's services to the English language, the article continues:

> But Dr. Webster has probably done less for the English language in our country by his dictionary than by his spelling book. But for the all-prevailing presence of this book throughout our wide extended country, nothing could nave[sic] saved us from as great a diversity of dialects as there is in England . . . And this is principally owing to the fact that nearly every one who has learned to read, has acquired his rudiments from Webster's Spelling Book, or some other spelling book compiled from Webster's.[39]

Chauncey Goodrich, who married Webster's second daughter, Julia, and who carried on the work of editing Webster's dictionary after Webster's death, attributed to the speller "more than to any other cause . . . that remarkable uniformity of pronunciation in our country, which is so often spoken of with surprise by English travelers."[40]

An examination of this extravagant claim, too often accepted at face value by Webster's biographers, will be deferred until later. It is enough, for our purposes, to accept the fact that Webster's assertion was not considered farfetched by his contemporaries. The ideal of fostering a truly "American language" would continue to inspire Webster long after he became disillusioned with American politics.

If Webster's contemporaries had no trouble with the notion that his spelling book would foster a national language, their reaction to his major innovation, the new division of syllables, was much more varied. Not unnaturally, those who recommended the book found his new approach an improvement over the old; but some who wrote to Webster privately had certain reservations—not so much about the syllabic division itself, as about its acceptability. Webster's friend, Dr. Elizur Goodrich, who had been sent a few sheets of the first part of the *Grammatical Institute* before its publication, warned Webster that "perhaps the alteration of the way of spelling" (that is, the division of words into syllables) "will operate against you more than any other prejudice, you have to contend with." He continued with a mild rebuke. "Mr. Dilworth followed the rules of spelling long established: He only improved on a system, that had been in being for ages before he was born." Dilworth's double accent, under the circumstances, was a real advantage. "Your zeal against this accent, in my opinion, is rather intemperate."[41]

If the new syllabic division gave pause to some, neither was Webster's treatment of the endings *-sion* and *-tion* as one syllable, not two, acceptable to all. The story goes that a Scottish elder from a secluded valley in Pennsylvania rode furiously into town one morning, calling out:

> "Have you heard the news, mon? Do ye ken what's gaen on? Here's a fellow with a book made by a Yankee lad called Wobster, teaching the children clean agenst the Christian religion!"
> "Ah, how so?"
> "Why, ye ken we canna sing the psalms of David without having *salvation* and such words in four syllables, *sal-va-ci-on*; and he's making all the children say *salvashun!*"[42]

Such criticisms must have been very much in the minority, however, for subsequent spelling book authors would adopt Webster's innovation.

Another point of departure from Dilworth was Webster's treatment of the tables. Dilworth's method of classification was to group together all words that were spelled alike, whether or not they were pronounced alike. Webster arranged words in tables according, not to their spelling, but their pronunciation.

Webster's most notable innovation, however, was a description of the sounds represented by different letters in the English language. Never before in a spelling book printed in America had there been so full and accurate an attempt to describe, categorize and compare the phonemic values that different letters indicated. Webster achieved this in two ways. First, he described each letter of the alphabet, giving a word as an example of the sound he was focusing on.

> *G* is also hard before *a, o, u,* as *gat, got, gum;* but sometimes hard and sometimes soft before *e, i, y.*
> *H* is only an aspiration or breathing and is often silent, as in *h*our.

Second, he designed a numerical "index" (or key) to the pronunciation of the vowels, which as he had pointed out in his introduction he considered difficult for the learner.[43] He modified this key slightly in his next major revision of 1787, and this latter key was virtually identical to the one used in all subsequent revisions of the speller until 1829.[44]

The principle underlying Webster's key was straightforward: with the exception of numerals one and two, every number represented a different vowel pronunciation. Long vowels all had a superscript *1*; short vowels the superscript *2*; while a superscript *3* represented the vowel heard in *bald, tall* and *law.* Webster evolved ten superscripts in this manner, which identified pronunciations such as the "oo short" in *book,* and included the diphthongs heard in *found* and *voice.* He instructed the pupil to read his lists of words downwards; a superscript over a vowel would indicate that this vowel and those in all the subsequent words were to be pronounced in the same way, until the student met another superscript. In addition, Webster printed "silent" letters in italics.

Here, for example, is the beginning of Webster's twelfth table.

1	9	1	. . .	8	3	10
Be	fun	fly		now	law	bay
pe*a*	gun	cry		cow	maw	day
se*a*	run	sky		how	raw	hay
te*a*	son	lie		bow	saw	lay
ye*a*	ton	di*e*		mow	paw	may
fle*a*	won	ey*e*		sow	awe	pay
ke*y*	on*e**	b*u*y		vow	*g*naw	say[45]

(A footnote for the asterisk reads: "Pronounced *wun.*")

As an analysis of the relationship between letters and sounds, all of this was, compared with Dilworth's, a giant leap forward. The value of Webster's book in this respect was appreciated very early by his contemporaries. Dr. Goodrich considered it "not only ingenious, but a real improvement upon former treatises of this kind."[46] Joseph Buckminster, Webster's tutor at Yale, who had been corresponding with his former student all along, thought that Webster's key to the vowel sounds was as simple as perhaps it could be, but wondered whether a child might not have to be eight or ten years old before he could understand it.[47]

Of all Webster's improvements over Dilworth, the Americanizing of the towns, boroughs and so forth was, for obvious reasons, the easiest to accept, and no voice appears to have been raised to attack the change. The publishing of the grammar as a separate volume was also an innovation that no one challenged, although there would be many criticisms of the grammar itself when it was published in the following year, in 1784.

It is to Webster himself, at the end of his life, that we should look for his retrospective opinion of the value of the innovations in his spelling book. A man with such a strong sense of his life's work might be expected to have a few comments on the work that originally made him famous, and sure enough, he has. There is an unsigned manuscript in the Webster archives at the New York Public Library. It is written in the third person, but the hand is that of Webster's old age:

> In this work [the spelling book], he [Webster] boldly departed from the plan on which similar books were then, & still continue to be, constructed in Great Britain.
>
> The principal improvements were
>
> 1 In the division of syllables. In English books words are thus divided, ha-bit, le-mon, va-lor, te-nor. In this case, the learner, at first, gives to the vowel of the first syllable its long sound; nor can he readily understand why the vowel should not be long in these words, as well as in po-em, la-bel, pi-lot, lu-nar. Webster's division, hab-it, lem-on, val-or, ten-or put an end to this difficulty.
>
> 2 In making one syllable of *tion, sion*. The English division is thus; mo-ti-on, na-ti-on, ab-lu-ti-on, in-tru-si-on. This division compels the public to go

through the process of m-o, mo—ti, si, mosi, on, motion—Websters [sic] division shortens the process.

3 The classification of words. The arrangement of words having a like vowel sound, though represented by different characters, in columns in succession, serves as a guide to the pronunciation; it greatly facilitates the acquisition of the language by the tyro, & lessens the labor of the instructor. The seperation [sic] also of the long & short sounds of the vowels, & of other distinct sounds into classes, contributes to the same end.

4 The collecting & arranging of words of irregular & difficult orthography in distinct classes is a great improvement.

5 A key to the pronunciation of the vowels, & some of the consonants. Webster's key is remarkably simple, & has been, in part, adopted by many of the compilers of a similar book, without an acknowl-edgment.[48]

Such was Webster's retrospective verdict on his own work.

* * *

Perhaps an overall view of this famous little spelling book is in order at this point. It is, like all the spellers of its time, a tiny book. This first edition is in very small print, which Webster would replace by a larger type, pica size, in the third and fourth editions. There are no illustrations, and no fables in the 120 pages. After the lengthy introduction, the work proper begins with the familiar alphabets (roman and italic), and the mono-syllables:

ba be bi bo bu by...
ab eb ib ob ub.

The text proceeds to "Words of three and four letters" in Table II, then progresses to "Easy words of two syllables, accented on the first," in Table IV. By Table IX, Webster has reached "Easy words of four syllables, accented on the first" (Ami a ble to vol un ta ry); Table X lists "Easy words of four syllables, accented on the second" (A e ri al ... vi cin i ty); and

Table XI, "Easy words of four syllables, accented on the third"
(Ac ci dĕn tal . . . u ni ver sal). Webster may well have been the
first spelling book author to identify secondary stress on the
longer polysyllables, for he adds a note to his Table XI: "N.B.
The half accent is on the first syllable." He finally leaves
polysyllables at words of six syllables in Table XXIII, with "ex
tra ȯr di na ry" and "con grăt u la to ry" as his parting shot.
Tables XXIV to XXVIII list words which exhibit unvoiced and
voiced *th* (faith ful, gath er); silent *ue* (vag*ue*); words ending with -
ow (fol *low*); those in which *ch* is pronounced like *k* (char ac ter);
words ending with -*sion*, which the children are directed to
pronounce -*zhun* (con fu *s*ion); those where *ci* and *ti* are
pronounced *sh* (gra cious, pa tient); "capricious" words in which
the vowel of the accented syllable is short (am bi tion); and words
where *i* is to be pronounced like *y* (fil ial as "filyal"). The
remaining tables include proper names, irregular words ("Written:
amour; Pronounced: a moor"), and the ever popular homophones:

> Bar*e*   naked
> Bear   to suffer
> Bear   a beast.

The tables end with lists of place names in the United States,
with a disproportionate amount of space allotted to Connecticut
towns.

Not until Table XXXVII is the child given any reading
matter at all. Here Webster used the famous first lesson from
Dilworth:

> No man may put off the law of God:
> My joy is in his law all the day.
> O may I not go in the way of sin.
> Let me not go in the way of ill men.[49]

(Note that, true to his scruples against using the name of the
Deity, Webster has modified Dilworth's original.) Other lessons
follow. One of them reads:

> The wick-ed flee when no man pur-su-eth; but the righ-
> te-ous are as bold as a li-on. Vir-tue ex-alt-eth a na-tion;
> but sin is a re-proach to any peo-ple.[50]

Another lesson offers the child "Familiar Phrases, and easy

Dialogues, for young beginners." They were certainly written by Webster himself, and they convey a flavor of the late eighteenth century classroom as nothing else in his book does:

> Have you learnt your lesson?
> I am almost master of it.
> It is almost time to repeat it.
> I shall be ready in about half an hour.
> Who took my penknife?
> Did it lie near your inkhorn?
> It lay on the table by my paper.
> Will you hand me a ruler and pencil?
> Do not blot your paper.
> Sit down in your place and be silent.
> Indeed I will not speak a word. I think of the ferule.[51]

This lesson also includes a very rare glimpse of what, in Webster, could charitably be termed a sense of humor:

> How came you so late at school?
> I stopped to pull off my hat to a Gentleman.
> How long did that hinder you?
> A considerable time.
> Pray, Sir, how do you make your manners?
> I parade myself with my face to the person, take off my hat with both hands, make several bows and scrape with my right foot.
> I do not wonder you are late at school; for surely if you meet several persons, it must employ most of your school-hours.[52]

The final lesson in the spelling book is the story of Tommy and Harry, who are classic, if early, examples of the good boy and the bad boy. Tommy is rewarded in this life by material prosperity and a happy marriage, while naughty Harry is subjected to destitution and public ignominy. The tale, which prefigured a hundred such others in the nineteenth century, was adapted by Webster from the same story in Daniel Fenning's *Universal Spelling Book* (like Dilworth's, an American reprint of an English publication.)[53]

The value system displayed by Webster's spelling book was, as Dilworth's had been, thoroughly religious. Notwithstanding Webster's declared intention of avoiding the name of the Deity, the scriptural loading of the contents is obvious. In fact, the material just quoted on children at school is really atypical and was, significantly, dropped in later revisions. Here is a more characteristic lesson, which appeared in the first edition, the revision of 1787, and the revised impression of 1804 and thereafter:

> Be not anxious for your life, what ye shall eat, or what ye shall drink; nor for your body, what ye shall put on; for your heavenly father knoweth that ye have need of these things.
> Behold the fowls of the air . . .[54]

Here, finally, is another lesson that survived all the editions of the spelling book verbatim, from 1783 until the drastic revision of 1829:

> When good boys and girls are at school, they will mind their books, and try to learn to spell and read well, and not play in the time of school.
> When they are at church, they will sit, kneel, or stand still; and when they are at home, will read some good book, that God may bless them.
> As for those boys and girls that mind not their books, and love not the church and school, but play with such as tell tales, tell lies, curse, swear and steal, they will come to some bad end, and must be whipt till they mend their ways.[55]

WEBSTER'S SOURCES

According to his own admission, Webster used the spelling books of Dilworth and Fenning in writing the first edition of his own spelling book. He also acknowledged using the dictionary of Samuel Johnson as his source for spelling and accentuation (a work he would one day take pains to repudiate), and mentions the grammar of Bishop Lowth. The only other source identified by Webster in his first edition was *Lectures on Elocution* by the English author Thomas Sheridan. Like Webster, Sheridan had devised a numerical scheme to indicate pronunciation in another work, his *Rhetorical Grammar*, available in an American imprint in 1783.[56] But Webster's key is by no means identical, and he would later claim not to have seen Sheridan's key until after he had completed his own first edition. If this is true (and it seems more likely to be true than not), Webster's key was the more remarkable in being of his own devising.

"Dilworth's Ghost" Controversy. If it is a little difficult for us to disentangle just what Webster's sources were, his contemporaries had many fewer doubts: charges of plagiarism were leveled at Webster in the context of a heated newspaper controversy. The controversy related both to the sources Webster had used and to the innovations he had made, and is reviewed here as a gauge to what Webster's contemporaries thought of his spelling book and of his grammar, which was published in March 1784.[57]

The opening salvo of the crossfire was a letter to a Hartford paper in June, 1784; it was signed, appropriately, "Dilworth's Ghost." (The author is believed to have been a former New York City schoolmaster named Hughes.[58]) Although Webster had the advantage of being a body, said Dilworth's Ghost, "yet have you not been able, even to transcribe and compile (for Transcribing and Compiling make the Bulk of your 'Institute') without a numerous Catalogue of Mistakes, &c." Dilworth's Ghost claimed that Webster's plan for syllable division had been previously suggested by others. He also ridiculed Webster for attempting to fix a standard of pronunciation, on the grounds that language was mutable. In addition, the Ghost trusted that Webster's equanimity would not be disturbed, "as you claim the Protection of the Law for what you *call your own* . . . should one of Doctor Lowth's Proxies—Ash's, Sheridan's, or Kenricks [sic], &c. &c. Agents commence an Action against you for Plagiarism, or *what is really theirs?*"[59] Webster responded to this that he would only take notice of such a publication if the author subscribed his real name, avoided scurrility, and expressed himself in grammatical language.[60]

Another unidentified writer, this one giving himself the pseudonym "Thomas Dilworth," wrote in Webster's support. "I am happy to see later writers improve on mine," commented this new Dilworth, and mentioned Lowth, Ash, Sheridan and Perry by name as among those who "had made many judicious remarks on the English language . . . [Yet] no one had attempted to reduce their observations to use for the benefit of schools, or to compile a Spelling-Book on a similar plan," until Webster.[61]

While this debate appeared to be focused simply on the

issue of Webster's little books, Webster himself thought
otherwise. Retreating from his position of disdaining an answer
until his antagonist identified himself, he wrote a lengthy letter
to the *New York Journal* in his own defense. He there suggested
that his political activities on behalf of the Federal government
had made him "some personal enemies who acknowledge my
influence by seeking revenge." He also answered the Ghost's
accusations point by point, calling upon older authors to bolster
his view that language became stationary once it had reached a
peak of perfection. As to the charge of his "compiling and
transcribing," Webster claimed that every grammar was a
compilation. He used stronger language to rebut the charge that
his syllable division had been suggested by someone else. "What
a barefaced assertion! I never knew till the Ghost informed me
that the attempt had been made." He had only made the
innovation after he had been assured by "the most eminent
scholars in America" that he might safely make the change. He
also denied that he had used the works of Sheridan, Perry or
Kenrick for his pronunciation key. "I have only to observe on
this point that I was wholly unacquainted with those authors till
after I had published the first edition. Entick's Pocket Dictionary
was the only work of the kind that I consulted while I was
compiling it!" He had acknowledged the assistance of these
authors for his second edition in the preface to that edition.[62]

More letters followed in various Connecticut newspapers,
some in oppositon to (of whom one signed himself "Entity")[63]
and some in support of, Webster's books.[64] Webster himself,
however, was not roused to respond until he was again attacked
by "Dilworth's Ghost," who charged that Webster, by publishing
a second edition of his spelling book, had acknowledged that the
first one was defective. He also assailed Webster's adaptation of
Fenning's story of Tommy and Harry for being flat and
repetitious.[65] Taking on all comers—"The Ghost has transmi-
grated into an *Entity* . . . . Probably the third form he will assume
will be a *non-entity*"—Webster wrote:

> I am under ten thousand obligations to that restless
> spirit, for his spiteful attempts to depreciate my
> publications. Had not his scurrilous remarks appeared,
> people would have taken less pains to examine, the
> design, the plan and the merit of the Institute. The

result of a critical examination has generally been in its favour, not only in Connecticut, but in other States, where people cannot be supposed to be partial.[66]

Other attacks followed, one of which accused Webster of "sanctimony" because of his scruples against using the name of the Deity in his spelling book.[67] Webster answered all these onslaughts in another long letter, which appeared on February 1, 1785. In it, he voiced a concern that some people had suspected that "I, or some friend of mine, wrote it [Dilworth's Ghost's first piece] with a view to excite public attention and increase the sale of my books." Webster denied this, as well he might, and absolved himself of the charge of "arrogance" in his choice of title, by saying, truthfully, that he had not given it that name himself: "it was christened by the gentleman who presides over literature in Connecticut [Dr. Ezra Stiles of Yale]." Perhaps his "arrogance" lay in not altering the title, added Webster ruefully: ". . . it may prejudice the work more than I imagine." As to his making a second edition, said Webster, "I ever thought, Sir, that it was the part of an honest man to correct his faults as fast as he found them." Dilworth's Ghost had suggested that Webster return people's money for his defective first edition.

> I thought then, and still think, that the *first* edition was much better than Dilworth's, and consequently the purchaser's money was well employed. Several thousand purchasers have thought the same; for not only the *first*, but the *second*, and several thousand copies of the *third* edition are sold, amounting in the whole to above 12,000 copies.

To remove all grounds of complaint, however, he enclosed some money to compensate Dilworth's Ghost for his supposed loss.[68]

Some of Webster's replies shed an informative light on his bookselling activities before his famous tour, which he would start in May of 1785. It is clear that he had sent his grammar, the second part of the *Institute*, to London for review, and that he now felt called upon to defend himself for selling his own books in the towns where he had been a schoolmaster.

> But you say that I have retailed the books in towns where I formerly kept school. Indeed, Sir, being on a

visit to see a sister in the western part of the state, at the particular request of some friends I carried a few books; some I gave to my friends, and some I sold . . . .

"I have trespassed on the generosity of friends," said Webster sarcastically, "and *consequently* my books are poor things." Then, citing "Dilworth's Ghost's" own comments on Dilworth's *New Guide,* Webster continued:

You say, "It proved a very pretty thing, for it has passed through forty editions" since its first publication, which is about forty years. This is an irresistible argument that the *New Guide* is the best book in the world, and mine is good for nothing. I have only to observe that unless you retard the sale of the *Institute* . . . it must, at the present rate of selling, pass through more than a hundred editions in the same period of time.

(On his copy of this newspaper, Noah Webster added a note some thirty years later: "AD 1818. The work has passed through twice that number.") We also learn from this letter that Webster's books had been introduced into all the New England states; that someone in the West Indies had applied for a gross; that Webster had had a request from South Carolina for several thousand; and that Hudson & Goodwin were selling from 500 to 1,000 copies of the speller a week.[69]

In what was in essence a continuation of the same letter, two weeks later, Webster defended his Tommy and Harry story, discussed various grammatical points, and reiterated his statement that he had "never heard the names of Sheridan, Kenrick or Perry" until he had published his first edition. He continued with a peroration on the lines of "history shall decide," which would be a blueprint for many such utterances in the years to come.

Proud and arrogant as you represent me, I have not a single wish to impose any thing on my countrymen. I offer them what I esteem a better system of education than that which has been generally used; and they have a sovereign right of receiving or rejecting it at their pleasure . . . . If the system I have proposed is on the whole good, neither printing errors nor your own petulant errors can overturn it. But if upon the whole it shall be found not preferable to those which have gone before it, you may be assured, Sir, that it will fall into neglect and oblivion without your assistance.

When I first formed the design, I had not an idea of deriving any pecuniary advantage even from success. And when I found I might make the work beneficial to myself, I set on foot a plan for procuring laws to secure to authors the copyright of their productions. In pursuance of the plan I have expended some time and much money....

With that ability to foretell the future that would be one of his hallmarks, Webster added, "and to me, among others, future writers... will be indebted for the security of their literary property." Webster's final word was an appeal to the republican spirit. If his books were only as good as European schoolbooks, which would Americans prefer? As for himself, he said, "I have too much pride to stand indebted to Great Britain for books to learn [sic] our children the letters of the alphabet."[70]

EDITIONS OF THE SPELLING BOOK IN 1787, 1804 AND 1818

It is convenient to treat here Webster's later editions of his spelling book, up to his entirely new edition of 1829, when he abandoned the title *American Spelling Book* altogether. As might be expected, his revisions were related to the exigencies of the copyright law. The first national copyright law was passed in the United States in 1790; it gave to authors the right to their own works for fourteen years, renewable for another fourteen. After Webster's initial edition in 1783, he made major revisions in 1787, when he was in Philadelphia, and republished the book under the title of *The American Spelling Book*. In 1804, when his first copyright expired under the new law, he revised the book again, and this version is called *The American Spelling Book*, "revised impression (or "revised copy"). This new copyright expired in 1818, when Webster was deeply involved in his dictionary. He therefore renewed the copyright after making minimal alterations. This last version, whose copyright extended to 1832, was identified as *The American Spelling Book*, "the revised impression," and usually has the addition of the words "with the latest corrections."[71]

Webster's bibliographer, Emily Skeel, has pointed out, however, that while the editions can be grouped into these three major versions of 1783, 1787, and 1804 (that of 1818 being virtually unchanged from the 1804 edition), nearly every edition, until the introduction of stereotyping, contained minor additions, corrections, deletions, and alterations, whether initiated by Webster or his printers.[72] Individual words in the "tables" were particularly vulnerable to change.

In many ways the revision of 1787 was the most far-reaching of any edition until that of 1829. Some changes seem to have been motivated by suggestions from Webster's friends, and some by his own reactions to the criticisms he had received from those who were not so friendly to him. One friendly correspondent, a schoolmaster who said he used the *Institute* for virtually all his lessons, wrote Webster in May, 1788,

> Do you not think that a few easy fables; and familiar allegories, where the application is so readily understood, that while the little mind is delighted with the story, it cannot fail of being benefited by the moral, would render it [the speller] more serviceable than it now is?"[73]

Webster had in fact anticipated this very just criticism by his revision in 1787, which his correspondent had obviously not seen. For the first time, in the 1787 spelling book, we see the eight fables, with illustrative woodcuts, that subsequent generations of schoolchildren would remember so well. The first fable depicts a boy in an apple tree, and begins, "An old Man found a rude Boy upon one of his trees stealing Apples . . . ." When the boy responds neither to words not tufts of grass, the old man says, "I must try what virtue there is in stones," which makes the boy climb down from the tree in a hurry. "MORAL," finishes the tale. "If good words and gentle means will not reclaim the wicked, they must be dealt with in a more severe manner."[74] The tough moral stance that this indicates would characterize Webster's ethical views all his life.

In addition to adding the fables to his 1787 revision, Webster reorganized the contents of the speller, placing the reading lessons among the tables, so that "No man may put off the law of God" now appeared early in the book. Webster also added to this edition a few proverbs, such as "Hot love is soon cold." His tables were improved and expanded, and he now indicated secondary stress, as well as primary stress, on polysyllables. He responded to the criticisms of the Tommy and Harry story by dropping it altogether, and substituted dull paragraphs about a "good boy" and a "bad boy." He also included an account of the creation of the world, which began, "In six days God made the world." One important change that Webster made could be attributed to his enemies rather than his friends: he abandoned President Stiles' unfortunate title, *A Grammatical Institute*, and returned to his original conception of the nationalistic title, naming the revision *The American Spelling Book*.[75]

Another new edition in 1804 produced no dramatic changes. The structure of the work is essentially the same; there are some alterations (chiefly additions) to the tables. The proverbs added in the previous edition are abandoned in this—they were presumably considered too frivolous. The "Hot love is soon cold" lesson now begins "The time will come when we must all be laid in the dust."[76]

The most notable difference from the 1787 edition is the inclusion of reading material which reflects the fact that Webster was, in 1804, the father of six children, Emily, Julia, Harriet, Mary, William and Eliza, born between 1790 and 1803. Each child has a portion of text with his or her name in it. "WILLIAM, tell me how many mills make a cent? Ten.—How many cents a dime? Ten." In a passage titled, "The Sisters," each sister recites a poem.

> Emily, look at the flowers in the garden. What a charming sight.... Julia, rise in the morning betimes, dress the borders of the flower beds, pull up the noxious weeds, water the thirsty roots.... Does the heart want culture? Weed out the noxious passions from the heart, as you would hurtful plants from among the flowers.... Harriet, bring your book, let me hear you read. What book have you? Let me see: a little volume of poems.... [Then, addressing Mary,] Your little fingers are very handy with a needle.... What small stitches. You shall hem and mark all your papa's handkerchiefs, and very soon you shall work a muslin frock for yourself.

It is no mere coincidence that all the reading matter associated with boys' names is on the lines of either arithmetic, or good behavior, or both ("John, keep your seat, and sit still. You must not say a word, nor laugh, nor play.... Charles, can you count?"), while the girls are associated with flowers, poetry, tidying chores, and needlework. This too would be a faithful predictor of Webster's views on differential education for each sex and was, of course, the widespread view of the time.[77]

Given the changes Webster made over the years in his spelling book, it is worth looking, once again, at one of the constants in the book—the famous first reading lesson. For generations it would be remembered by the young as their first introduction to reading, as opposed to spelling. "And what a day that was," wrote one who learned to read from Webster's spelling book, reminiscing in 1890 about his youth,

> when we stood on the hilltop of human greatness and grappled with our first reading lesson!
> 'No man may put off the law of God;
> My joy is in his law all the day.'
> See that boy in his mighty wrestlings to spell out the words! Lips move vigorously; brow knit; book turned this way and that, to give room for the great idea to come in; his whole frame writhing and screwed down hard and tight to the supreme task. Perhaps he will "fetch it," perhaps not....[78]

Or, as Thomas Palmer, who by no means felt so warmly toward his first reading experience, described it in 1840,

> Let us examine a line with which we are all familiar—the initiatory sentence in Webster's old spelling book.... The manner in which we were taught to read this—and this manner still prevails in most of the schools—was as follows: 'En-o, No, emm-ai-en, man, emm-ai-wy, may, pee-you-tee, put, o-double eff, off, tee-aitch-ee, the, ell-ai-double you, law, o-eff, of, gee-o-dee, God.'[79]

A GRAMMATICAL INSTITUTE, PART II AND PART III

It is not possible to discuss the second and third parts of the *Institute* (the grammar and reader) in any detail here. Like the speller, Webster's grammar was offered as a rival to Dilworth's, for as we have seen, Dilworth's *A New Guide* had a section devoted to a discussion of grammar. Webster criticized earlier authors for superimposing Latin constructions upon English, and said that the merit of his own grammar lay in the fact that he was shedding the trappings of Latin grammar. He objected, for example, to the notion that English nouns decline. Instead, said Webster correctly, whether nouns were in what others had called the "nominative" or "objective" case was actually a function of their position before or after a verb.[80] Nonetheless, despite his criticisms, Webster's grammar bears many more similarities than dissimilarities to its English predecessors.

Webster's purpose in composing his reader was genuinely original. He aimed to put within the reach of schoolchildren a collection of speeches and writings like James Burgh's *Art of Speaking*, that had been available to colleges or academies but was too big and too expensive for younger students. Instead, children had all too often graduated from the spelling book to the Bible; Webster deplored the use of the latter as a school text.[81] The content of his reader was very mixed. After eleven chapters of "select sentences" from Swift, Shakespeare and Johnson, there were a couple of stories lifted from an Edinburgh newspaper; Webster's own (but unacknowledged) "Character of Juliana" (presumably inspired by Juliana Smith, who thought less well of Webster than he of her); two unattributed extracts from the unpublished epics of Joel Barlow and Timothy Dwight; various chunks from Shakespeare, and two Congressional addresses. The book ends with an extract from a letter by Thomas Day, which states that men should admit the consequences of their own principles and argued that Americans were "reduced to the dilemma of either acknowledging the rights of your Negroes, or of surrendering your own."[82]

Neither the grammar nor the reader was destined to achieve the popularity of the first part of the *Institute*. Webster's grammar "had its run," as Webster put it in 1807, "but has been superseded by [Lindley] Murray's."[83] Webster's reader, too, was vanquished. Its first successor was *The American Preceptor*, written by the Bostonian Caleb Bingham in 1794.[84] This in turn succumbed to another work by Lindley Murray, *The English Reader*, which was available to Americans after 1799.[85] It is the more remarkable that Webster's reader never became the leading book in its field, because, at the time it appeared, it had no competitor. It was, in fact, a pioneer work in a type of text that was rapidly recognized as an essential element in a school's curriculum.[86]

III

Family Life and Financial Problems
1783 to 1818

By the time the second part of the *Grammatical Institute* had come off the press in March 1784, Webster was back in Hartford and unemployed. He had a few court cases in the summer; otherwise, he seems to have been without an income. He passed time pleasantly enough by sending off volleys of letters to local newspapers, either unsigned or under a pseudonym. One batch was on the hotly disputed topic of congressional commutation: Congress had voted to commute the half-pay promised Revolutionary officers to five years' pay in a lump sum.[1] In another batch, Webster again made some "Observations on the Revolution of America."[2] These, and pseudonymous articles like them, discussing controversial issues of politics and economics, would pour off Webster's pen for the whole of his life.[3] He was selective about what he signed his name to: as we have seen, he did sign his name to several letters in the Dilworth controversy. He also published under his own name, early in 1785, a document titled *Sketches of American Policy*, which was a strong statement in favor of allocating more power to the central government.[4]

Meanwhile, the spelling book was selling very nicely. As we have seen, by January 1785, Webster was able to claim that over 12,000 copies had been sold. This was clearly a promising start. That same month, Hudson & Goodwin were busy selling the third edition of the speller, and in February they were able to advertise the reader, the third part of the *Grammatical Institute*, as ready for sale.[5] Webster, with his three-volume work now complete, made the necessary preparations for a long trip. Like so much else he had done in the previous year or so, this would be a foretaste of things to come.

A TOUR, MAY 1785 TO NOVEMBER 1786

On May 2, 1785, Webster left Hartford on the first leg of an eighteen-month tour. He had shipped copies of the *Institute* ahead to Baltimore and Charleston. The trip, which Webster recounted in a daily journal, was undertaken with two purposes in mind.[6] In the first place, Webster wanted to extend the copyright protection which had already been won in most of the eastern and middle states; and secondly, he wished to promote the *Grammatical Institute* in the middle and southern states.

Webster traveled to New Haven, then New York and Philadelphia by various conveyances, which ranged from horseback to carriage. By May 13 he was in Baltimore, and by the 19th in Alexandria, Virginia. There he laid before a member of the legislature, David Stuart, his proposals for copyright legislation. (Far in the future, Webster's son, William, would one day marry Stuart's daughter Rosalie.)[7] That same afternoon, Webster proceeded to Mount Vernon, home of General George Washington where, according to Webster's own account, he was "treated with great attention" and spent the night. (He played whist with the General and his wife, "who is very social.")[8]

After this heady introduction to the most important man in the country, young Webster returned to Baltimore, where he listened to Dr. Moyes lecture on sounds. The experience would lead him, somewhat later, to design his own series of lectures as a source of badly needed income. At the time, however, he turned to the hope of financial aid provided by his usual standby, teaching, and placed an advertisement in a local newspaper for a school where his pupils were to engage in the "Study of our native Language."[9] Baltimore was central enough to serve him as a base for operations, and he was obviously not planning on opening the school immediately, for he set out from Baltimore a few days later on a sea voyage south to Charleston. In Charleston, Webster set his books out for sale, advertised them in local newspapers, and registered the *Grammatical Institute* in the Secretary's office. He had begun "those activities," as his bibliographer and great-grand-daughter put it, "for pushing his books into notice, which eventually became a life-long pattern."[10] He presented the Mount Sion Society with 200 copies of the first part and 100 copies of the second part, of the *Institute*.[11] An announcement of his donation appeared in the newspaper (it was almost certainly put there by Webster himself): "Three hundred copies... by the ingenious Mr. Webster to the Mount Sion Society for the benefit of Winnsborough College."[12] He also visited the local grammar school and gave the gentlemen in charge of it some examination copies of the *Institute.*[13]

Back in Baltimore on July 15, Webster opened a singing school.[14] At the end of August, he decided to try his hand at lecturing, and from August 25 to October 6, he wrote a series of "remarks on the English Language," to be presented as five lectures.[15] When he began his lectures, charging a fee for admission, they were successful enough to embolden him to go on a lecture tour around the country. He set off again for Virginia, once again visiting with General Washington. Washington provided him with letters of introduction to the Governor of Virginia and to the Speakers of both houses, to further his quest for copyright legislation.[16]

By November 17, Webster was reading his first lecture to an audience of thirty people in no less grand a setting than the Capitol in Richmond, Virginia.[17] New Year's Day, 1786, found him in Annapolis, Maryland, where he again read his lectures in the State House. He wrote to Timothy Pickering, as he made his way back to Baltimore, that he had finished his business in those states, "having secured the copyright of my works and introduced them into schools. I have also read Lectures in the Principal Towns in Virginia and Maryland...."[18] At the end of January, Webster set off for Dover, the capital of Delaware, where he presented a petition to the Assembly for a copyright law for himself.[19]

Now he proceeded north to Philadelphia. There he met the aged Benjamin Franklin, whose permission was needed as President of the Trustees of the University in order for Webster to use a room in the university for his lectures.[20] The two men had much in common. Decades earlier, Franklin had printed primers and spelling books. In addition, he had always been interested in exploring ways to mitigate the difficulties of English spelling, and had invented a phonetic alphabet.[21] The meeting proved to be the start of a rather touching friendship— in view of the huge disparity in their ages—between Webster and Franklin. Webster was inspired by their encounter to ponder about forming a phonetic alphabet, although it would be May before he actually committed it to paper.[22]

Another fruitful meeting in Philadelphia was a dinner with Colonel Timothy Pickering, who had first written to Webster the previous October.[23] Before he had even met Webster, Pickering had done what many friends —and relatives— of Webster would do: he had used his personal influence to attempt to introduce the first two parts of the *Grammatical Institute* into a local school, in this case the recently opened Episcopal Academy of Philadelphia. Pickering had reported a poor reception at the time: "One of the trustees informed me they were fearful of injuring the school if they should introduce a spelling book with which the people were totally unacquainted."[24] His remarks are indicative of the kind of difficulties that Webster was facing in introducing his textbooks. Pickering proved as valuable in person as he had on paper. "One of the best of men—" wrote Webster in his diary.[25]

In Philadelphia, Webster started his course of lectures, giving one every other day.[26] On March 19 he gave a farewell dinner for his Philadelphia friends and set off in the direction of his home. He went by way of Trenton, New Jersey, and New York, then detoured to Albany, everywhere lecturing and registering the *Institute* under the states' copyright laws. At the end of May he was at last back in Hartford, dining with his good friend Joel Barlow.[27] He had been on the road for thirteen months. The attendance at his lectures made him sanguine of success: "There is no longer a doubt that I shall be able to effect a uniformity of language & education throughout the continent."[28]

Far from being content to relax after his arduous tour, Webster set off again after only a short stay, this time to the east. He paid a call on Isaiah Thomas, the printer and publisher, in Worcester.[29] Webster was still lecturing: from July to October he gave his lectures in Boston, Salem, Portsmouth, and after a reprise in Boston, went on to deliver the series in Newbury Port, Providence, Newport, New London and Norwich.[30]

Back home in Hartford on November 1, Webster assigned the copyright of his *Institute* for the New England area to his old publishers, Hudson & Goodwin, "for the whole term granted me by the laws of the several states."[31] If Hudson & Goodwin thought that, by this assignment, they would be spared Webster's constant oversight of his books, they were soon to be disillusioned.

Webster's promotional and lecture tour of the United States

had lasted fully eighteen months: it had kept him on the road from May 2, 1785 until November 1, 1786. It proved to be a precursor of many similar trips that Webster would take throughout his long life. By any standards, this first one had to be judged a success. It certainly was so on the personal level: after all, he had made the acquaintance, and in some cases even won the friendship, of some of the most influential men in the country. It was also a success on a professional level: he had used the time to promote his textbooks in a variety of ways, as well as to secure their protection by copyright legislation. It might even be considered a success at a national level: for Webster's championship of copyright laws was of assistance in persuading every state in the Union, with the exception of Delaware, to pass some kind of copyright legislation by January 1787.[32] And even Delaware, thanks to Webster's urging, had appointed a committee to introduce a bill on copyright by March.[33] All in all, it was a good start for someone who had been an unknown country schoolmaster, and a none too successful lawyer, only two years earlier.

Ironically, there was one level on which Webster's tour had not been of permanent value to him—the financial. Despite everything that happened, he was still a man without a job or a regular income. At the end of November, he set off again for the middle states, "to seek a living."[34]

WEBSTER THE PATRIOT, 1787 TO 1789

Webster tarried in New York until the end of December, and it was not until Christmas Day that he set off from there for Philadelphia, to keep an appointment with Benjamin Franklin that he had already postponed for three months.[35] He visited Franklin three days later.[36] Webster would make his home in Philadelphia until the following October.

His earlier discussions with Franklin soon bore some fruit: Webster gave a lecture at Philadelphia in February, 1787, on reforming the English alphabet.[37] He and Franklin had frequent meetings.[38] From April on, he kept himself financially solvent by teaching first math, then English, at Philadelphia's Episcopal Academy—the institution that had looked so askance at his new spelling book eighteen months earlier.[39]

Controversies that occurred during Webster's stay in

Philadelphia illustrate the ambiguous position he held in the
public esteem, and the antagonism he aroused as a young man, in
both the political and educational arenas. In a letter published as
from "a Citizen of Philadelphia," Webster opposed the funding
of domestic debt. The letter drew forth a volley of others, both
in support and in opposition to the proposed fund. As was the
custom of the day, authors of an unpopular viewpoint were
treated as roughly as their views.[40] Meanwhile, Webster was
attacked from another quarter, by a former teacher at the
Episcopal Academy, who, under the pseudonym "Seth," satirically
sympathized with Webster, who "had been flourishing through
the United States with lectures and a new grammatical
publication," but had now "suddenly sunk into the humble
office of a teacher of children!"[41] Webster, under the pseudonym
"Adam," defended himself, as he also did under his own
signature when the third edition of his grammar came in for
some harsh criticism in yet another set of letters to the local
press.[42] The charges against Webster of vanity that were a
common thread in all these separate, but certainly interrelated,
controversies were not dissipated by Webster's turns of phrase.
In defending himself in the funding dispute, for example, he
wrote the following:

> Had I not a thousand testimonials of my patriotism,
> love of government and justice; had I not written the
> substance of volumes in support of the Revolution and
> of federal measures; had I not crushed, almost with my
> single pen, a state combination against those measures;
> did not almost every weekly or other publication in
> America contain proofs of my sentiments . . . . I might
> have had some apprehensions from the malevolent
> charges and suspicions of the *Pennsylvanian*.[43]

News of the controversies in Philadelphia made their way
back to Webster's home. "I have had a hint Son from some
Gentlemen and some Newspapers as though you had made some
unfriendly to you by some of your writings and done yourself
damage," wrote his father. He counseled his son to temper
courage with prudence.[44] How well Webster took this advice to
heart may be gauged by a story propagated years later, on the
subject of Webster's 1787 arrival in Philadelphia. Dr. Benjamin
Rush, who would become a close friend of Webster, thanks to

their correspondence on Webster's history of epidemic diseases, is said to have met Webster and cried, "How do you do, my dear friend. I congratulate you on your arrival to Philadelphia." Webster, according to the story, replied, "Sir, you may congratulate Philadelphia on the occasion."[45]

If Webster was publicly abused in the Philadelphia press, he was faring much better on a personal level. On March 1st, 1787 he was introduced to a young woman with the romantic name of Rebecca Greenleaf. Rebecca actually lived in Boston but was visiting a sister in Philadelphia. By the time Rebecca left at the end of June, she and Noah had what used to be known as an "understanding."[46] Their prospects for an early marriage were not good, as Webster had no assured income or settled place of residence.

With Rebecca gone back home, Webster had more time to spend on his other interests; he oversaw the first Philadelphia edition of his spelling book. This was a thoroughly revised edition, the seventh in terms of the total editions that had appeared so far, and it was called, in tune with the excitement of the locale, *The American Spelling Book.*[47] He also published an "amended and improved" edition of the *New England Primer.*[48]

Webster was to be given the opportunity to use his gifts as a writer to further the cause of the American government. For Philadelphia, from mid-May to mid-September 1787, was the scene of the Constitutional Convention, which under the strictest conditions of secrecy, was hammering out the new Constitution of the United States. General Washington was presiding officer over the delegates' anguished debates.

When the constitution was finally finished, and a propagandist sought for it, Thomas Fitzsimmons, a member of the federal convention, turned to Webster for help. He wrote ask Webster to exert himself "as a friend to your Country."[49] It was Webster's *Sketches of American Policy*, published in 1785, that had brought him to the attention of the members of the Constitutional Convention, as well as to the public at large.[50] Fitzsimmons' plea did not, of course, fall on deaf ears. In a remarkably short space of time, Webster wrote his *An Examination into the Leading Principles of the Federal Constitution.*[51] It appeared in October, just before he left Philadelphia for New York, having spent some of his last evenings there with Benjamin Franklin.[52] The essay was attributed to "a citizen of America." (Presumably Webster wished to avoid antagonizing the public by using his own name.) His tract was credited with helping to create a climate favorable to the adoption of the new constitution.

Webster now engaged in the extraordinarily ambitious undertaking of publishing a magazine out of New York City.[53] Titled *The American Magazine*, the journal was a compendium of news, articles and stories of all kinds. It was an enormously expensive undertaking, and Webster financed it initially by selling the rights of the spelling book to Samuel Campbell of New York for five years.[54] The magazine did not prosper and by the following December, 1788, Webster was "happy to quit New York."[55] Despite his preoccupation with the magazine, he had found time to begin a "Philological Society" in New York,[56] and had rashly undertaken to assist his friend Jedediah Morse in writing a geography for schoolchildren.[57] He also managed to fit in a swing through New England in the spring of 1788, to see how his books were faring.

December 1788 found Webster in Boston, close to Rebecca. Ever able to combine business with love, he put the revised version of his lectures to the press, now titled *Dissertations on the English Language*. He dedicated the book to Franklin.[58]

Webster was now thirty years old and anxious to marry Rebecca. Her brother, Noah's friend James Greenleaf, whose mercantile business with Europe appeared to be flourishing, wrote to Webster from Amsterdam that he was concerned that his sister should be supported in the manner to which she was accustomed.[59] He, with others, encouraged Webster to return to Hartford to practice law in earnest. In the spring, when Webster did indeed return to Hartford, James generously gave him a thousand dollars to set up house.[60] "I have taken a house in the center of the town & of business," reported Webster, "where I hope to find a home & domestic happiness. It is impossible for me to foresee my fate; but judging by the success of other beginners, I calculate upon getting a living the third or fourth year, til which time, I must depend in great measure on my books."[61]

Early in October, Webster wrote Rebecca that he was getting ready to "recieve [sic] *my bride*. Becca, does your little heart flutter at the name?" He expected some palpitations for his own, he said, "for, my sweet girl, knows how we poor grave bachelors feel on such occasions."[62] On October 19, he left

Hartford for Boston "on an important errand," as he informed his diary.[63]

Four days later the whole of Boston turned out to greet President George Washington, who was paying the city a ceremonial visit. Webster was not among them. Smitten by flu— or was it pre-wedding nerves?—he recovered just in time for his wedding day, October 26, 1789. "I am united to an amiable woman," he confided to his journal, "& if I am not happy, shall be much disappointed."[64]

The newlyweds left Boston for their new home in Hartford. Not everyone was sanguine about their prospects of financial security. "Webster has returned," a friend wrote from Hartford to Oliver Wolcott, Webster's Yale classmate, "and brought with him a very pretty wife. I wish him success, but I doubt in the present decay of business in our profession, whether his profits will enable him to keep up the style he sets out with. I fear he will breakfast upon Institutes, dine upon Dissertations, and go to bed supperless."[65]

HUSBAND AND AUTHOR

On November 7, 1789, Noah and Rebecca Webster began their married lives together in their Hartford home.[66] Webster borrowed $200 from his brother-in-law, James, to purchase books for his law library. Although his legal practice was making a slow start, this was a prolific period for Webster as an author. He sent off a battery of articles to the papers, ranging from comments on women's education to the excise laws of Connecticut. When Benjamin Franklin died in April of the following year, Webster published in the *American Mercury* the long letter Franklin had written him in praise of his *Dissertations*, as part of a series of fourteen articles on the corruptions and errors which prevailed in the English language.[67]

That same year, 1790, saw a number of publications of Webster's on a variety of topics. In March, *Rudiments of English Grammar* appeared (it was to serve as an introduction to his larger grammar); in June, Thomas & Andrews published his *A Collection of Essays and Fugitiv* [sic] *Writings*, which was based on articles that had already appeared in newspapers during his lecture tour.[68] (Parts of this were printed in very innovative spelling, which was destined to be poorly received.) In July Webster financed the printing of Governor John Winthrop's *Journal*, and in October saw his small book, *The Little Reader's Assistant*, come off the press.[69] He intended it to be a transitional book between his spelling book and the reader. He also wrote a number of essays in homely, Franklin-style prose, which he published anonymously under the title *The Prompter*.[70] His motives for this secrecy on his authorship were surely those he had expressed to President George Washington on a different topic. Asking for his communication to be kept secret, Webster said that "any doctrines I might advance, under the signature of my name, would not meet the consideration they might deserve . . . . The prejudices of many men are against me. I have written much more than any other man of my age in favor of the Revolution and my country, and at times my opinions have been unpopular."[71]

Webster's other activities lie outside the scope of this book. He wrote on the utility of banks, discussed the economic conditions of Connecticut, and involved himself in such causes as the establishment of a charitable society on behalf of the families of laborers who had died in job-related accidents. He also became active in the Hartford anti-slavery society and served as its secretary in 1792. He was elected to the Hartford Common Council for two successive years, in 1792 and 1793.

Despite such hard work on so broad a range of fronts, Webster found himself deeply in debt. He had lost $400 on the publication of the *Dissertations*, and by July 1793 had debts amounting to some $1,815.[72] James Greenleaf and some of Webster's other friends began making overtures in New York to Federalists there, to see if Webster could publish a newspaper in the Federalist cause. They were successful, and in September 1793 Webster formed a business partnership with George Bunce. Bunce was to print the paper; Webster was to be its editor. In addition, Webster would be able to supervise personally the publication of his spelling book, grammar and reader, as Samuel Campbell's license to print them in New York had just expired.

Webster and his family, who now included his daughters Emily, born in August 1790, and Julia, born early in 1793, moved to New York. On December 9 Webster noted in his diary, "Begin a Daily Paper."[73]

WEBSTER AS A NEW YORK NEWSPAPER EDITOR, 1793 TO 1798

The *American Minerva* was a four-page sheet and was the first daily newspaper in New York City. For five years, through its columns, Webster supported the policies of the Washington administration, covered the excesses of the French Revolution, and included articles that ranged from city planning to forest conservation.[74]

Webster had difficulties with the printing side of the paper from the first. Bunce proved to be an incompetent and Webster dissolved the partnership in February 1796.[75] Webster's new partners, Hopkins and Webb, were not much of an improvement: Webb turned out to be dishonest, and yet another partnership had to be set up with Hopkins as the publisher.

While Webster was immersed in his exacting work of editing two papers (for he was also putting out a semi-weekly), he tried to oversee the publication of his textbooks. But his financial difficulties with the newspapers were increasing. "Our business was never so productive as now, but collections were never so difficult," he complained in May 1796.[76] His efforts first to publish, then to sell, his own books were also unsuccessful. He had to resort to obtaining his spellers from Hudson & Goodwin, who shipped them to him from Hartford. "The books are not all sold," Webster told the firm in January 1798, "& some which are, are not paid for, & I wish you not to draw on me at all, for I can make no promises."[77] On April 1, 1798, Webster, financially embarrassed and politically disillusioned, handed over the management of the newspapers to Hopkins and left New York for New Haven. As a commentator has said, it was a symbolic, as well as a physical, withdrawal from active involvement with the political life of his country.[78]

During the five years in which Webster managed his New York newspapers, his opinions on the American Republic had undergone a dramatic change. The young idealist and the ardent supporter of the American Revolution, who had worked for human freedom and based his beliefs on the doctrine of the Enlightenment, was now a figure of the past. The excesses of the French revolution, the rise in party and in party passions, as well as the anxiety he shared with so many others on the future of the American experiment, had altered Webster's vision of man's nature itself. "We see in our new Republic, the *decrepitude* of Vice," he wrote in 1797.[79] Richard Rollins, Webster's most recent biographer, has suggested that from this point on Webster's support of progressive social change virtually vanished.[80]

WEBSTER IN NEW HAVEN, 1798 TO 1812

Webster's choice of New Haven for his home was no accident: Connecticut was the last bastion of Federalism. There, others beside himself looked to a respect for law and order as the essence of civil liberty.[81] But however dismayed Webster was by the national scene, he nonetheless still chose to be active in local affairs. Now established in Benedict Arnold's house in New Haven, site of his alma mater, he flung himself into new activities. He was appointed a member of the school visiting committee and, dissatisfied with what he saw, organized a group of leading citizens to open a new school. The Union School opened in 1799; it was a brick schoolhouse with two rooms, one for boys and one for girls. By 1801 Webster was president of the school, which had an enrollment of fifty-two boys and sixty-three girls. Among the girls was Webster's oldest child, Emily.[82]

Webster had watched his little daughters suffer from scarlet fever in the epidemic of the spring of 1793, and had received eye witness accounts from his friend Oliver Wolcott of the terrible yellow fever epidemic that had ravaged Philadelphia that same year. Only ten days after he resettled in New Haven, he began to collect materials for a history of epidemic diseases. Webster's two-volume work appeared in 1799.[83] While his conjecture that epidemics were a result of the turbulence in the elements was incorrect, the work is today considered valuable for its pioneering emphasis on the compilation of statistics and for its historical approach. At the time, it sold a mere 200 copies and Webster lost money on the work.[84]

Once his history of epidemics had been completed, Webster was able to turn his attention back to educational matters. Mindful of the statement he had made many years before, that spelling books did not constitute the whole of a child's education, Webster embarked on yet another set of educational texts. Over the course of the next six years, he wrote three volumes on American history and geography and added a fourth in 1816. The whole series was titled *Elements of Useful Knowledge*.

The first volume, published in 1802, was, said Webster, "the beginning of a system which has been, for many years, in contemplation; but the execution of which has been heretofore delayed by other necessary employments."[85] It involved a historical and geographical account of the United States, covering the history of America up to the American Revolution. The second volume, which appeared in 1804, continued the history of the United States up to the organization of the national government in 1789.[86] His third volume, which was published another two years later, contained a historical and geographical account of Europe, Asia and Africa.[87] The fourth and last volume was not printed until 1816, and was a textbook of biology.[88]

There was still, however, an element missing from his scheme of education. When the spelling book was first published in 1783, Dr. Elizur Goodrich, of Durham, had suggested to Webster that he publish a dictionary on a similar plan.[89] Now, Webster felt, the time had come. His reorganization of the contracts for the spelling book in 1804 at least guaranteed him an income of a penny a spelling book. Since 1800 he had been preparing for the greatest and most exacting undertaking of his life, a new dictionary of the English language. In 1806, he issued a stop-gap dictionary, titled *A Compendious Dictionary*, as an earnest of what was to come. It already contained an additional 5,000 words over John Entick's *Spelling Dictionary*, on which it was based.[90] Webster marked the pronunciation of words by his placement of the accent and introduced some of his pet spelling reforms, which ranged from *theater* to *melasses*. It was largely thanks to the latter, coupled with Webster's announcement of his plans for a yet larger and more comprehensive dictionary, that the publication aroused a flurry of sarcastic comment that would have permanently discouraged another man.[91] The following year he saw through the press a small dictionary for schools, condensed from his *Compendious* dictionary.[92]

How Webster felt about his long-term plans for American education is summed up in a letter he wrote a year after his *Compendious Dictionary* appeared. "My views comprehend a *whole system* of Education—from a Spelling Book through Geography & various other subjects—to a complete Dictionary—beginning with *children* & ending with *men*." It was not fame and emolument that he sought, he said, but the introduction of permanent improvements into the language.[93]

A personal episode occurred at this time which rooted him, never a disbeliever, in Calvinistic Christianity for the rest of his long life. In December 1807 there was a revival in New Haven. Webster was rather opposed to such meetings, as he was afraid they induced "enthusiasm or fanaticism." Rebecca and the two oldest girls became involved in the revival, to his alarm, and he unsuccessfully tried to persuade them to accompany him to some Episcopal services. He did not make the break to Episcopalianism, however, as he was so reluctant to separate himself from his family in worship. A conversation with his Congregationalist pastor, the Rev. Moses Stuart, removed some of Webster's objections to Calvinism. Yet he found himself becoming more and more agitated, and unable to concentrate on his work: "at all times of the day, & in the midst of other occupations, I was suddenly seized with impressions, which call my mind irrestibly [sic] to religious concerns & to the awakening . . . . I closed my books[,] yielded to the influence, which could not be resisted or mistaken & was led by a spontaneous impulse, to repentance, prayer, & entire submission & surrender of myself to my maker & redeemer." In April, with Emily and Julia, he made a profession of faith, which he called the "most solemn and most affecting of all transactions of my life."[94] (From this moment on, Webster would look to religion as the sheet anchor in all life's vicissitudes, and as the only guarantor of the safety of the American Republic.)[95]

His new serenity of mind would stand him in good stead in the trials that were to come. Now that he was devoting himself solely to writing, he was finding it harder and harder to support his family, despite the fact that, by 1810, the speller was bringing him some $2,400 a year.[96] He had hoped to support his lexicographical work by a good income from the first three volumes of the *Elements of Useful Knowledge*.[97] This had not materialized, and he now made a vigorous effort to raise money for his work by soliciting subscriptions. He only succeeded in getting an advance from a few interested persons, and what he thought was the first of three installments turned out to be the last of one.[98] As he wrote to a friend early in 1811, "My own resources are almost exhausted & in a few days I shall sell my house to get bread for my children. All the assurances of aid which I had rec^d . . . have failed & I am soon to retire to a humble cottage in the country."[99]

WEBSTER IN AMHERST, 1812 TO 1818

The site for Webster's cottage in the country was Amherst, Massachusetts, where he moved in September 1812. His family now numbered seven children, of whom the three youngest had been born in New Haven: Mary in 1799; William Greenleaf, his only surviving son, in 1801; and his fifth daughter, Eliza, in 1805. An infant son had survived only nine weeks in 1806, and Webster's last daughter, Louisa, born in 1808, was tragically mentally retarded as a result of an illness. The older girls were by no means happy to leave the bustling college center of New Haven, but their beaux pursued them to Amherst. By 1816 the three oldest were all married: Emily to William Wolcott Ellsworth, Julia to Chauncey A. Goodrich, and Harriet to Edward Cobb. In 1818, Mary married Horatio Southgate, a widower in Portland with four children.[100]

In Amherst, Webster experimented with crops in his ten acres of land, and doggedly pursued his tracing of twenty different languages to their roots. He still found time for local affairs, running successfully for a seat in the Massachusetts legislature in 1814. He took an active part in the First Congregational Church, organizing, with his older daughters, the choir. Somehow he also found time and energy to be one of the moving spirits behind the foundation of Amherst Academy, now Amherst College. It was he who gave the oration when the cornerstone was laid in 1820.[101]

A decision that Webster made in November 1815 made a material difference in his involvement with the sales of his books. His 1804 copyright, which was paying him a cent per spelling book, was due to expire in March 1818. Under the United States 1790 copyright law, it was renewable by the author for another fourteen years. Webster was in urgent need of cash, and made the decision that his work on the dictionary would proceed better if he divorced himself entirely from the whole process of keeping an eye on the sale of his books. He also hoped to provide a profession for his only son, William. In November 1815, Webster made a preliminary draft of a letter that he planned to send to his publishers. In it, he offered to sell the spelling book for the whole term of fourteen years to just one purchaser. He was still asking a cent a copy. "Many publishers have made estates from it already, while at times, I have not had the means of subsistence. As the work has a sale which was perhaps never before known, in any country, it is but reasonable that I should derive more profit from it than I have hitherto done." He pointed out that the average sales of the *American Spelling Book* for the previous eleven years had been 241,000 annually, and that for the last two years it had averaged 286,000 a year. It would rise, he predicted, to some 300,000 annually. He would give the contract, he wrote, to whomever made the best offer.[102]

Hudson & Goodwin had been his first publishers, and had now been printing the spelling book continuously for over thirty years. It was to George Goodwin, of that firm, that Webster made the first offer.[103] Hudson & Co., as the firm had become, was not slow to take advantage of it. On April 19, 1816, Barzillai Hudson and Henry Hudson signed, with Webster, a contract which gave them "sole & exclusive right of printing, publishing & vending" the *American Spelling Book* for a term of fourteen years, beginning March 14, 1818. Webster's son, William, now fourteen, was to be an apprentice or clerk to the firm until the age of twenty-one, with a view to becoming a partner. In return for the sole rights to the spelling book, Hudson & Co. was to pay Webster $3,000 annually.[104] In fact, Hudson & Co. advanced Webster $3,000 in July 1817,[105] and on April 20 the following year paid him twenty thousand dollars in advance, in full satisfaction for the entire contract.[106] It was a costly discount for Webster, for he received a total of $23,000 then, instead of a sum of $42,000 over a period of fourteen years. It was not the first time in his life that he had sacrificed future income for present needs.

His financial concerns were now alleviated, at least for the time being, and his only son was apparently positioned on the first rung of the ladder to a successful business career. Webster had reminded the public of his ongoing dictionary work the year before, in 1817, by reissuing the school dictionary that he had first put out in 1807. Now he turned his full attention to his extraordinary lexicographical endeavors.

IV

Webster the Businessman and His Speller, 1783 to 1818

In order even to begin to appreciate the efforts that Webster put into nursing his works along the road to educational and commercial success, we must return to the early years and take up Webster's activities as a promoter from the time that he first saw the three parts of the *Institute* through the press.

When the three parts of the *Institute* were initially published, between 1783 and 1785, each of them bore the rubric, "for the author."[1] At this time, the very beginning of his long career as an author of educational books, Webster was in essence his own publisher. Hudson & Goodwin had printed the first two parts of the *Institute*, Barlow & Babcock the third, but it is clear that Webster was in charge of the show. We have seen how Webster had been retailing the speller in the towns where he had once been a schoolmaster, and that he had received purchasing orders from other states.[2] It was he who had made the arrangements for sending books out of Connecticut. Early in 1784, for example, he was in touch with Isaiah Thomas of Worcester, the well-known publisher, to tell him that he would send him seven dozen copies of the first edition of the speller.[3] And it was Webster who went to New York in May 1784 to check on how the books were selling there. (He was dismayed to discover that his spellers were "kept in the box in a back room" instead of being exposed for sale.)[4] This early involvement with the business aspects of his books, coupled with a keen appreciation of the factors that enhanced or detracted from a book's sales, would characterize Webster's entire life.

WEBSTER AND HIS PUBLISHERS

The first edition of the spelling book fared so well that when Webster had completed its second edition he no longer had to have it printed at his own expense. In June 1784 he announced that the second edition was ready for sale, and told prospective purchasers to apply to Hudson & Goodwin, to whom he had assigned the "sole right of printing and vending" the speller.[5] (As we have seen, until this point Webster had been doing much of the vending himself.) Hudson & Goodwin would also become the publisher (not just the printer) of the grammar and reader once each reached a later edition.[6]

While Webster was on his lengthy and successful tour of the middle and southern states from May 1785 on, Hudson & Goodwin's monopoly suited him well. As time passed, however, and he saw what a market there was for the speller, he decided to reassert some control over it. Hudson & Goodwin were willing to forgo their market outside New England if they could still control their own area, and sent Webster a proposal to this effect in July 1786.[7] Webster was not altogether happy with it. "By giving you the whole right of printing all parts," he grumbled from Boston, where he was in the thick of the eastern leg of his tour, "I make all the printers & Booksellers here enemies to its progress."[8] He was appeased by Hudson & Goodwin's reply— "your explanations have indeed removed all my objections"— but insisted that some Boston bookseller be supplied with the *Institute.*[9] Hudson & Goodwin evidently decided that the market could bear another printer besides themselves, and they softened their stand: Webster wrote them at the end of August that he was glad to hear that an application had been made by the Boston firm of Edes to print the spelling book and that Hudson & Goodwin had agreed to it.[10] "Much depends on Printers & Booksellers in introducing a School Book—afterwards it may rest on itself or on custom or prejudice," Webster continued, demonstrating his fine grasp of the realities of textbook adoption. "Get it introduced & you then have the advantages in your own hands."[11] The new contract was drawn up with the aid of Joel Barlow[12] and signed in Hartford by Webster and Hudson & Goodwin on November 1st, 1786.[13]

This new contract did not make provision for any other publisher to print the books in New England. It did, however, leave Webster free to sell the copyright to whomever he wished in the southern and middle states. He assigned Hudson & Goodwin the copyright of his *Institute* "for the whole term granted me by the laws of the several states."[14] The firm was to have the "exclusive right of printing & vending all parts of the Institute in New England & Vermont." They also agreed to pay Webster £5 worth, in actual books, for every 1,000 copies sold of any of the three parts of the *Institute*, on condition that the "coppyright" [sic] (right to copies) be reduced proportionately if they had to reduce the price of the book.[15] If other New England firms wished to print any part of the *Institute*, they would have to purchase the right from Hudson & Goodwin.

Webster was in Philadelphia, as we have seen, from February to October 1787. Despite all his other involvements—his pursuit of Rebecca Greenleaf, his teaching at the Episcopal Academy, and his writing of a defense of the new federal constitution—he found time to revise his spelling book thoroughly and just before he left the city, signed a contract for its publication with a Philadelphia printer, William Young. For the sum of £42, he gave Young's firm the exclusive right to print and vend the *Grammatical Institute* in the states of Pennsylvania, Delaware, Maryland and Virginia for a term of three years. Furthermore, he also gave them the right to vend, but not to print, the book in New York, New Jersey, both North and South Carolina, and in Georgia. Webster himself was to receive 1/20 of all copies, in sheets, of the spelling book, and 1/15 of all copies of the second and third parts of the *Institute.*[16]

The American Spelling Book, as this edition was called for the first time (a title that was in tune with the stirring events that had resulted in a new constitution for the country), was the first of Webster's books to have "cuts," or illustrations. The engraver, Isaac Sanford, engraved plates to accompany the fables.[17] From then on, all Webster's spellers would have illustrations.

Now in New York, and about to pursue another nationalistic interest (the publication of the *American Magazine*) Webster, as we have seen, raised more ready cash by selling the right to print his spelling book in New York to Samuel Campbell.[18] Campbell was to have the exclusive right to print the work in New York State, and a simultaneous right to vend the work in New York and other states, for a term of five years.[19] Webster's assumption in this and previous contracts—that it was possible to authorize sales in one state and not another— would soon lead him into considerable difficulties. In addition, the contract with Campbell made no provision for giving Webster any benefits related to the number of copies of the work that were sold.

Despite his involvement with the *American Magazine*, Webster managed to get away from New York in the spring of 1788 to take a look at what was happening to his books in New England. He was aware that the impending ratification of the United States Constitution would enable him to alter his future contracts. "Literary property" would now come under congressional jurisdiction, and he anticipated a national copyright law which would supersede existing state laws.[20] (Such a law would indeed be passed two years later.)

Webster's swing into New England confirmed his conviction that he needed to increase the number of his publishers in the east. In Vermont, for example, he found that 2,000 spelling books had been sold, and "the printers say they could have sold 5000 more. The demand is great & no supply." People were not about to travel to Hartford to buy books, Webster told Hudson & Goodwin, and if the market were not supplied nearer home, the printers would introduce a rival spelling book. Indeed, the firm of Russel and Haswell had already begun to "compile one on my principles, but so different as to evade the laws."[21] He had also received an application from another printer in Boston, Mr. Folsom, who wanted to print 5,000 or 6,000 copies of the speller.[22]

It was with relief, then, that on his return to New York, Webster found a letter from Hudson & Goodwin awaiting him, expressing their willingness to make a new arrangement. "Messrs Hudson & Goodwin have, after much persuasion," he wrote triumphantly to Isaiah Thomas, "consented to resign the monopoly of it [the *Institute*], and let other printers have a share."[23]

Webster therefore proposed a new arrangement to Hudson & Goodwin. They would keep the monopoly of printing in Connecticut but could sell anywhere they wished. Webster would then "give to some booksellers in Boston the right of printing for their own market, which will extend to New Hampshire. I will give the right to but few companies, but in such places as to leave little room for interference." He suggested selling the rights for £4 per 1,000 for the time being, but offered to sell the rights for the whole term of fourteen years, without reference to the number of copies sold, once the new copyright law was passed.[24] (He subsequently asked Hudson & Goodwin for £250 for the entire fourteen-year contract.)[25]

Hudson & Goodwin agreed to these new terms,[26] and Webster went to Boston in August to combine, as was his wont, business with pleasure. He saw Rebecca, of course, and made arrangements with the firm of John Folsom to print an edition of the spelling book there.[27] (He was unable to make any arrangements for the second and third part of the *Institute* to be printed.) From New York, he made overtures to Russel and Haswell of Bennington, Vermont, whom he had discovered printing a pirated edition. In an effort to legitimatize it, Webster offered the firm a five-year contract: £10 for the current year and £15 a year for the next four years, after which a new contract would be made. His terms provided that the Bennington firm could "print & sell as many of the books as you please and where you please," and even offered to accept produce instead of cash.[28] Not until the following year would Webster settle the question of a permanent publisher for the Boston area.

The terms of Webster's contracts were now different from the terms he had negotiated earlier with Hudson & Goodwin. In the earlier contract, he had stipulated that Hudson & Goodwin was to have the exclusive right to sell, as well as to print, in the New England area. His new terms were less exclusive. This move away from exclusivity was made, presumably, on the basis of experience: it was possible to know who was printing what and where, but it proved to be quite impossible for anyone to control where the works, once printed, were sold. Bound books or books in sheets were shipped freely from state to state. This freedom of vending proved financially most unfortunate for both Webster and Hudson & Goodwin, for it could be, and was, easily exploited by an unscrupulous printer.

Such a printer was Samuel Campbell of New York City. In order to raise ready cash for his magazine venture, Webster had, it will be recalled, sold Campbell the right to print and sell the *Institute* in New York for a term of five years.[29] Mere months after his contract began, Campbell started to defraud Hudson & Goodwin by shipping Webster's books to Connecticut, where Hudson & Goodwin had the sole right of vending under the existing state law which forbade the importation of books from out of state.[30] By February 1788, Webster was suggesting to his publishers that Mr. Hudson (who was presumably the senior and more experienced partner) be the one to "transact all business with those gentlemen—I should like, if possible, to see them [illegible]."[31]

A year later, in February 1789, when Webster was again in Boston, he had to take time off from his courtship of Rebecca to sign affidavits detailing Samuel Campbell's violation of Hudson & Goodwin's copyright.[32] Campbell's defense was that Webster had given him the right to sell in New England. Webster's suit was not made easier by his having obviously indulged in some rather loose talk, at the time when he was persuading Campbell to take the contract. Webster wrote a rather panicky letter to Hudson & Goodwin about Nathaniel Patten, who was the Hartford bookbinder and bookseller to whom Campbell had sent his books, and whom Hudson & Goodwin had taken to court. "Patten, I find rests his defence, mostly on what I have said to one & another about the country, in a cursory conversation, as 'that you [i.e. Hudson & Goodwin] have given up your contract;' 'that any person might sell in New England &c.' It is possible I have said so repeatedly, without having the remotest suspicion, that a right of selling would be claim on such declarations, which are still true with respect to all the states but Connecticut."[33]

Hudson & Goodwin won their case against Patten early in 1790,[34] but their victory seemed only to inspire him to greater efforts. In May, anticipating the federal copyright law which would allow complete freedom to vend across state lines, Patten advertised a "proposal" to the citizens of Connecticut. As, he said, the consumption of Webster spelling books in their state was about 20,000 annually, he could save the public over £330 a year by selling imported Webster spellers at 6 shillings a dozen, instead of Hudson & Goodwin's 10. "The monopoly of printing and vending them, being only in one printer, keeps the prices so high."[35]

Webster's lawsuit against Campbell dragged on for years, and Campbell continued to print huge editions of the spelling book, shipping them in sheets to Patten in Hartford, where Patten bound and sold them under the noses of Hudson & Goodwin. In 1792, Campbell published his fourteenth edition of the speller. Webster declared it, in a letter to the (Hartford) *Connecticut Courant*, "the *most incorrect* edition I have ever seen."[36]

When this letter was reprinted in a New York paper, Campbell countercharged that it was injurious to his license. A heated correspondence ensued, during which Campbell called Webster "a pedantic grammarian... full of vanity and ostentation."[37]

So, despite the lawsuit, Webster had to bide his time until the five-year contract with Campbell expired in 1792. Campbell wound up his five years with an incredible printing spree, putting out 90,000 copies, of which he sold some 25,000 in sheets to Patten. Patten not only sold them in Hartford, but shipped some of them back to New York for Campbell to sell.[38] Two years later Patten still had spelling books on the market: "Patten cannot plague you, I think, much longer—" Webster wrote Hudson & Goodwin; "his supplies must be exhausted."[39] This optimism turned out to be premature. In 1796, Campbell and Patten were still flooding the market,[40] and Webster complained from New York that "Patten sells some thousands here every year—he gives them for goods & thus injures me materially."[41] Not until 1797 was the suit closed; Webster recovered $250 in damages, with costs.[42]

If Webster was singularly unfortunate in his dealings with Samuel Campbell of New York, he had better luck with the firm of Thomas & Andrews of Boston. Webster's correspondence with Isaiah Thomas dated back to February 1784, when he was sending him copies of the first edition of the spelling book.[43] In 1788, when Hudson & Goodwin agreed to relinquish their monopoly of the eastern market, Webster reopened his correspondence with Thomas, and the following year Thomas undertook a package deal: he published Webster's *Dissertations on the English Language* and produced his first edition of Webster's spelling book in Boston.[44]

Thomas' adoption of Webster's speller was important to Webster for a number of reasons. In the first place, Thomas was, even as early as 1783, already established as one of the leading and most influential printers in the United States. With outlets in Worcester and Boston, his firm had access to booksellers all over New England. The work Thomas did was of a high standard, as he was a perfectionist, and his editions of Webster's book would prove no exception.[45]

More important, however, as far as Webster's ambition for his work to be the textbook of the nation was concerned, was the fact that, since the appearance of Webster's spelling book,

Thomas & Andrews had been printing not one, but two, competing textbooks. Isaiah Thomas, with his acute business sense, saw the enormous possibilities of Webster's spelling book from the first. He had even declared it, if we are to believe Webster, "the *best spelling* [book] *extant*."[46] When Thomas failed to obtain any rights to its publication, he brought out his own *New American Spelling Book* in 1785, in what a commentator has called "an obvious attempt to capitalize on Webster's success."[47] He also published an imported work, William Perry's spelling book, that same year. (Significantly, Perry's speller had an elaborate diacritical marking system to indicate letter-sound correspondences.)[48]

Not only did Thomas print Perry's speller; more threatening still, early in 1786 he advertised his intentions of publishing Perry's dictionary. It was Timothy Pickering who warned Webster of the perils that this involved: in so far as "that or any other work, differing from your principles of pronunciation, shall spread, so far will it interfere with the adoption of your plan."[49] Perry's tandem of spelling book and dictionary, written on the same principles, represented a powerful combination—a point that Webster would take note of, and one day use to his own advantage. That Thomas would forgo this combination in favor of Webster's work was both a tribute to its excellence, and a healthy indication of its promising commercial future.

So Thomas & Andrews printed their first edition of Webster's speller in 1789, purchasing the copyright from him for a term of fourteen years for the sum of £200. (They paid £50 each for the *Grammar* and the *Selections*.)[50] In those fourteen years they would print thirty editions of the spelling book, ending their contract in 1804 with no fewer than five editions within that one year. During their term they would expand their outlets to Baltimore and Albany.[51]

In 1790, the year after Thomas & Andrews began printing the *American Spelling Book*, the United States government passed a national copyright law which gave authors the right to the copyright of their works for a period of fourteen years, and the right to then renew it for another fourteen. Aware that such legislation would be passed, Webster had made his licenses out to his major publishers, such as Hudson & Goodwin and Thomas & Andrews, for the full term of fourteen years.

By 1790, then, Webster had printers producing his spelling

book all over the country.[52] Thomas & Andrews had just started printing his speller in Boston for the eastern market; Samuel Campbell was printing it—with a vengeance—in New York; Hudson & Goodwin, of course, was still printing hard in Hartford for the Connecticut market; William Young's firm was still printing in Philadelphia, although its contract was about to expire; and Russel and Haswell, after a couple of unauthorized editions, was now printing the speller legitimately in Bennington, Vermont.[53] There was even a lone Providence edition.[54] In the seven short years that had passed since the spelling book first appeared, there was not a state in the union to be found where the speller was unavailable.

Between the years 1790 and 1804, when the copyright for the major publishers was due to expire, Webster's printers continued to be Hudson & Goodwin and Thomas & Andrews. Mathew Carey, the well-known Philadelphia publisher, had hoped to purchase the expiring Young license.[55] He balked, however, at Webster's price,[56] and the Philadelphia slot remained unfilled, in spite of Timothy Pickering's efforts.[57] Haswell of Bennington put out another couple of editions in 1794 and 1796, after the death of his partner Russel, and in 1794 the firm of Charles and George Webster, up in Albany, printed what was to be the first of their three editions.[58] (These Websters were Noah's second cousins once removed.)[59] In 1802, the Wilmington firm of Bonsal & Niles printed two editions under a short-term contract that ran from November 1797 to June 1804.[60] Although Bonsal & Niles made overtures to Webster in 1803, asking him to renew their contract for the middle states of Pennsylvania, Delaware, and Maryland, Webster refused to do so. He had good reason: Bonsal had openly vowed to print all he could before the first of June, when his contract expired,[61] and had managed to sell at least 50,000 copies after the first of June.[62]

There was another publisher in addition to those in Hartford, Boston, Bennington, Albany, and Wilmington: Webster himself. His attempt to be his own publisher was none too successful, however, and lasted only a short time. It arose from the circumstance of his being in New York at the time that Samuel Campbell's contract finally expired. From November 1793 on, Webster was in New York to publish the *American Minerva*, as we have seen. He had hopes of printing his own edition of the *Institute*, which was to be a flawless edition, coming out as it did under his own supervision. It was to be printed by George Bunce, his business partner, who was already printing the daily newspaper for him. Bunce's work, however, proved to be of such poor overall quality that Webster dissolved the partnership, as we have seen, in a costly settlement, early in 1796.

Copies of the three parts of the *Institute* did come off Bunce's press in 1794 and 1795, but after the dissolution of the partnership with Bunce, Webster throttled down his book-publishing activities.[63] When he had exhausted his own stock of spelling books, he purchased them in bulk from Hudson & Goodwin and retailed them for a couple of cents profit in New York. He also sold a good number to several Philadelphia booksellers.[64] His New York edition, therefore, was but a drop in the large bucket of the nation-wide production of the speller.

Up to this point in his life, Webster had conducted his business arrangements almost entirely in one way. It was his practice to sell his copyright (that is, a license to print) to a given printer for a certain term of years, at a set lump sum. The number of books printed and sold by the publisher did not affect him financially, except when he received a set percentage of the books printed, as he did, for example, from William Young. It was his publishers, not Webster, who were getting rich. By 1791 he reckoned that the rights to his books were worth $2,000 a year to their publishers. "Could I have kept my copyright in my own hands till this time," he complained to his brother-in-law, "I might now have rid in a chariot."[65]

As time went on, and with the awful example of Samuel Campbell fresh in his mind, Webster belatedly realized that his financial future lay in his somehow tying the sum he was to receive to the number of copies that were to be printed. As early as 1789, therefore, he seems to have made some arrangement with Isaiah Thomas whereby he shared in the income from his own books;[66] and from 1796 on, if not earlier, we find Webster selling licenses to different printers to print a specific number of books: a license to print 150,000 copies was auctioned off in March 1796, and in 1802 Martin & Ogden of North Carolina was given a license to print 25,000.[67]

A license to print a set number, however, proved no more capable of enforcement than had the right to sell only in certain states. The firm of Martin & Ogden, just mentioned, had, in fact, printed a much larger number than their license had entitled them to. In 1803, now back in New Haven, and faced by the fact that the first fourteen years of copyright was due to expire the following year, Webster determined to improve his control over his work, as well as his income from it. "The business of printing this book will hereafter be placed on a different footing," he warned his Wilmington printers.[68] He undertook a major revision of his spelling book, which was itself essential if he was to protect his work under a new copyright. The words "revised impression" or "revised copy" were now added to the title *The American Spelling Book.*

The American Spelling Book, revised, 1804-1818. In addition to revising his work, Webster revamped his entire procedures for selling licenses.[69] A printed indenture now set out the terms for the licensee. The party was given the sole and exclusive right to print the book in such and such a state, together with the right to publish and vend the book—Webster threw in the sponge on this issue entirely—anywhere in the United States. (In fact, he had no choice since freedom of vending was provided for in the U.S. copyright law.) The number of copies that were allowed to be printed under the license was stated, and for the first time a procedure was built in to monitor exactly how many books were printed: the number was to be reckoned from the amount of paper used, calculating 22 quires of paper per 1,000 copies.[70] The grantee was to render Webster an account of the number of copies printed annually, each June. One cent was to be paid Webster for every copy. A written license was needed to print over the stipulated number, and—a move in the direction of consistency—the speller was to be printed from standing type. Even the price was set: the book was to be offered for sale at not less than "ten cents for each copy in quires or sheets, and sixteen cents for each copy in common binding with scaleboard, covered with blue paper." An allowance was permissible, however, to bulk purchasers.[71] (This "blue paper" would be responsible for the speller's later nickname of "Old Blue-back" in its final form after 1829.)

Although Webster still depended upon the honesty of his printers in being truthful as to the number of books printed (or the number of quires of paper used), this 1804 contract represented a large leap forward for him as far as his financial benefit was concerned. For the first time, he would directly profit from the number of his own books that were printed. He may well have been the first American author to do so on so large a scale. Because the number of copies printed now affected him personally, he kept accounts, meticulous as always, of the number of copies each printer reported annually, from 1804 to 1818.

In addition to tightening up the form of his contract in 1804, Webster reassigned his licenses. He had four main grantees: Jacob Johnson was the licensee for Philadelphia and its environs; Webster's relations, the twin brothers Charles and George Webster, took care of Albany and its environs; Hudson & Goodwin still preserved the right to print in Connecticut, of course; and after considerable dickering, a flurry of letters, and some behind-the-scenes activity in Boston, the right to print for Boston was removed from Thomas & Andrews and given instead to the Boston publisher John West.[72] (There was a Greenleaf in West's firm—Greenleaf was Rebecca's maiden name—and Webster liked to keep his business dealings in the family when he could.)

Only a year passed before Webster expanded his network of publishers. in Utica, New York, Asahel Seward printed the first of his annual editions of the revised *American Spelling Book* in 1805. The following year Charless of Lexington, Kentucky began a 7,000-copy edition of the speller. In 1807, spellers again began to roll off the presses of a Vermont printer. Published first by the Bennington firm of Wright, Goodenow & Stockwell, then by Holbrook, Fessenden & Porter of Brattleboro, these Vermont editions would prove to be the largest yet. Webster's own accounts show that successive Vermont firms purchased licenses for a total of just over 950,000 spellers by 1818. Next in volume came the West firm in Boston, which printed about 700,000 copies between 1804 and 1818; then came Webster's Philadelphia publishers, with 657,000 spellers in all, while Hudson & Goodwin at Hartford printed 590,000. The Websters of Albany had reached a total of 168,000 spellers by 1814; Seward of Utica put out only small editions of the speller for a total of some 157,500 by 1818. Bradford & Read of Boston was given a license to print up to 100,000 copies, not in New England, but in the south: one such edition was printed in Charleston, South Carolina, in 1815. At about the same time "two small impressions" amounting to some 6,000 copies were printed in Ohio and New Orleans. The sales of

Webster's speller were growing in both numbers and extent, at a steadily increasing tempo. Webster kept track of them all by means of his new licensing system.[73]

In summary, then, from the day that the spelling book first came off the press in 1783, until the day that he assigned all rights to the speller to the firm of Hudson & Co., in April 1816, Webster was closely involved with the question of who should publish his work. As we have seen, he kept in touch with every one who printed his speller, and over the years evolved a system to keep yet closer control over who was printing what and how much of it.

Price. We would be mistaken, however, if we were to assume that Webster's concern for his books ended with his finding the right publisher. Second, perhaps, only to his care over who published his books, Webster was concerned with how much the books should cost. As we have seen, even when he was receiving the royalty of one cent per copy for his spelling book, after 1804, his income was based on the number of books sold, not on any percentage of the price of the book. So his interest in price was strictly related to whether or not a given price improved the chances of the book's sale. Like modern publishers, he knew that there was a narrow line between selling the book for too high a price, which made it unattractive, and for too low a price, which meant that it became unattractive to its publishers since they could not make money out of it. In addition, he was early aware of the vital importance of there being a uniform price for his works nationally, so that publishers did not begin a destructive policy of undercutting each other's sales.

At the beginning of his long career as an author, Webster was dismayed at the high prices that were being charged for the spelling book in relation to its competitors. "It is not at all strange than [sic] the Institute sells so slowly when we find what price is set by the booksellers," he grumbled to Hudson & Goodwin, writing from New York in 1784. "Mr. Hodge sells both parts at 18/ [18 shillings] York money per dozen—." He told Hodge that they should be cheaper and suggested to Hudson & Goodwin that they make a contract with Hodge, either giving him a 15 per cent commission on sales or letting him have the books at 14 shillings a dozen to sell them at a price to be set by Hudson & Goodwin. He recommended 15 or 16 shillings: "They will sell very well at 15 or 16/ [shillings] York currency—At any rate please to see them exposed to sale & for a lower price—They are much in estimation here & will soon be in general use, if properly managed."[74]

Two years later he was writing again to Hudson & Goodwin: "I wish the first part [of the *Institute*] might be disposed of at 10/ per dozen in Boston—Other books of the kind are sold so & mine at 12/. This is a great injury to the sale. Is it not possible to have them sold at that!" Letting the booksellers purchase the books in sheets, rather than already bound, was often a way to reduce the cost to the booksellers, because as Webster put it, "The Booksellers are most of them bookbinders." Webster therefore continued, "If not I wish Mr Hastings might be furnished principally in sheets, & the booksellers will sell them lower than 12/."[75]

It was a remarkably short time, however, before the position was reversed: Webster became preoccupied with keeping the price of the spelling book up. In 1789, referring to Samuel Campbell's flooding the New York market with cheap copies, Webster said, "One thing is certain, when the right in N York returns to me, no man shall have it—I will keep it in my own hands & keep up the price."[76] A month later he was writing Hudson & Goodwin from Boston: "By the way, I wish you would raise the price of the Spelling books to 11/ a doz. & of the 3d part to 20/. They will sell just as well, & all the Boston edition of the Spell^g books are sold at 11/. The said sale of both is encreasing [sic], & the booksellers complain that the price is not uniform."[77] As we have seen, Webster took the opportunity occasioned by a new copyright agreement, in 1804, to write a minimum price for the spelling book into the contract: ten cents for each copy in sheets, sixteen cents if bound.

Contract or no, it still proved impossible for him to control the price the publishers set. His Brattleboro publishers were particularly delinquent in this regard. "I have long ago remonstrated with Mr Fessenden on the subject of underselling," he wrote to Hudson & Goodwin in 1810, in response to a complaint from them. "I do not like lawsuits; but I have just wrote to Mr Fessenden, that if he does not desist from this practice, he will cut himself off from any renewal of the contract. I hope this will have the effect."[78] Unfortunately, as we shall see, the battle to keep the price up, and uniform among all the publishers, was one that Webster would eventually lose.

Uniformity. Just as Webster appreciated the importance of having a uniform price for his work, so too he was early aware of how important it was for all the editions of his spelling book to be uniform at any given time. As he aspired to its becoming the standard elementary school book for the entire United States, he rightly insisted on consistency of editions among the different printers. His interest in this aspect of the book can be documented as early as 1786. "In order to render Loudon's, Edes' & your future editions alike," he wrote to Hudson & Goodwin, "it is necessary that a copy should be corrected by the one I have left with you . . . ."[79] Once he had decided that the new version of the spelling book, titled *The American Spelling Book* after 1787, should have pictures, it annoyed him to discover that the Boston printer, Folsom, had begun an edition without them. "This I object to," he wrote, "for all the future editions must be alike." He even told Hudson & Goodwin how to correct this lack: they were to send their own set of plates to Folsom in Boston by the next stagecoach, either loaning them or selling them and getting replacements for themselves.[80] He reiterated this point in a letter to Russel & Haswell of Bennington that same year, 1788: "If the work is to be reprinted in Bennington in future, it must be copied from the last edition, which is corrected by the Philological Society, & recommended as the elements of a federal language. I shall insist upon it that all the future editions be alike."[81]

As we have seen, the spelling book was constantly undergoing revision. When Webster saw the first editions of his spelling book through various presses from 1783 on, he saw to it that successive editions were numbered sequentially, even though they were published in different parts of the country. The situation rapidly got out of hand, however, and in 1789 Webster abandoned the attempt to keep the editions straight nationally, and instead the printers in the several states called their own edition "the eighth Connecticut edition," or "Thomas and Andrews' twelfth edition."[82]

When the opportunity presented itself, as it did when a new copyright agreement was made in 1804, Webster took advantage of it to write into his contract the stipulation that the printer should use standing type. That is, the type from which the speller was printed was not to be dismantled for use on another work, but left set up for a subsequent edition. Eventually Webster's printers would take advantage of the new process of stereotyping, which was introduced into the United States in 1813. (This process, a revolutionary improvement in printing technology, involved casting a plate from the hand-set type. A page would then be printed from this single plate.) A printer in Charleston, South Carolina, seems to have been the first of Webster's printers to strike copies of the speller from a stereotype in 1815.[83]

In addition to his constant watchfulness over the uniformity of the spelling book's editions vis-à-vis different publishers, as well as over editions coming from the same publisher, Webster took pains over every aspect of an individual edition. No detail of production or of the finished product was considered insignificant. The paper that the books were printed on was a topic for concern. Webster discussed its quality with Hudson & Goodwin in 1786: "There ought also to be a change respecting the kind of paper & goodness of the work, for these are now an injury to the sale."[84] He was testy about the binding: "I wish that all books you send to N York may be sewed—the present mode of bestobbing[?] injures the sale."[85] He gave instructions on the kind of type that was to be used—Pica for the spelling book, but a smaller type (he would prefer a fair Long Primer) for the *American Selection.* "It is large enough for children & I want the work to contain as much as possible," he wrote in 1787.[86] He often supervised, by letter, the purchase and transfer of an actual font of type,[87] or he would go himself to a city to procure type, as he did in Philadelphia in 1803, when he was undertaking his major revision.[88]

Webster was also constantly concerned with the internal quality of the work, making minor corrections particularly when a new edition was in the offing: "I percieve [sic] you are about beginning another edition; for which reason I send you a copy, with some corrections in Spelling &c."[89]

Not unnaturally, Webster considered accuracy of spelling in his spelling book to be of prime importance. While he had revealed his notions on orthographic reform to an astonished and unappreciative public in his *A Collection of Essays and Fugitiv* [sic] *Writings* in 1790, at no point did he attempt to introduce these unorthodoxies into his spelling book. But there were certain minor innovations about which he felt so strongly that he introduced them early into his work. We find him writing to a

printer in 1804 with a list of corrections that he wished attended
to: "p. 111 in two places *practice* is spelt practise—this is the
common mode, but there is no reason for the difference between
the noun & verb—any more than in notice—both should be spelt
alike—"[90]

In addition to those words that he felt should be spelled
differently from the common practice, there were a number of
words, particularly place-names, about which there was general
disagreement . Webster would make a decision on these, often
after considerable research.

> Piscataway is spelt two ways—but I believe the more
> correct spelling of the first syllable is Pas—& so I will
> thank you to spell it.... I have often been embarrassd
> to settle the true orthography of many words, &
> especially of Allegany—the Laws of Pennsylvania have
> it Allegheny; but Mr Jefferson, Mr Elliot, & most writers
> spell it Al-le-ga'-ny, which is also warranted by the
> pronunciation—& is most simple. After much research
> & reflection, I have determined on the latter—Al-le-ga'-
> ny,—& will thank you to alter the word in page 123, at
> bottom.[91]

Webster's innovations in syllabic division meant that he had
to pay particular attention to this aspect of the spelling book. In
the same letter he writes, "page 106 credit & creditable should
have the *d* in the first syllable—cred-it."

Besides those corrections which were a function of Webster's
orthographical philosophy rather than simply typographical
errors, there were, of course, genuine errors that Webster had
made himself when he sent along his original copy. He tried to
set these right, but showed that he was aware of the constraints
of the printer's art. "The word *prowl*, page 35, is misplaced;
please to substitute for it *k*noll; prowl should be inserted in page
40, last column, but there is no place for it—let it be omitted—"[92]
"Page 40 Col 5. for *bowl* insert *owl* i.e. remove *b*."[93]

Because of his system of denoting the pronunciation of
certain letters by using different type—as, for example, italicizing
"silent" letters—Webster was also preoccupied with typefaces.
"It seems necessary to the uniformity of my scheme of
pronunciation, in the Spelling Book, that *ay* and *ai* should be
both printed in Roman Letters, wherever they occur—as they are

in the 16th Table."[94] "In page 35 of Spl Book, do insert an Italic i in *Juice*. It is in the last column."[95]

As he included topical references in his spelling book—such as the number of inhabitants in each state!—some of the content at the end of the book was subject to change. Webster would provide these corrections, once making the rather airy comment, "everything respecting the civil & political affairs of America are [sic] necessarily changeable—but these changes may easily be attended to."[96]

PROMOTION OF THE SPELLING BOOK

In addition to involving himself with every aspect of the printing of his books, and with every detail of form and content in the finished product, Webster undertook a continuing publicity campaign that would not have discredited a modern public relations expert. His efforts in this regard date from 1783, the first edition of his spelling book, until 1816, when as we have seen, he signed away the entire contract for the spelling book to one publisher, so that he could devote himself full time to his dictionary.

Recommendations. His first approach to boosting his work was to obtain recommendations for it. This was then a very common practice. The assumption was, then as now, that a work's prestige was enhanced by having an "expert" praise its merits. Webster was looking for recommendations for the first part of his *Institute* before he had completely finished writing it. "I have not procured many recommendations;" he wrote to John Canfield early in 1783. "There are no judges of extensive characters [sic] in this neighborhood & I am too much confined to go abroad for them."[97]

When the first part of the *Institute* actually appeared in the fall of 1783, we find that Webster had made a virtue of necessity. In his introduction, one may recall, he had lamented the custom of the patronage of great names and said that he had adopted it only in part. If his work had merit, he said, "it will make its own way in the world."[98] Just how specious this disavowal was became clear very soon. A month after the spelling book's publication, the *Connecticut Courant* printed the first advertisement of the speller: it featured recommendations signed by no fewer than nine prominent citizens.[99] And when the speller appeared under the new title, *The American Spelling Book*, as it did from 1787 onwards, we find that Webster had incorporated into his frontispiece a host of recommendations: Oliver Wolcott, Ezra Stiles, Joseph Buckminster, Chauncey Goodrich and Joel Barlow, to name but a few, had all put their names to a statement that said the work was "far preferable, in the plan and execution, to Dilworth's or any other Spelling-Book."[100]

The recommendations Webster obtained were of several kinds. Those he sought most avidly were from university professors. It is notable that never, in all of Webster's correspondence, is there a suggestion that an elementary work was unworthy of the consideration of academics. As we have seen, Webster traveled around the country in 1782 to show his *Institute* to the heads of several collegiate institutions. He had several birds to kill with his one stone: he wished to get suggestions for the improvement of the spelling book; to solicit aid in his fight for copyright protection; and to obtain recommendations to enhance its chances of being acceptable to the public.

Webster had a recommendation in hand from Princeton a year before the first part of the *Institute* was even published: Samuel S. Smith, of that institution, wrote that he had looked at Webster's plan for reforming Dilworth's spelling book, and thought that "he proposes many useful improvements in a book of that kind; & that he has executed with judgement that part which he has already finished—Every attempt of this nature undoubtedly merits the attention of the public; because it is by such attempts, that systems of education are gradually perfected in every country."[101] Archibald Gamble of the University of Philadelphia added his signature to this letter. Webster's alma mater, Yale College, was a natural target. Yale's president, Timothy Dwight, wrote, "You are perfectly welcome, Sir, to make use of my name, in the manner you mention, if you imagine it will be of the least service to your design."[102]

A second source for recommendations were, of course, Webster's personal friends. Joel Barlow, Webster's classmate, who had lent him $500 to finance the cost of printing the first part of the *Institute*, readily lent his name. Oliver Wolcott, another classmate, did the same.[103] Joseph Buckminster, Webster's old tutor with whom he had kept in touch, was another willing subscriber.

But Webster looked further afield than his college friends and acquaintances. He sought recommendations from a third source: famous persons of all and every kind. He solicited the blessing of the political luminaries of his day, asking both George Washington and Benjamin Franklin to endorse the spelling book. They both had the prudence to refuse. Washington said that he was not qualified to pass judgment on the book's merits.[104]

Once the first part of the *Institute* was published, Webster had access to a fourth source of recommendations: the satisfied schoolteacher. Benjamin West, the American astronomer and teacher, was genuinely pleased with the speller. He thought it "the best plann [sic] for the instruction of youth of any that has yet been published. I have introduced some of them into my school, and perhaps shall be able to introduce more . . . I shall do all in my power to encourage the sale of your Books."[105] Soon Webster was able to collect a number of names of satisfied schoolmasters and insert them after his advertisements in local newspapers.[106]

While written recommendations of his work were valuable to Webster, because they could be printed up in both newspapers and the speller itself, he also solicited word-of-mouth recommendations. He was acutely aware of the value of getting prominent citizens to sponsor his books in their communities. Once again, no one thought it beneath his notice to examine a work of this nature. Webster's bookseller at Springfield wrote to him in the fall of 1783 that the court had sat there the previous week, and that the "Gentlemen of that order" had come to examine the book. They had recommended it highly, according to Webster's contact, to the people of the several towns they lived in.[107]

Webster made strenuous efforts to contact leading citizens and obtain their approval of his work when he was on his long promotional tour that took up his time from May, 1785 until November, 1786. "I am making men of literature, & particularly clergymen, friends to my publication & designs," he wrote triumphantly to Hudson & Goodwin from Salem. "I shall get to the windward of the Printers yet, before I quit the undertaking."[108] Most valuable of all were the commendations of the local teachers. Webster usually turned these into names that he could add to his list of printed recommendations. "The Gentlemen who have the care of the Grammar-school in Charleston, are much pleased with the Institute, & promised to give me their names after they had examined it with attention," he reported to Hudson & Goodwin earlier on the same tour.[109]

When he was in New York three years later, Webster was instrumental in founding the Philological Society, which was ostensibly dedicated to the furtherance of American English. With a sleight of hand that would be characteristic of him in later years, Webster prevailed upon this society to endorse the spelling book. (He failed, however, to win the support of its members for his heretical grammar.) A recommendation from the Philological Society carried with it the enviable aura of approval from linguistic experts, and it must be counted as one of Webster's more prestigious recommendations. Webster wasted no time in asking his publishers to incorporate the recommendations in the next advertisement for his spelling book. "It may be useful to notify the public," as he worded it, "that it is the wish of many leading men in America that all the children in the different states should learn the language in the same book, that all may speak alike. The Philological Society in New York recommend this work, with a view to make it the *Federal school Book* [sic]."[110]

Lectures. During most of Webster's tour across the country from 1785 onward, he was earning some much needed money by giving his series of lectures on the English language. These lectures were viewed by Webster as just one more aspect of his promotional campaign. "The influence & prejudice of foreigners are all against me," he wrote on the New York leg of his tour, "and I find Lecturing is the best method of exciting the attention of people and of overcoming prejudices." The spelling books would "sell whilst I am here—My Lectures will make them an object of notice."[111] (Not all of the notice was favorable. Even Webster's ally, Timothy Pickering, felt that Webster exhibited too much conceit in the delivery of his lectures, and urged upon him more "diffidence," as "essential to the art of pleasing.")[112]

Advertisements and Notices. Another major facet of Webster's promotional campaign was advertising. He was keenly aware of its value. "One great reason why they [the spelling books] have sold no better, is, they have not been properly advertised."[113] Being in so many towns on his nationwide tour had enabled him to place advertisements for his books, along with the notices of his lectures, in the local newspapers. "I will advertise the Books in some of the eastern Papers," he wrote back to Hudson & Goodwin from Salem, in 1786, towards the end of his tour.[114]

It was obvious that many, if not the majority, of the advertisements can only have been written by Webster himself, for they consist of extracts from letters written to him by those answering his requests for recommendations. (His citations, incidentally, are models of accuracy.) One such advertisement, which appeared in a New Haven paper in the fall of 1784, quoted Joseph Willard, who at the time was president of Harvard College. Webster had sent him several copies of the first part of the *Institute*. The advertisement quotes Willard's letter verbatim; the errors in the copy are those made by the printer, not by Webster:

> I have perused it myself, and put into [sic] the hands of several friends for their perusal. We all concur in the opinion, that it is much superior to Mr. Dil*worth's New Guide*; and that it may be very useful in schools.[115]

According to Emily Skeel, Webster's bibliographer, extensive advertising for the *Grammatical Institute* began with the third edition of the first part, which was ready for sale in January 1785. She reports having located scores of advertisements after this date.[116]

As the years passed, Webster continued to use this method of exposure to attract attention to his book. But in addition to advertisements—which had to be paid for—Webster availed himself of a technique that would today be called a press release—which was free. He rapidly became a master at inserting into papers the anonymous review, or notice, of either himself or of his works or both. He would also use his friends as intermediaries, sending them a copy of his remarks so that they, not he, should be the ones to submit it to the newspapers. As his handwriting soon became familiar to the editors of newspapers, he would even go to the length of having someone else copy his notice over. "Make two fair copies," he suggested to Hudson & Goodwin, as he enclosed some remarks for publication in the eastern papers, for "I do not wish to appear in person." Hudson & Goodwin were to send them to John West or Jedediah Morse (friends of Webster) "in confidence—stating the reasons which induce my friends to offer these remarks to the public—&

requesting him to get them inserted in a newspaper at Newbury Port & Portsmouth."[117]

Donations of Books. In addition to advertising, both directly and indirectly, Webster used a technique for the promotion of his books that is well known today: the handout, or free copy. Colleges were his first target. For example, in 1784 he gave three copies of the first part of the *Institute* to Harvard; two of them were put in the library, and the third circulated among the president's friends.[118] (This gift, as we have just seen, generated a publishable recommendation.) In Charleston on his grand tour in 1785, when he donated 200 copies of his spelling book and 100 copies of his grammar to the Mount Sion Society (an organization formed for the encouragement of literature) for use by the newly founded Winnsborough College, Webster was well aware of what he was doing. This fact emerges from his self-satisfied comment to Hudson & Goodwin about this donation: "This is the best step I have ever taken—They cost me about 12 pounds & are worth £25 to them; & I am secure of their encouragement."[119]

Webster's second and even more important target was secondary schools. He left sample copies of the *Institute*, in 1785, at the local grammar school, as noted earlier, and gleefully reported it to Hudson & Goodwin.[120] When Webster reorganized his licenses in 1804, he had a revised version of the spelling book to promote. "It will be well for you," he wrote to one of his publishers the following year, "to spread the new books as far as possible, & you may have some effect by *presenting* a copy to all the eminent teachers in your part of the country. A little liberality in this respect may have a good effect."[121]

Another technique Webster used on at least one occasion was the donation of his works as a school prize. In 1790 he gave two sets of the third part of the *Institute*, bound, gilt, and lettered, to three Boston schools.[122] In this case Webster's gift may have been inspired by gratitude for services rendered rather than a desire to promote his works, as the town committee had just adopted his speller and reader for the Boston schools.[123]

One type of donation that appeared much less suspect—in the sense that Webster had apparently nothing to gain from it—was his gift of a certain proportion of the income he derived from his books to worthy causes or institutions. The year the *Dissertations* was published, Webster made arrangements for a percentage of his income from the book to be donated to the Pennsylvania anti-slavery movement.[124] In addition, in 1804, he gave the Connecticut Academy of Arts and Sciences 50¢ on every 1,000 copies of *The American Spelling Book*, and a handsome $2.00 for every 1,000 copies of both the *American Selection* and the first two volumes of the *Elements of Useful Knowledge*.[125] He gave a similar donation to Princeton[126] and another to the Missionary Society of Connecticut that same year.[127] But precisely how keenly aware Webster was of the public relations aspect of these charitable efforts appears from a letter to his Philadelphia publisher in 1790, in which he discussed just such a donation. "My books having become almost the universal school books in these States, I have made a donation to three colleges of a certain percent on the annual sales, for the purposes of encouraging literary improvements. You will doubtless see the beneficial consequences of interesting such large bodies of men in the sale of the books." He went on to urge his publisher to give one percent of all the books he sold in Philadelphia to some public purpose. "The sum is small & the benefit will be great."[128] So much for charity!

Agents. It was a characteristic book-marketing practice of the time for a publisher to employ agents to assist him in selling his books. Mathew Carey of Philadelphia, for example, had over fifty agents working for him by 1790. They ranged from printers and booksellers to postmasters, general merchants and private individuals.[129] In a sense, Webster was his own best agent at this period in his life, and it was not until decades later that he would employ paid agents. Until 1816, however, he regularly availed himself of the free services of his friends and relations, who undertook all kinds of chores on his behalf. Timothy Pickering, in Philadelphia, single-handedly attempted to introduce Webster's spelling book and grammar into the Episcopal Academy in 1785.[130] He saw the primer through the press the following year,[131] and in 1791, after the deal with Mathew Carey failed to materialize, he put himself to considerable trouble investigating Philadelphia printers, to see if he could find one who would print the spelling book for a reasonable fee.[132].

After Webster's marriage in 1789, a new resource of unpaid agents opened up: his brothers-in-law. Thomas Dawes, a Boston judge, was the behind-the-scenes actor in the delicate negotiations that took place when Webster was choosing his Boston publisher for a new fourteen-year contract in 1804.[133] Nathaniel Appleton, who like Dawes lived in Boston and was married to a sister of Rebecca Greenleaf, was Webster's contact in his dealings with the Boston School Committee,[134] and in general kept a weather eye open for the quality of Webster's Boston books.[135] Daniel Greenleaf, Rebecca's brother and a resident of Quincy, was similarly pressed into service.[136]

Attacks on Competitors. Of all Webster's promotional activities, whether conducted by himself or by his friends and relations, the most important perhaps was his struggle to combat rival spelling books. As we have seen, Webster knew that the only serious competitor his first spelling book would face was Dilworth's *New Guide*. Before Webster's spelling book had even been put to press, he had been warned by his friend Joel Barlow of the problems he would face with this rival (that is, the attachment Americans had for Dilworth's book, and the large number of cheap editions that the printers were able to make). Barlow had said at the time:

> Now if you make an impression, unless it be very large, you can't afford it so cheap as they do: even if you get nothing for your copy, if it is large the novelty of the book will make it lie on your hands. If the impression is small, the greatness of your necessary price will be another reason why it will lie upon your hands.[137]

From the printer's point of view, Dilworth had the important advantage of being cheap to publish; for, in the absence of international copyright legislation, an American printer could reproduce it or any other foreign work without paying a cent to its author. "All the printers in every State will print & sell all they can of Dilworth—this is expectable," wrote Webster in 1786, three years after his own speller first appeared.[138] The difference in price between a Dilworth and a Webster spelling book could be considerable. For instance, in 1790, when the court case brought against him by Hudson & Goodwin was decided in their favor, Nathaniel Patten printed up a huge edition of Dilworth, which he sold for ten cents; the price of the Webster speller at the time was fourteen cents.[139]

It is a mark of Webster's genius as a salesman that he turned *A New Guide*'s enormous popularity, which offered such stiff competition to his own work, deftly to his own advantage; for, as

we have seen, he produced what was in effect an improved
version of Dilworth. His work, therefore, had the charm of
familiarity for the public; yet, at the same time, he was able to
treat Dilworth as his most deadly rival, delivering a blistering
denunciation of the book in the introduction to his first edition.

There were those who thought he overdid such attacks.
Joseph Buckminster, Webster's tutor from Yale, thought that
Dilworth had introduced some improvements over earlier
works, and told Webster astutely, ". . . it is a wonder if an ill
natured world does not ascribe some of [your] observations not
so much to his deficiencies as to a desire to give a currency to
your Institute."[141] So rapid was the success of the first part of the
Institute, however, that when Webster revised it in 1787,
Dilworth's name had virtually outlived its usefulness. Although
the recommendations bound into the book still claimed that
Webster's speller was superior "to Dilworth's or any other,"
Webster (perhaps heeding Buckminster's comment) mentioned
Dilworth only once in his new preface.[142]

The only other spelling book of any popularity that
antedated Webster's speller was Daniel Fenning's *The Universal
Spelling Book* which had appeared after 1769.[143] Fenning had been
no rival to Dilworth and proved to be no rival to Webster.
"Mr Carter [a Providence bookseller] finds his Fennings a drug
[worthless]," Webster was able to report to Hudson & Goodwin
in 1786.[144]

A rival that was published two years after the appearance of
Webster's own work was William Perry's *The Only Sure Guide to
the English Tongue*. Like the Dilworth and Fenning spelling books,
the Perry speller was a reproduction of a British work. Perry was
a professor at Edinburgh, and the speller had originally been
published there in 1776.[145] As we have seen, the Perry speller was
first published in America by the Thomas firm in 1785, when
Isaiah Thomas realized that Webster's spelling book was
becoming a best seller. In addition, Thomas actually composed
his own spelling book and marketed it, also in 1785, under the
title of the *New American Spelling Book*.[146] Similarly, Mathew Carey
wrote and published his own spelling book when he decided in
1791 that the price Webster quoted him for the Philadelphia
license was too steep.

Neither Thomas' *New American Spelling Book* nor Carey's
Columbian Spelling & Reading Book seems to have lost Webster any

sleep. The threat from Isaiah Thomas was averted when the Thomas firm purchased a fourteen-year license to print the Webster speller in 1789, and although Carey's book went into at least nine editions, it seems not to have sold widely.[147] "Not agreeing to my price," Webster related later, with characteristic reluctance to hide his light under a bushel, "[Carey] determined to compile a similar book himself. He made his book & printed it. But he told me afterward that his examination had convinced him that I had so well done my work that no great room for improvement remained. His book proved a failure."[148]

Generally speaking, a publisher would publish one spelling book exclusively. (Isaiah Thomas was a notable exception to this rule, and his continuing to put out an annual edition of Perry may well have been one of the reasons why Webster denied the Thomas firm a renewal of their contract for his own speller in 1804). Any printer, therefore, who was putting out feelers to Webster for the potential purchase of a license could always hold over Webster's head the threat of publishing a rival speller if the deal fell through. When Folsom of Boston was seeking a license to print the Webster speller in 1788, Webster urged Hudson & Goodwin to grant him one, "otherwise he will print an edition of Perry."[149]

By 1804, Webster was very favorably situated, with publishers for his revised *American Spelling Book* all across the country. This, from his point of view, was just as well, for after this date we begin to see for the first time, in his correspondence, references to new rivals. The editions by Thomas and Carey, with their nationalistic titles, had been harbingers of what was to come. "Two or three spelling books have appeared the last year in N York & Phil^d," Webster warned one of his publishers in 1805 (after a reminder that he had a "family whose subsistence depends chiefly on sales of my Sp. book"), "& more will appear as long as profit is to be made by them."[150] From now on, spelling books would be authored by Americans; the time for reproducing British imports was long over. There was no change, however, in the threat that a potential purchaser of a Webster license could hold over Webster's head. In 1806, for example, a Kentucky printer informed Webster that he would purchase a license if "you will render the payments less speedy." Otherwise he would strike off an edition of Carey's *Columbian* spelling book.[151]

If a publisher lost the right to print Webster's spelling book, he naturally turned at once to printing and promoting another. When Thomas & Andrews lost their license in 1804, they immediately set about to "usher Alden's Spelling Book into notice," as Webster put it. (Webster was not alarmed: Alden's work was a two-volume affair, and so more expensive than his own.)[152]

One rival that would not easily be scared from the field was *The Juvenile Spelling-book* of Albert Picket. Twenty-five years later, Webster's own son William would meet up with Picket in Cincinnati. But in 1810, Picket's book had only been on the market for two years, and Webster was not concerned: "I have long known Mr Pickets Book & the efforts making to spread it," he wrote that year. He thought little of it. The only valuable part of the book, in his opinion, was the reading lessons, which were lifted wholesale from Murray's *English Reader*. (Lindley Murray's book was one of the most popular readers at that time and would continue to be so. Murray, though American by birth, lived in England, and his work was therefore, in Webster's words, "free to be published by any person.")[153]

OTHER BOOKS

It is not without interest that Murray's reader was so popular, for Webster, of course, had a reader on the market himself: the third part of his *Institute*. As he correctly opined later, it was the first collection for reading published in this country.[154] Like the speller, it had been considerably revised in 1787, and like the speller, given a patriotic title, *An American Selection of Lessons in Reading and Speaking*. The revision sold somewhat better than the original version, and always did better than the second part of the *Institute* (the grammar), but never approached the speller in popularity.[155]

Even before Webster had made his major revisions to all three parts of his *Institute* in 1787, he decided to bolster his textbooks by adding other texts: he came to see a need for a primer to precede the speller, and for an intermediary book to follow the speller but to precede the reader. His decision to print a primer was prompted by Timothy Pickering, who had suggested just such a step in his first letter to Webster in 1785, which had heralded the beginning of their long friendship.[156]

Webster liked the idea, and an abbreviated version of the spelling book was seen through the press by Pickering the following year. (No other edition of the primer is known besides this lone Philadelphia printing.)[157]

A few years later, however, Webster published his own version of the colonial favorite, *The New England Primer*. Its title claimed that it was "amended and improved." Perhaps Webster felt that he needed the popularity provided by such a well-known title, and that he could work this to his advantage, just as he had used the public's affection for Dilworth. The public, however, was not pleased with such a drastic revision of colonial America's best-selling work, and after revising his own revision to make it conform much more closely to the original, Webster ceased to take an interest in the book.[158]

A more imaginative—and in its way equally heretical—work was Webster's *The Little Reader's Assistant*. As we have seen, Webster first published the book on his return to Connecticut from New York in 1790, but it only ran to a few printings.[159] It has been suggested that the work marked a new departure, constituting "the first set of consecutive readers in the history of American reading instruction."[160] Certainly Webster saw it as "a step by which children will rise with more ease to the *American Selection*, or other books used in schools," and said that he had published it in response to requests from instructors, who felt the need of a book for the benefit of children "when they first begin to read without spelling."[161]

This intermediate work fell into four sections: stories on the history of America; rudiments of English grammar (actually an abridgment of the second part of the *Institute*); a federal catechism; and general principles of government and commerce. The book opens with the story of Columbus. Some of the material is unexpected: it includes tales of the Indians and does not mince accounts of Indian atrocities. It also includes an outspoken attack on slavery: so much so that Webster's most recent biographer has labeled the work "an early abolitionist tract."[162] After a blood-curdling description of the capture of Africans, the text reads, "Shall this barbarous and unlawful practice always prevail? Are the negroes *brutes*? Or are they *men* like ourselves? ... If there is justice in heaven, vengence must fall upon the heds [sic] of men who commit this outrage upon their own kind." As if this material were not provocative enough, the book also includes some Websterian innovations in spelling, such as *nabors*, *yung*, *giv* and *catechizm*. Alongside this material are much more conventional stories, such as the heroic actions of two dogs who apparently teach men to be "faithful, generous and kind to each other."[163]

Promotion of Other Books. These three works—the *American Selection*, the revised *New England Primer*, and *The Little Reader's Assistant*—all fell within the area of reading instruction. Full documentation of Webster's efforts to promote his works in this area, and his books of more general interest, would take us too far afield. It is enough, for our purposes, to note that virtually every effort he made on behalf of the speller was reduplicated by the attention he paid to his other books.

The *American Selection* of 1787 (the revised version of the third part of the *Grammatical Institute*) may be taken as an example of Webster's concern. He asked Benjamin Franklin for his advice on the book at the time; discussed the price with Hudson & Goodwin the following year and was personally responsible for getting sheets sent from Hartford to Boston for sale there; gave instructions to printers on spelling, in line with his concern for uniformity ("Spell honor," he told Isaiah Thomas, "without *u* public &c without *k* luster theater &c *e* before *r*"); and saw that the book was extensively advertised.[164] He gave copies of the *American Selection*, as we have seen, to Boston schools as prizes. He asked his Philadelphia booksellers to let him know "the opinions of the public" on the work,[165] and he used his relations to keep an eye on it. Rebecca's brother-in-law, Nathaniel Appleton, kept Webster posted on the quality of various editions (Edes' Newport edition of 1789 was "shockingly printed")[166] and upon the reactions of schoolmasters (one considered certain expressions in the work "indelicate & improper to be read, especially by Misses.")[167]

At all times, Webster sought to upgrade his reader by revising it. When Jedediah Morse's *Geography* appeared, for example, as it had by 1796, the geographical portions in Webster's *American Selection* were no longer needed, and Webster decided to eliminate them and substitute something else. His correspondence about this proposed revision reveals an occasion in which the businessman in Webster proved stronger then the perfectionist. He was in New York at the time, in the spring of 1796, struggling with his newspapers. His new version of the

American Selection was, in his opinion, so much better than the published version that it would "destroy the sale of the present impressions. I have on hand 3000 copies, in sheets—& I cannot consent to have an improved impression offered to the world, until these are off my hands." He could not allow the new edition to be published, he said, unless his publishers would exchange at least 2,000 of his old for their new.[168] (As the revised edition did appear, the problem must have been resolved in some manner.)[169]

This version was the basis of the *American Selection*, ("a new edition,") which was the form the reader took when Webster revised it for the sake of copyrighting his new edition in 1804. After this time, however, the work was no longer published by Thomas & Andrews of Boston. This was not to be wondered at, as Webster had removed the spelling book from their care. More noticeable is the absence of Hudson & Goodwin as the book's publishers. In fact, the book was printed spasmodically until 1816, chiefly in Philadelphia. After that there was no edition until Webster tried once more to get it into the market, now under the title *Lessons for Youth*, in 1835.[170]

We could cite other examples of Webster's concern for his books. The *Elements of Useful Knowledge*, which appeared in four volumes between 1802 and 1816, was a major text, from Webster's point of view. In his correspondence about the work, all his usual interests emerge: his concern with the typeface used for it; his wish to have recommendations for the work bound right into the book itself ("This I believe to be a better mode than to print them in Newspapers which are soon destroyed"); and his attempts to introduce the work more widely.[171] But perhaps just one letter will serve to demonstrate his involvement. It is a classic of its kind, which he wrote to Websters & Skinner, of Albany, in 1807.

> I have sent to your care for sale 100 copies of the first & 100 do [ditto] of the second volume of "Elements of Useful Knowledge." Please to offer them for sale at 37 cents single—& 30 cents by the doz^n—Inclosed is a recommendation which I will thank you to insert in your paper, under an advertisement of the work—two or three times.[172]

One such recommendation reads:

> From three years constant use of the "Elements of Useful Knowledge," in my school, & from the benefits which my pupils have derived from it, I do not hesitate to recommend it to the use of schools, as surpassing anything of the kind which has come to my knowledge.[173]

Despite all Webster's solicitude, the *Elements* was not a commercial success. No more than 5,000 copies were printed at any one time, and even the most popular volume, the first, only ran to six editions.[174]

Only a man of Webster's energy could have found time to involve himself, as fully as he did, with the commercial aspects of all his books. For as early as 1800, as we have seen, he was starting on another path of enquiry altogether, one which would lead to his great dictionary. As time went on, it became clear, even to Webster, that he needed a mind free of all other distractions so that he could devote his full attention to this colossal undertaking. By 1816, the moment had arrived. The last volume of the *Elements of Useful Knowledge* appeared that year, and it also was then that Webster completed negotiations with Hudson & Co. over selling the firm the rights to the spelling book for fourteen years. It marks the beginning of a hiatus of twelve years, during which, almost without exception, Webster would neither write new books nor revise his old.[175]

V

The Dictionary of 1828

As we have seen, on April 20, 1818 the Hartford publishing firm of Hudson & Co. paid Webster the princely sum of $20,000 for rights during the entire fourteen-year copyright of his spelling book. Young William Webster was apprenticed to their firm, with a view to eventually becoming a partner.

At no other time in Webster's life was he so divorced from the commercial aspect of his own speller. There is no evidence from these years—in marked contrast to both earlier and later years—that he continued his supervision of his book. No accounts appear in his account book, for there were none to keep: he had received the whole sum in one large prepayment. He now had other things to do with his time than focus on his spelling book.

With his usual energy, Webster persisted with his incredibly ambitious, self-set aim, of tracing over twenty languages to their roots, from Anglo-Saxon to Chaldaic, which he considered a prerequisite to undertaking his enlarged dictionary.[1] For years he had been laboring on his unpublishable "Synopsis of Words in Twenty Languages." He had a semicircular table, two feet wide, on which lay his reference books. Working from right to left, swiveling on a chair with casters as he did so, he would methodically trace an individual word in each of twenty languages, making notes as he went along. At four o'clock each afternoon, Rebecca would bring him fruit or nuts and cake, and he would take a break.[2]

The work went well, if slowly, and in 1822 Webster decided to return to New Haven to complete the dictionary.[3] His family

came with him. Eliza, William and Louisa were still in the family—
William's apprenticeship had ended in disaster. Harriet had
returned to her parents' home, after losing both her husband and
her child. Mary was dead. In 1818 she had married a widower,
Horatio Southgate, with four children; she died, presumably of
puerperal fever, shortly after her little daughter was born. The
baby, also named Mary, remained with her father in Portland
until there was a scandal: the lonely Southgate, now widowed for
a second time, apparently took to his housekeeper. She became
pregnant and was quick to take advantage of the situation. The
family was now considered unsuitable for a Webster granddaughter, and she was whisked away to her grandparents' home.[4]

Julia and Chauncey Goodrich were delighted to have the
senior Websters back in the same town: Chauncey had been a
tutor in philosophy at Yale since his marriage. They rented a
house for her parents,[5] which the family occupied until their new
house, specially designed for them (twenty-three windows with
Venetian blinds, painted green), was completed.[6]

Webster felt that a trip to Europe was necessary for the
completion of his dictionary. He needed access to foreign
dictionaries and wanted to clear up some terms abroad,
particularly scientific ones. In June 1824 he packed up the bulky,
handwritten pages of his dictionary, and boarded ship for
Europe. William, now twenty-four and still unemployed, accompanied him. He would do valuable secretarial work for his father.

Father and son kept the family posted on their trip—the first
European trip that either had ever undertaken. Poor William was
desperately seasick; Noah never lost a meal. By the time they
reached France three weeks later, Noah was "so tanned I look
like a Spaniard." French cuisine was not to his liking: "I cannot
endure most of the dishes of French cookery—but I generally
find something that I can eat."[7] He even had the classic American
complaint: "none of the baker's bread will make good toast."[8]

From the other side of the Atlantic came good news: the
widowed Harriet was engaged to be married. Webster gave his
consent "most cheerfully. You know I have always chose [sic] to
have my daughters please themselves," he wrote to Rebecca,
"& in doing that, they have hitherto pleased me. I sincerely wish
them all the happiness of which the married state is susceptible.
My love to Both."[9]

In Paris, Noah Webster steeped himself in what the

Bibliothèque du Roi had to offer, with its 800,000 books and 80,000 manuscripts. In his black coat and black silk stockings, this "curious, quaint, Connecticut-looking apparition" stood out in such striking contrast to the rest of Paris that Samuel Goodrich (better known as Peter Parley, the author of children's books) recognized him: "I said to myself—'If it were possible, I should say that was Noah Webster!' I went up to him and found it was indeed he. At the age of sixty-six, he had come to Europe to perfect his Dictionary!"[10]

After three months in Paris, the two Websters left for England, reaching the university town of Cambridge in September. "The colleges are mostly old stone buildings," was Noah Webster's verdict on this ancient university seat, "which look very heavy, cold & gloomy to an American, accustomed to the new public buildings in our country." There were consolations, however: "it is a pleasant thing to get among people that look & dress & eat & cook & talk like our own people—"[11]

They found themselves modest, but comfortable lodgings in the center of Cambridge, where they settled "very snugly" for the winter.[12] Noah was enjoying excellent health, and his work progressed faster than he had anticipated. In January 1825 he came to write the last definition of the last word in his dictionary. "When I had come to the last word," he recalled later, "I was seized with a trembling, which made it somewhat difficult to hold my pen steady for writing. The cause seems to have been the thought that I might not then live to finish the work, or the thought that I was so near the end of my labors. But I summoned strength to finish the last word, & then walking about the room, a few minutes, I recovered."[13]

William spent most of his time laboriously copying over the remainder of his father's 70,000 entries.[14] In February Webster went up to London to see if he could find a printer for his massive work. He knew that there were no American printers with the typefaces for all the languages he had in his work. He had anticipated difficulties both "from the prejudices of the English—and from the interest which the principal booksellers have in Johnson's Dictionary by Todd."[15] (Since 1818, London publishers had been printing the Rev. Henry Todd's enlargement of Dr. Samuel Johnson's famous dictionary.)[16]

Webster's fears proved to be all too well founded. One after another, potential printers gave him the cold shoulder. Messrs.

Baldwin of Pater Noster Row informed him that, quite independently of their own involvement in Todd's dictionary, their other obligations were too weighty to undertake such a project. They put a price tag on the work for Webster of £4,000.[17]

This was a blow, for Webster had been so sure that he would have the work printed in England that he had already obtained Daniel Webster's assistance in getting a special act of Congress passed which would have enabled him to import his dictionary into the United States without incurring duty.[18] Undaunted as ever, however, he parceled up the manuscript of his dictionary once again, and he and William sailed back to New York, landing on June 18. At New Haven, there was a hero's welcome awaiting them. America had finally caught up with what Webster was accomplishing.[19]

Sherman Converse of New York agreed to publish the dictionary and sent for types from Germany. Pages of the two-volume work started to come off Hezekiah Howe's press in New Haven on May 8, 1827. The last of its pages was printed eighteen months later. The *American Dictionary of the English Language*, some twenty years in the making, finally graced the national scene.[20] Webster presented it to his fellow citizens, "not with frigid indifference, but with my ardent wishes for their improvement and their happiness; and for the continued increase of the wealth, the learning, the moral and religious elevation of character, and the glory of my country." He paid tribute to the "great and benevolent Being" who had given him the strength and resolution to bring the work to a close.[21]

VI

Orthography and Pronunciation

There are four essential ingredients to any dictionary, over and above the words it contains: its definitions, etymologies, pronunciations and orthography. It is generally agreed today that *An American Dictionary of the English Language* excelled in two respects. In the first place, its 70,000 entries easily surpassed the number of words included in any of its competitors. At the time of its publication, Henry Todd's second edition of Samuel Johnson's dictionary, published in London the previous year, was the largest English language dictionary in print; it had, as Webster was quick to point out, a vocabulary of only 58,000 words.[1] In the second place, Webster added a new dimension to the art of defining. His definitions, though verbose, were "more accurate, more comprehensive, and not less carefully divided and ordered than any previously done in English lexicography."[2]

On the other hand, Webster's conversion to a fundamentalist Christianity affected his work to its detriment. As Rollins has demonstrated, it influenced the wording of some of his definitions and is most evident in the sentences that Webster used to illustrate the words he had defined. For the verb *love*, for instance, Webster wrote, "the Christian *loves* his Bible"; the noun *love* is illustrated by "the *love* of God is the first duty of man."[3] Moreover, because Webster now took the Bible literally, he accepted the biblical version of man's origins, and believed that, just as all mankind had descended from Adam and Eve, so had all languages descended from one single language. Adam's language itself was, he thought, probably the "immediate gift of God." As Webster had a preconceived theory to which he had to fit his facts, he dismissed as worthless work in philology that was being done in Europe, because he could see that it threatened his notion of one primal language.[4]

It was not, however, Webster's promotional efforts (as it were) on behalf of "Quiet Christian behavior," as Rollins has characterized it, nor his flawed etymologies, nor his positions on pronunciation that aroused the ire of his contemporaries. Instead, it was the area of orthography that drew the most fire from his critics, who were quick to charge him with inconsistencies within the work itself.

Webster himself realized that this was a weak spot in his great quarto dictionary. He had been so much occupied, he admitted, with the more difficult part of the work, the etymologies and definitions, that some errors in orthography "escaped observation, which an exclusive attention to that subject would have prevented."[5] He speedily began to make amends by turning to a revision of his *American Spelling Book*, even before the copyright was due to expire, and produced an entirely new work, in conjunction with a New York educator named Aaron Ely.[6] He titled it *The Elementary Spelling Book*; it was published in 1829, a year after the *American Dictionary*. The following year he abridged the *American Dictionary* to make a duodecimo volume of 40,000 words "for the use of primary schools and the counting house."[7] Discrepancies would be found in his dictionaries, he said—for there was another edition, abridged by Joseph Worcester, which he had been unable to supervise himself.[8] But this small dictionary for schools was, he informed his readers, "all written and corrected by myself, [and] is to be considered as containing the pointing, orthography, and pronunciation which I most approve."[9]

CONFLICTING VIEWS ON THE NATURE OF ORTHOGRAPHY

To appreciate Webster's views on orthography, and his shifts over the decades, one first has to know what an orthography is about. To oversimplify greatly, there have been two major views on English spelling.[10] The first and much older view is that an ideal orthography is one that presents one, and only one, symbol for every phoneme in the language. Only the most cursory inspection of the English orthographical system is needed to convince one that the traditional orthography of the English language is singularly deficient in this regard. "How would a child or a foreigner learn the different sounds of *o* in these words, *rove, move, dove*," Webster asked rhetorically in 1783.[11] His was not a new complaint. Discourses on the irregularities of English spelling date back to at least 1551, when John Hart, in England, had deplored "the vices, and faultes of our writing: which cause it to be tedious, and long in learnyng; and learned hard, and evill to read."[12]

This view of written English as a mirror of spoken English, and an imperfect one at that, has continued down the centuries. Some who deplored the inconsistencies of the system have proposed a reform of the alphabet, to get a better match between sound and symbol. These reformers trace their lineage back as far as 1569, when John Hart proposed his own phonetic alphabet[13]; and they include in their ranks such figures as Benjamin Franklin, George Bernard Shaw and, of course, Noah Webster himself in his idealistic youth.

Discussions of English orthography, up to and including the early nineteenth century, were vitiated by a confusion between the spoken language and the written at the level of letters. Thomas Dilworth expressed the prevailing viewpoint of the eighteenth century when he wrote that letters were "the Foundation of all Learning, as being those Parts of which all Syllables, Words, Sentences and Speeches are composed."[14] Webster himself was, of course, a victim of this view, which regarded the spoken word as a bundle of letters, not of sounds. The great contribution of the linguists of the early twentieth century was to disentangle, once and for all, the written from the spoken language system. They pointed out that the spoken was the primary system; not all cultures even had a graphemic system.

Even though they hesitated to jettison the English alphabet in favor of a new one, most linguists of the early twentieth century believed that English spelling was defective.[15] This point of view was unquestionably aided by behaviorism, to which Leonard Bloomfield, the most influential of American structuralists (structural linguists), was converted. Bloomfield regarded language itself as falling within the stimulus-response paradigm: he considered it a linguistic substitute for a practical response.[16] Writing was not language, but merely a way of recording language by visible marks. Reading was the habit of "responding to the sight of letters by the utterance of phonemes."[17] No wonder Bloomfield sided with those who excoriated the English alphabet for its imperfections.[18]

There is another view of English orthography, however—namely, that it performs, rather successfully, other functions than that of transcribing speech. It is significant that such a position could only be suggested after there had been a revolution in the theory of language: in 1957, Noam Chomsky published his *Syntactic Structures* and reintroduced mentalism into language.[19]

Those working within the framework of this new theory—transformational generative grammar—have posited an abstract level of representation within the phonological system, and have described the general rules by which these underlying abstract forms are converted into their phonetic realizations (that is, the words we produce in normal speech.)[20] It is to this abstract, or "lexical" level, they suggest, that English spelling, for the most part, corresponds.[21] English orthography strips away the surface phonetic differences and depicts language at this deeper, and more abstract, level. It ignores, for example, the difference that stress makes to the phonetic realization of adjacent syllables. If one takes the group *phótograph, photógraph-y* and *photográph-ic*, it is plain that the shift in stress produces a wide range of schwas, in different syllables, in the various forms of the word. Our spelling ignores these schwas, whereas a one-to-one sound-symbol system would have to take them into account and spell each *photograph-* differently. To put it in Carol Chomsky's succinct summation, "on the lexical level and in the orthography, words that *are* the same *look* the same."[22]

Richard Venezky, the modern authority on English spelling, has taken a similar position. He sees English orthography not as a letter-sound system riddled with imperfections, but as a more complex system in which phoneme and morpheme share leading roles.[23] He argues that the spelling of base words tends to be phonemic, while compounds and derivative words tend to be morphemic, in that the spelling of the base word is retained as much as possible. He has also pointed out that the English spelling system includes, thanks to a systematic use of letters as markers, additional aids to indicate pronunciation of words in their derived or inflectional form.[24]

Here, then, are two opposing views of the structure of English orthography—the ancient, which states it is an unmitigated disaster as a symbol-sound system; the modern, which suggests that it successfully performs other functions, representing an abstract level of language in a manner helpful to the reader, instead of specifying irrelevant surface phonetic features. Turning back to Noah Webster, we can now use these two views to illuminate what Webster thought about spelling throughout a long life, the greater part of which was devoted to words in their written form. It will turn out that while Webster was of course the product of a century which adhered to the ancient view, his innovations in American orthography would eventually make a major contribution to the modern view.

Orthographic Reform: Benjamin Franklin and Webster. It is easy to see that, in 1783, when he published the first version of his spelling book, Webster aligned himself firmly with the ranks of those who maintained that the English spelling system was a defective and inefficient portrayal of English phonology, which fell far short of the ideal of having one and only one symbol for every sound. As others had done before him, Webster criticized the conventional orthography for both the inadequacy and the superfluity of its notational system: "Several of our vowels have four or five different sounds; and the same sounds are often expressed by five, six or seven different characters. The case is much the same with our consonants: And these different sounds have no mark of distinction."[25] He spent several pages, in the first edition of his spelling book, elaborating upon this point. The sound of the first, or long *a*, he pointed out, was expressed in six different ways:

by a	in hate
ai	fair
ay	day
ey	they
ei	vein
au	gauge

Yet some letters represented a variety of sounds. *Ch* had three sounds, for instance:

ch	in chase
sh	chaise
k	chorus.[26]

Webster had used Dr. Samuel Johnson's dictionary as the source for his spelling, and made no attempt to alter the traditional orthography at this time. He does make one comment on it, and it forms an amusing contrast to what he would hold, with great conviction, later in his life. Some writers, he said, wished to alter the spelling of certain words by expunging superfluous letters: they recommended writing *favour* and *honour* without the *u*. "But it happens unluckily that, in these words, they have dropped the wrong letter." The words should be written, according to Webster, *onur* and *favur*. Nor did he approve of dropping the *e* in *judgement*, "which is the most necessary letter in the word; it being that alone which softens *g*." That the language was pronounced very differently from the spelling, he said, "is an inconvenience we regret, but cannot remedy." To try to change spelling little by little would keep the language in perpetual fluctuation (once again, he was confusing the spoken with the written language); to attempt to change it completely would render the language unintelligible.[27]

That was Webster's view before he met Benjamin Franklin. As we have seen, they met for the first time in Philadelphia in February 1786. It proved to be a heady encounter. Franklin had long been interested in spelling reform and had gone so far as to prepare his own orthographical system; he had even procured for it the special types it required.[28] Webster departed from their meeting in a starry-eyed glow that was a combination of linguistic and national patriotism. A month later he wrote to General George Washington, to whom he was recommending an instructor for his children, "I am encouraged, by the prospect of rendering my country some service, to proceed in my design of refining the language & improving our general system of education—Dr Franklin has extended my views to a very simple plan of reducing the language to perfect regularity."[29]

By May Webster had sounded out other interested persons for their views, as he continued his lecturing and traveling. He had completed his design, and he sent it from New York to Franklin. His covering letter reveals how influential his meeting with Franklin had been. He had not hoped for success in altering the conventional alphabet, he said, but "your Excellency's sentiments upon the subject, backed by the concurring opinion of many respectable gentlemen, and particularly of the late Chairman of Congress [Dr. David Ramsay], have taught me to believe the reformation of our Alphabet still practicable." He enclosed his plan "for redusing [sic] the orthography of the language to perfect regularity, with as few new characters and alterations of the old ones as possible." A large number of new characters would, he thought, probably defeat the attempt. He asked Franklin to adopt, amend or reject his effort, and submit this, or some other plan, to Congress. He believed that General Washington would support it and stressed the urgency of the moment. The minds of people were in a ferment and disposed to accept improvements. Once this had passed, lethargy would set in again. Webster, never one to let slip an opportunity for promoting his books, closed his letter with a characteristic postscript: "P.S. It would be esteemed a singular favor, if your Excellency would publicly recommend the Institute—it would facilitate its introduction, and confer a peculiar obligation on me."[30]

In his covering letter to Timothy Pickering, to whom he had entrusted the task of handing over the letter to Franklin, Webster dashed off his reasons for alphabetical reform:

> 1st. It will render the acquisition of the language easy both for natives and foreigners. All the trouble of learning to *spell* will be saved.
> 2. When no character has more sounds than one, every man, woman, and child who knows his alphabet can spell words, even by the sound, without ever seeing them.
> 3. Pronunciation must necessarily be uniform.
> 4. The orthography of the language will be fixed.
> 5. The necessity of encouraging printing in this country and of manufacturing all our own books is a political advantage, obvious and immense.
> 6. A national language is a national tie, and what country wants it more than America?[31]

Webster's new alphabet met with Franklin's approval. But he had so much to say on the subject, Franklin replied, that he wanted to see Webster "as that would save much Time and Writing. Sounds, till such an alphabet is fix'd, not being easily explain'd or discours'd of clearly upon Paper." Their ideas were so similar that Franklin had no doubt that they could agree upon the plan. As for recommending Webster's *Institute*, canny old

Franklin tied it in with support of the plan: "you may depend on the best Support I may be able to give it [the plan] as a Part of your Institute."[32]

Webster was not able to leave for Philadelphia then, as he had engagements to read lectures in Boston and Portsmouth, and asked Franklin if the meeting could be deferred till the fall.[33] Franklin fully understood: "I think with you that your Lecturing on the Language will be of great use in preparing the Minds of People for the Improvements proposed, and therefore would not advise your omitting any of the Engagements you have made."[34] Webster finally kept his appointment with Franklin in December,[35] and gave a lecture on reforming the alphabet two months later, in February 1787.[36]

One of Webster's key motivations at that time for reforming the traditional alphabet was nationalistic; he genuinely believed that the time was ripe for America to separate herself from England linguistically, as well as politically. Americans should not only have one language across the entire continent; they should also have one that differentiated them from the British. When he came to revise his lectures for publication, as he did in 1789, Webster called them *Dissertations on the English Language* and, significantly, dedicated them to Franklin. In them, he stressed the relationship between political and linguistic independence: "Our political harmony is therefore concerned in a uniformity of language. As an independent nation, our honor requires us to have a system of our own, in language as in government."[37] He correctly anticipated the future for the English language on the North American continent, predicting a population of a hundred million people all speaking the same language.[38] He also thought that the separate circumstances of the two countries would "produce, in a course of time, a language in North America, as different from the future language of England, as the modern Dutch, Danish and Swedish are from the German, or from one another."[39]

Many years later, he abandoned that view, and actually attempted to increase the cultural unity of England and America by introducing his spelling reforms into the language on both sides of the Atlantic. On his own copy of the *Dissertations*, he annotated the passage quoted above with a large X in brown pencil, and a "No" in the margin.[40] At the time, however, with his nationalistic fervor yet undimmed, he believed that "we have ... the fairest opportunity of establishing a national language, and of giving it uniformity and perspicuity, in North America, that ever presented itself to mankind."[41]

He presented his reforms, to achieve this worthy object, in an appendix to his *Dissertations*. He had three main thrusts. First, he would omit all superfluous silent letters, such as the *a* in bread, giving *bred*. Second, he would substitute a character with what he called a "definite" sound, for one that was "more vague" (in modern terminology, he would replace an "unpredictable" correspondence by a "predictable" one.[42]) *Grief* would become *greef*. Third, he proposed altering letters in "trifling" ways, by adding a stroke or a point to distinguish different sounds. *Th*, for example, would have a small stroke across it to differentiate its voiced from its unvoiced form.[43]

He launched these innovations upon an unappreciative public the following year, in 1790, when he published *A Collection of Essays and Fugitiv* [sic] *Writings*. "The following Collection consists of Essays and Fugitiv Peeces, ritten at various times, and on different occasions, az wil appeer by their dates and subjects," he informed his readers. "The reeder wil obzerv that the orthography of the volum iz not uniform." This was because it was too laborious, he explained, to change the orthography of the essays published earlier. "In the essays ritten within the last yeer, a considerable change of spelling iz introduced by way of experiment." Anyone who had approved the change of *mynde* to *mind* should also approve the changes to *helth, breth, rong, tung,* and *munth*.[44] Indeed, his new spelling appears about half way through the work and is continued to the end.[45] It is the vehicle for sentiments such as these, addressed to "Yung Ladies: ... let the prime excellence of your karacters, *delicacy*, be discuvered in all your words and actions."[46]

Even his friends found these innovations hard to accept. "I suspect you have put in the pruning knife too freely for general acceptance," wrote Ezra Stiles, President of Yale College, and long one of Webster's staunchest supporters.[47] Nathaniel Appleton, Webster's brother-in-law, even while responding to the latter's condolence letter for the death of his daughter, felt called upon to remark that "The Novelty of spelling the word give without the e final, struck me disagreeably."[48]

A total stranger, however, named Daniel George, was overcome with admiration: "I was pleased with your useful and approved *Institute*: I admired your learned *Dissertations on the English Language*; but with your late 'Collections of Essays and fugitiv writings,' I am pleasingly astonished. Go on, Sir, and make a *thoro* reform in our orthography, the irregularity of which, must give every *American* pain." He suggested that Webster compile a dictionary to incorporate his new spellings.[49] Webster responded that he was doubtful whether the public was prepared for the reception of such a dictionary.[50]

Indeed, the public mind was not. A full ten years later, Webster announced his plans for "completing the system for the instruction of youth, which he [Webster] began in the year 1783." His plan included a dictionary of the American language, a small dictionary for schools, one for the counting house, and a "large one for men of science." Such a dictionary was necessary because of the differences between the American and English languages: new circumstances gave rise to new words and rendered other words obsolete.[51] (Webster had made this point rather more gracefully eleven years earlier in a quotation from Horace: "Words . . . are like leaves of trees; the old ones are dropping off and new ones growing.")[52]

The editorial reaction to this seemingly innocuous announcement was brutal. It should be borne in mind that Webster was by then back in New Haven, having abandoned his New York newspaper, which had supported Federalist policy so loyally until 1793. The editor of the Philadelphia *Gazette of the United States*, although not unsympathetic to Webster's political views, did not relish the thought of an entire dictionary being devoted to Webster's spelling innovations, and published witty satires on his conception of the new orthography.

> To Mr. Noab Wabstur
> Sur,
>   by rading all ovur the nusspaper I find you are after meaking a nue Merrykin Dikshunary; your rite, Sir; for ofter lookin all over the anglish Books, you wont find a bit of Shillaly big enuf to beat a dog wid. so I hope you'll take a hint, and put enuff of rem in yours, for Och 'tis a nate little bit of furniture for any Man's house so it 'tis.
>   PAT O'DOGERTY

As I find der ish no DONDER and BLIXSUM in de

English Dikshonere I hope you put both in yours to
oblige a Subscrybur

HANS BUBBLEBLOWER[53]

Webster's reply was, under the circumstances, a model of
restraint.[54] But the editor had a point: if one regards spelling
solely as a medium for reproducing speech, whose speech (or
dialect) is one to reproduce?

Yet even these attacks were not as vicious as the one that
appeared in the *Aurora* of Philadelphia (a violently anti-Federalist
publication) in 1800, which declared of Noah Webster that

> his spelling-book has done more injury in the common
> schools of the country than the genius of ignorance
> herself could have conceived a hope of, by his
> ridiculous attempts to alter the *syllable* division of words
> and to *new model* the spelling, by a capricious but utterly
> incompetent attempt of his own weak conception.

The reasons Webster gave were preposterous, the editorial went
on. "The plain truth is . . . that he means to *make money*" by the
scheme.[55]

Webster's announcement of his plans turned out to be
premature, as well as unfortunate. His *Compendious Dictionary* did
not appear until 1806.[56] In his preface to the work, he discussed
orthography at length and rewrote a little history by saying that
he had not been tempted by Franklin's scheme of a Reformed
Alphabet. "In the year 1786, Dr. Franklin proposed to me to
prosecute his scheme for a Reformed Alphabet, and offered me
his types for the purpose. I declined accepting his offer, on a full
conviction of the utter impracticability, as well as inutility of the
scheme. The orthography of our language might be rendered
sufficiently regular, without a single new character, by means of
a few trifling alterations of the present characters, and retrenching
a few superfluous letters."[57] Opinions had run into extremes on
the issue, according to Webster, but those who would not alter
the orthography at all were as mistaken as those who would
introduce new characters. A living language must undergo
changes in its words, not only in meaning, but in pronunciation,
with the result that fixing the orthography destroyed the
benefits of the alphabetical system. The solution lay between the
two extremes, and gradual changes should be made to accommo-
date the written to the spoken language.[58]

This view was an advance over Webster's earlier view that languages reached a certain stage of perfection, and then either had to remain stationary or deteriorate.[59] His attitude toward the relationship of the spelling system to the spoken language was also a more moderate position. He now stated clearly that one of the functions of an orthography was to reveal etymology, and he argued that his reforms (such as *tung*), far from obscuring the original etymology, restored it. He included in his 1806 dictionary idiosyncratic innovations such as *determin, melasses* (for *molasses*), but not *hed, giv* or *nabor*. He kept the *u* out of words in the class of *honour*, the *k* out of words like *musick*, and terminated *theatre* and analogous words with *-er*.

What is of interest here is not, however, Webster's wide range of respellings of different words,[60] but the extent to which he felt free to include them in his spelling book. Even at the height of his enthusiasm for the most radical of his reforms, he was prudent enough not to introduce them into the speller. In his preface to a 1789 edition of the *American Spelling Book*, he declared that he had followed the orthography used by approved authors in this and the last century, although he would have preferred *publik, favor, nabor, hed, proov, flem, hiz, giv, def, ruf* and *wel*.[61] He did include his trio of preferred spellings, words in the class of *honor, music,* and *theater*, but these were not considered as revolutionary, because the spelling of the first two, at least, was familiar from the words in their derived form, such as *honorable* and *musical*. (The derivative *theatrical* was better preserved, in contrast, in the British spelling of *theatre*.) In short, he showed himself fully sensitive to the public's conservatism, which made drastic orthographic reform unlikely to be acceptable in a textbook aimed at children.

Webster's Final Orthographic Decisions. Over twenty years later, with his great dictionary behind him, Webster turned his attention once again to orthography, which he had admittedly somewhat neglected in his struggles with definitions and etymology. The fruit of his renewed thinking on the topic, and the crystallization of his deliberations on how the written language should relate to the spoken language, may be seen in his introduction to his dictionary for common schools, which was published in 1830. We have seen how the spelling conformed to that of the *Elementary Spelling Book* (1829), and that it represented Webster's best thinking on the subject.

He had followed certain principles, he said, in making decisions on orthography. He stated that he had taken, for a general rule, "*uniformity* in words of like formation." He listed classes of words and elaborated on the motivations for each spelling as follows:

1. *Favor, candor, arbor, labor,* and so forth should be spelled without the *u*, so that the pupil need not be troubled by *u* in *labour*, but not in *laborious.*

2. The spelling of *music, public* and similar words from the Latin and Greek was similarly motivated: Webster wished to avoid *k* in *musick*, when there was none in *musical*. There were three general exceptions to this rule: first were words of this class used as verbs, such as *traffick*, which needed the *k* in *trafficking*. Second, he excepted words he believed to be of Teutonic origin, which had never lost *k*, such as *hemlock, fetlock*, and *wedlock*. Third, he excepted monosyllables, most of which were used as verbs.

3. *Defense, expense, offense,* and so on had the *s* in the original Latin, and their derivatives were written with *s*, as in *defensive, expensive,* and *offensive.*

4. *Blamable, debatable, movable* should be spelled without *e*, except after *c* and *g*, as in *noticeable* and *changeable*. (This was presumably motivated by a wish to follow the analogy of *blaming* and *debating*.)

5. *Befall, miscall . . .* should retain the second *l*, because if it were omitted in the radical form, it would have to be inserted in the participial form, *befalling.*

6. *Foretell, distill, fulfill* were similarly motivated.

7. *Connection, deflection, inflection, reflection* follow the spelling of the verbs *connect, deflect, inflect* and *reflect*. (*Complex* and *reflex* were considered to have a different derivation.)

8. All verbs that had, according to Webster, been formed from Latin and Greek *izo*, and others formed on analogy, were to be written with the termination *ize*, as *generalize, legalize, moralize.* Words from the French *priser* generally retained the *s* as in *surprise, enterprise.*

9. Verbs of two or more syllables, ending in an unaccented vowel-consonant, were not to double the final consonant. Examples were *appareled, canceled, caviling. Dull, skill, will, full* should retain *ll* in their derivatives.

Finally Webster listed the spelling innovations on which he

would not relent. "The orthography of a few words, the etymology of which has been mistaken, has been corrected." The list included *furlow, chimist, melasses, mold, cigar, redout, redoutable* and *controller*.[62] They were holdouts in the last stronghold of Webster's reforms.[63]

That virtually all of the classes of spelling innovations, other than the final list of idiosyncratic spellings such as *chimist*, should appear so familiar to us is due, of course, to the fact that these were the spelling reforms that have been accepted, since Webster's time, as standard American spelling. Of all the forms he listed, only *traffick* is not today listed as the preferred form in the contemporary modern American dictionary. Words on the lines of *favor, defense* and *generalize* (not to mention *theater*, a major reform, which Webster omitted from his list, presumably because it did *not* altogether conform to his principle of uniformity) are the standard American spellings which today distinguish an American from a Briton. The British spelling would be *favour, defence, generalise* and *theatre*.

Singlehandedly, Webster had succeeded where so many other spelling reformers had failed: he actually introduced permanent spelling changes into the written language. It is thanks to Noah Webster, in short, that in so many cases, "words that *are* the same" do in fact "*look* the same" in American spelling.[64] His major classes of reforms had all appeared previously in the *American Spelling Book*; now they and these lesser reforms would be available to millions of schoolchildren through the medium of his *Elementary Spelling Book*. They would fix themselves in the minds of the young as the correct spelling, and in time become self-perpetuating.

It was through no fault of Webster's that the orthography of Great Britain was not also affected by what we can only characterize as his improvements. In December 1824, when Webster was in England finishing his dictionary, he had made overtures to linguistic experts at the university centers of Oxford and Cambridge to see if he could unify the two countries in their pronunciation and spelling[65]—a far cry from his youthful days of wishing to create a language that was as different from English as American politics were from British. Thanks to British disdain, he failed, on that side of the Atlantic, to win for his reforms the acceptance they deserved.

All the innovations Webster pioneered in orthography were

achieved by deleting, transposing or substituting a letter in a given word. These were not, however, the only changes in the written language that Webster wished to make. He had another plan in mind, which was, he said in the same letter addressed to scholars at Oxford and Cambridge, one "for correcting the evils of our irregular orthography, without the use of any new letters."[66] As we shall see, it was a device for indicating the pronunciation of the language that would prove to be a dramatic and original advance over his earlier system. It is to Webster's views on pronunciation that we now turn.

NOAH WEBSTER AND PRONUNCIATION

Webster's lifelong interest in orthography was accompanied by an equally longterm interest in what he called pronunciation.[67] In the small, stopgap dictionary that he issued in 1806, he devoted even more pages to a discussion of pronunciation than he had to his analysis of orthography.[68]

Webster, after all, first wrote his spelling book in 1783 in order to "introduce uniformity and accuracy of pronunciation into common schools."[69] He regarded his spelling books all along as instruments for the improvement of children's speech.

From his earliest pronouncements on the subject it is clear that Webster was prescriptive in his approach to pronunciation. He held, very strongly, that there was one, and only one, correct way to pronounce virtually every word in the English language. In the very first edition of his speller in 1783, he issued instructions on how certain words were to be pronounced and specifically pointed out how they were *not* to be pronounced. *Perfect, negro,* and *humor* were to be pronounced so, not as *parfect, neger,* or *yumor.*[70] It is clear that he regarded such pronunciations as socially unacceptable. *Fetch* was pronounced *fotch* in several states, "but not among the better classes of people." *Cotched* for *caught,* he said, "is more frequent and equally barbarous."[71] Webster was no less censorious about what he called "local peculiarities," such as the New England *marcy* for *mercy,* but was more tolerant of the variants of *leesure* and *lezhure* (as he spelled them) for *leisure.*[72] This kind of discussion made up a large proportion of his lectures when he was on his tour of the country to obtain copyright legislation and to promote his *Institute* in 1785 and 1786.[73]

When, much later in his life, Webster came to writing his dictionaries, he would include, as a staple element in the larger works, a discussion of the errors and inconsistencies in pronunciation committed by rival lexicographers. In the 1806 dictionary, for example, he lists the differences in pronunciation for selected words, such as *bench*, that were to be found in the dictionaries of Sheridan, Walker and Jones.[74] (*Bench* was pronounced *bentsh* by Sheridan and Jones, but *bensh* by Walker.) In his 1828 dictionary, Webster listed discrepancies at much greater length.

Throughout the rest of his life, Webster would fulminate against lexicographical directions for what he considered an incorrect pronunciation. Yet it is possible to detect a change of heart. In what are apparently notes that he made for a lecture, late in his life, he discussed the discrepancies among authors of dictionaries, naming Sheridan, Walker, Stephen Jones, Perry, Jameson and Knowles, and claimed he had found 1,100 differences in directions for pronunciation among them. But, he went on, it was questionable whether any good could proceed from dictionaries. "The higher classes of society in England never consult books—they are governed wholly by the usage most prevalent in educated circles." In practice, he continued, there was very little difference between the pronunciation of wellbred men in England and in America.[75] It may be said, then, that by the end of his life Webster had taken up the stand that *usus est norma loquendi*—provided, at least, that it was the *usus* of the educated. (As to when custom became the standard for speech, Webster was less sure: it was not easy to say, he wrote, when "*usus* in language becomes norma loquendi.")[76]

Syllabic Stress and Syllabic Division. Syllabic stress was, of course, a linguistic phenomenon that had been well understood by English-speaking educators for centuries before Webster's time. All the spelling books, it will be recalled, categorized polysyllabic words into groups, according to whether the stress fell on the first syllable, the second, and so forth. Webster, in his earliest speller, had followed this well-trodden path.

Webster wrote his most elaborate discussion of syllabic stress in his *Dissertations*, in 1789. There, as he would later, he emphasized the regularity of the English language and talked about the "rules of the language itself."[77] If we examined the structure of any language, he said, we would find a principle of analogy running through it. In considering accent (which he defined as "that particular stress of voice which should distinguish some syllable of a word from others"),[78] there were three factors to take into account: the importance of the syllable; the derivation of the word; and the terminating syllable.

1. One could discover which syllable was the most important, Webster claimed, by reducing the word to its radical, or root. *Sensible*, for example, was derived from *sensus* (Latin), or *sense* (English). Meaning was therefore derived from the first syllable, which thus required the accent.

2. As far as derivations were concerned, all words that had the terminations (suffixes) *ing, ful, less, ness, ed, est, ist, ly*, retained the accent on the primitives (roots). *Proceed*, for example, retained the accent on the same syllable in *proceeding*.

3. Finally, the stress was determined by the terminating syllable. There was a principle involved, which Webster called "the ease of speaking or the harmony of enunciation." This principle took precedence over the two others in cases where they conflicted. He stated his rule: "words, having the *same* terminating syllable, have the accent at the *same* distance from that termination." For example, the terminations *-tion, -sion, -cion, -cial, -cion* had the accent on the penultimate syllable. Words ending *-ty*, if they had more than two syllables, were accented on the antepenult, as in *probity*.[79]

In addition to the principal accent, Webster pointed out correctly, there was an "inferior accent laid on the third or fourth syllable from the principal." He laid it down as a rule that "we cannot pronounce more than two unaccented syllables with perfect ease." Compound words, because both units bore meaning, were equally stressed, as in *earthquake*.[80]

Webster himself soon abandoned the rules on accent that he had included in early editions of his spelling book, on the grounds that they were "found to be too lengthy and complex" to be of value in a work for children.[81] But, of course, he included markings for syllabic stress in every work he produced, both for children and adults. In his 1806 *Compendious Dictionary*, he simply marked the stress by putting an accent over a vowel (*vócal*), or after a consonant (*hab'it*), to indicate that the vowel was, respectively, long or short. (In neither his 1806 nor his 1828 dictionary did he divide words into syllables, other than by the placing of the accent.) Webster claimed that the accent alone was sufficient to teach pronunciation. "The accent being laid on the right syllable and letter, and the accented vowel correctly pronounced, the pronunciation of the unaccented vowels is extremely easy; so easy indeed, that it is more difficult to be wrong than right."[82] (This, although not clearly put, is actually an acknowledgement of the vowel reduction that occurs in unstressed syllables.)

In the works that Webster produced specifically for children, however—that is to say, in all the versions of his spelling book and in his 1830 dictionary for schools—he divided polysyllabic words into syllables, using the approach to syllabic division that had been an innovation in his 1783 spelling book and which had since become standard for the great majority of spelling books in the United States. In the dictionary, the item was hyphenated; in the speller, the word was in the familiar columns, divided by a space. Because polysyllabic words in the speller were classified according to where the stress fell, there was no need to mark the accent of every word. Instead, the first entry in each table showed the accent. In the dictionary, the accent appeared after the relevant syllable in the dictionary entry.

Diacritical Marks as Indicators of Letter-Sound Correspondences. Webster's innovation, in his new works for children—that it, his *Elementary Spelling Book* (1829) and his dictionary for schools (1830)—was to indicate pronunciation, not by numbers, as he had done in all earlier versions of his speller, but by diacritical marks. He had in fact introduced a diacritical marking scheme to the public in his *American Dictionary* (1828); the one in these new books for children was a modification of this initial version. The only remnants of the system that had appeared all this time in the *American Spelling Book* were the numerals 1 and 2, which still indicated long and short vowels respectively. He now indicated the pronunciation of variant vowel sounds by "points" (dots), single or double, over or under the vowel. The breve, familiar to us today, was used only over the short *i*. Unmarked vowels were to be considered short, unless they ended an accented syllable.

In addition, Webster actually attempted to modify the alphabetical characters themselves: across every page of both speller and dictionary were printed the key words exhibiting both his diacritical marks, and his revisions of certain letters:

Bär, fạll, whạt, prey, marïne, pin, bïrd, möve, bọọk, döve, fụll, u∿se, ꞓan, c̆haise, ġem, aʂ, this, t̶hou.[83]

Such was the scheme, one must assume, that Webster had intended to suggest to the disdainful dons at Oxford and Cambridge.

Webster's innovations in the actual characters of the graphemes *u*, *c*, *s* and *t*, (u∿, ꞓ, ʂ, and t̶h) did not survive. It had taken centuries to add two letters to the original twenty-four of the Roman alphabet; people proved unwilling to add little marks to any of the current twenty-six.

If Webster failed to win acceptance for his reforms in English graphemes, he also failed on a broader front. Dictionary makers would not, as the years passed, choose to indicate pronunciation by making marks on or over the dictionary entry itself. Instead, lexicographers resorted to re-spelling a dictionary entry in some kind of phonetic spelling, to indicate pronunciation. This approach was early familiar to Americans from such a dictionary as the *Pronouncing Dictionary* of John Walker (one of Webster's bêtes noires, as we shall see). Here is Walker's entry for the word *disaster*, in an 1836 edition of his dictionary:

DISASTER, dĭs-ăs'tŭr. s 454. The blast or stroke of an unfavourable planet; misfortune, grief, mishap, misery.[84]

Contrast an entry from Webster's 1830 school *Dictionary*:

Diʂ-äs-ter, *n.* calamity, unfortunate event.[85]

Webster's "pointing" system would make a numerical system of indicating pronunciation virtually obsolete, but his belief that the pronunciation could be satisfactorily indicated by his graphemic innovations, diacritical marks, and the placement of syllabic stress on the dictionary entry itself was not to be shared by the lexicographers who would succeed him.

THE ELEMENTARY SPELLING BOOK (1829)

All these innovations in indicating pronunciation were first introduced to the public by Webster in his *Elementary Spelling Book* of 1829. The work, as we have suggested, represented the culmination of his decades of thought on the subject of conveying to children the pronunciation of the English language. He named it the *Elementary* because he believed it taught the child the elements of his language.

Quite apart from the alteration in the method of marking pronunciation, there were other changes in the *Elementary Spelling Book* which, as we shall see, were so striking that many who met the work for the first time were skeptical as to whether Webster had actually authored it. (As we know, he in fact had been assisted in the writing but the work was constantly under his supervision.)

Of all the revisions that Webster made to his spelling book over the decades, those in this new edition of 1829 were the most far-reaching. The physical appearance of the *Elementary*, just to take the most obvious contrast, was very different from that of the old *American Spelling Book*. The book was wider, the type larger, some of the letters innovative, and pointed instead of numbered; but perhaps what struck the devotee of Webster's books the most was its absence of pictures (except for a frontispiece by Alexander Anderson) and the disappearance of its fables. The book still has columns of words to be spelled ("tables," which are printed in Webster's innovative type, with diacritical marks). These are followed by reading matter ("lessons," printed in traditional orthography). But the lessons are no longer familiar. The awesome "No man may put off the law of God" has vanished. Instead, the lessons are strings of sentences with no connecting meaning. They serve to provide a context for words that have appeared in the preceding tables.

Even the basic organization of the speller was changed. The number of tables increased from 54 to 149. Where the *American Spelling Book* and its predecessors had proceeded steadily up the number of syllables, so that you could be sure that words of three syllables, accented on the second, would precede words of four syllables, "the primary accent on the first and the secondary on the third," this was no longer true in the *Elementary*. There, although the progression was still from short words to long, it was much more uneven.

The *Elementary* was, however, undoubtedly more comprehensive than its predecessor. The book now included words of seven and eight syllables; a table of words beginning *gn* and *kn*; a table of words like *dead*, in which *ea* is to be pronounced as /ɛ/, and many other refinements, all of which were lacking in the old book.[86]

If the change in form is striking, so too is the change in content. As we have seen, all the reading matter has been sacrificed to sentences, whose sole purpose is to illustrate how words are used in context. (It is tempting to see in this the influence of over twenty years of defining, but we cannot be sure how much was Webster's work and how much Ely's.) There is no passage, in the entire book, that could legitimately be called a story, for the sentences bear no relation to each other. In addition, the choice of content was much more practical and child-oriented than in the earlier book. Here, for example, is a table of monosyllables in the *Elementary*:

bit pit jot got nut vix fox ean . . .

Ann can hem my cap
She has a new fan
He hid in his den

A table of "Words of two syllables, accented on the first," begins:

Làd' der shel ter chär ter chär nel . . .
The farmer hatchels flax; he sells corn by the bushel, and butter by the firkin.

(The vocabulary control in the sentences is far from complete. For example, *hatchel* and *bushel* have been introduced in the table, but not *firkin*.) But a close scrutiny reveals that there has been no fundamental change in Webster's value system; for the sentences that illustrate "im ma te ri àl' i ty," and the climax of the work, words of eight syllables, accented on the sixth: "un in tel li ġi bìl' i ty" and "in eom pre hen si bìl' i ty" read:

The immateriality of the soul has rarely been disputed.
. . . We cannot doubt the incomprehensibility of the divine attributes.

And the closing words of the book, printed in Webster's special type, read

For God shall bring every wŏrk into judġment, with every seeret thing, whether it be gọod, or whether it be evil.[87]

There is certainly, however, a change in overt religious content. The proportion of religious material in the *Elementary* has been calculated to be 10 per cent, in contrast to the 47 per cent of the *American Spelling Book*, revised impression.[88] But a decline in religious content did not make the *Elementary* a book of amusement. All in all, one is inclined to agree with Webster's son-in-law, Chauncey Goodrich, who wrote to Webster, after examining the *Elementary* with great care, that he had found it "not so *amusing* as the old one; but it is far more instructive."[89]

We have noted that this is the first of Webster's spelling books to introduce some of his more idiosyncratic spelling reforms. They were destined to be poorly received. In the same letter to his father-in-law, Chauncey Goodrich suggested to Webster that many of the attacks on the new spelling book were motivated by the public's uneasiness with the spelling of just a small number of words. He cited *maiz, sleezy, melasses, ribin, gimblet, porpess* and *steril* as examples. His advice to Webster was to sacrifice these in order to preserve his spelling improvements in whole classes of words (such as *theater* and *honor*).[90] Webster listened to this advice (not something he was in the habit of doing), and the later editions of the *Elementary Spelling Book* show that he retreated on about half of these highly unusual spellings.[91]

The public would also be unhappy with the *Elementary's* lack of pictures and connected prose. As Corey & Fairbank, a Cincinnati publisher, put it in an 1833 letter to Webster, "The objections which you have named as having been made to your Elementary book are the same that have been made to it here, viz: the want of a *due proportion* of *reading lessons*, and of some *pictures*."[92] Webster's only concession was to restore four of the original eight fables to the book. From 1831 on, the familiar "of the Boy that stole Apples" and "The Country Maid and her Milk pail" appear, with illustrations, in most editions of the *Elementary*.[93]

To understand the environment in which Webster planned the *Elementary Spelling Book*, and the reasons for such a radical alteration of his old book, we must return to the moment when Webster was at last able to divert his attention away from his *American Dictionary of the English Language* and think once again about his primary textbook.

VII

The Revised Speller of 1829

When Webster at last emerged from his heroic lexicographical endeavors in 1828, with the publication of his *American Dictionary of the English Language*, he once again had the time and energy to devote to his other works. The most pressing and urgent task was the revamping of his spelling book. As we have seen, the *American Spelling Book*, which had been in the hands of the publishing firm of Hudson and Co. since 1818, no longer conformed to Webster's decisions on orthography and pronunciation, which had matured during his years of working on the dictionary.

Webster had long been planning to revise his speller. True to form, as one who liked to keep the public abreast of his grand plans for American education, he had written a letter to the *American Journal of Education*, in 1826. He had completed his dictionary, he said in this letter (little suspecting that it would take another two years to see it into print) and his spelling book "will be adjusted to a uniformity with the dictionary in pronunciation." He also took advantage of the occasion—characteristically—to attack the dictionary of John Walker.[1]

The *American Journal of Education*, to which Webster wrote his letter, was itself a symptom of how the educational scene had changed since Webster first started writing spelling books. The national interest in education was now considerable. In particular, the rise of the common school had led to a flood of textbooks. The *American Journal of Education* had been started in 1826 by William Russell, who favored an "enlarged and liberal" view of education.[2] Textbook publishers were quick to take advantage

of Russell's review section, and in the same issue that carried
Webster's remarks, the editor noted that there were nearly fifty
textbooks on hand for review.[3]

No mean proportion of these textbooks were spelling
books, readers or primers. Spelling books, in particular, lay thick
on the ground. In the first three years of its existence, from 1826
to 1828, the *American Journal of Education* reviewed spelling books
authored by Thomas J. Lee, James H. Sears, William Bolles,
Elihu H. Marshall, Lyman Cobb, Noyes P. Hawes, Hall J. Kelley,
and B. D. Emerson.[4] These works were produced, by and large,
for the eastern market. The western market held other threats to
Webster's supremacy, such as the Cincinnati speller by Martin
Ruter, which had the effrontery to title itself *The New American
Spelling Book.*[5]

All of these spelling books had been published, either for
the first time or in a revised edition, since 1825. Worse still, from
Webster's point of view, many of them followed the pronunciation
of Walker's dictionary. So important was pronunciation held to
be—because, as we have seen, spelling book authors believed
themselves to be teaching the child to speak—that no less than
six of the works included a reference to the Walker dictionary in
their very title.[6] James H. Sears' work, *A Standard Spelling-book, or
the Scholar's Guide to an accurate Pronunciation of the English Language*,
proclaimed itself as *Designed as an Introduction to the use of Walker's
Pronouncing Dictionary of the English Language*. If this were not bad
enough, the reviewer of this work in the *American Journal of
Education* took it upon himself to point out its incompatibility
with Webster's speller, without mentioning the latter by name.
"It has unaccountably," ran the review, "been customary to
make use, in the youngest class, of a spelling-book entirely at war
with Walker's principles." This incompatibility, the review
continued, had been the cause of much trouble and waste of
time, which this new work would set right.[7]

The Walker dictionary to which all these works referred was
A Critical Pronouncing Dictionary of the English Language, first
published in London in 1791, and in its twenty-eighth British
edition in 1826. John Walker, its English author (1732–1807),
had a varied and rather exotic career. He entered the stage in his
youth and married an actress. When he had forsaken acting in
1768, he made a good living by giving lectures on elocution and
by writing books. His *Critical Pronouncing Dictionary*, the most

important of his works, was first published in America in 1803, and frequently thereafter.[8] As neither being an actor nor being British were characteristics dear to Webster's heart, and a London stage pronunciation had long been anathema to him, Walker was not a natural candidate for Webster's approbation, even in the best of circumstances.

Webster had known for a long time that Walker's dictionary posed a real threat to him. When he was in Amherst in 1820, battling with his own dictionary, Webster had received a letter from the superintendent of common schools for the State of New York. In his letter, the superintendent asked Webster, civilly enough, whether he could arrange the tables in the *American Spelling Book* so that they would conform to Walker's pronunciation.[9] Taken up with the dictionary as he was, Webster was roused to a lengthy reply. He numbered his responses, some of which contradicted each other. In the first place, his speller did in general, he responded, conform to Walker's pronunciation and to that of all good speakers. Second, there were pronunciation differences between his own work and Walker's dictionary which would make it impossible to introduce conformity without introducing disorder into the tables. In the third place, all the copies of his books agreed with each other in their pagination, so it was impossible to change one edition without changing all. Fourthly, he added, even if all these objections were removed, any alteration which would destroy the sale of the books previously published would be unfair to the book's owners. (This was very much an ad hominem argument, as, had Webster for one moment believed it, he would never have initiated revisions of his work. What is more, he was to set in train, seven years later, a plan that would indeed threaten to make the *American Spelling Book* obsolete.)

Webster had not finished. Fifthly, he asserted, many literary men would not accept Walker's pronunciation (shamelessly contradicting his first point). Sixth, he did not approve of Walker's pronunciation of *bench* as *bensh*. "In two or three other classes of words, Walker has entirely mistaken the genuine sound of English Letters & absolutely perverts the pronunciation." For this reason, it would do violence to his principles to adopt Walker's or any one else's scheme. In the seventh place, a plan to fix the pronunciation was premature. Eighth, no one state or district should adopt a standard of speaking—it should come from literary men across the country, perhaps through the medium of something similar to the French academy. Lastly, he himself, Webster said, had been working on a dictionary of the language, which would be more complete than anything yet published.

Webster closed this exercise in high dudgeon with a classic peroration: "Should my health continue, this work, the fruit of twenty years labor, will be offered to the public. Whether it will be an improvement on the best English dictionaries, whether it will be subjected to the revision of an Academy of literary men, and by them approved as a standard work; or whether the labor of a large portion of my life, & an expenditure of $30,000 of my private property are to be thrown away—I do not presume to decide." But he would not, Webster said, alter his elementary works until his dictionary was completed and "its fate determined."[10] (The superintendent of the common schools of the State of New York must have been exceedingly sorry that he brought the matter up.)

Webster had never, of course, been one to sit around waiting for fate to determine anything. In March 1826, he took the offensive and attacked Walkerisms (which had the effect on him, he once told a son-in-law, of "a box on the ears,"[11]) on the grounds that they were an un-American activity. He deplored the "overwhelming reverence for foreign opinions and authority," he said, regarding it as a *"species of slavery."* It was a theme he had struck in the first edition of his spelling book, when he had urged Americans to cast off their ties to Britain. Now he noted the restoration of all things British, in the intervening forty years, to the good graces of the American people. "Nothing now will be received and countenanced which is not *British*, or sanctioned by British authority."[12]

In June 1826, as we have seen, he announced that he was planning to revise his spelling book to bring it into conformity with his dictionary. For the first time in his life, he sought assistance in rewriting the speller. He first employed Daniel Barnes, a New York City schoolmaster, for the revision. Barnes was killed in an accident and Webster turned to Aaron Ely, also of New York.[13] In December 1828, Ely and Webster signed an agreement which stipulated that Ely would use materials prepared by Webster and himself to "compile a spelling book for said Webster, submitting the same to the revision of said

Webster." The fee was to be $1,000, to be paid in March 1832.[14]

With the revision of the spelling book in hand, Webster turned his attention to all the other aspects of producing a speller that had engrossed his attention almost fifty years earlier, when he was preparing to send his *Institute* off into the world. This time there was no grammar or reader involved with the spelling book. Instead, there was Webster's dictionary for schools. Webster regarded this, together with the spelling book, as his final word on the pronunciation and orthography of the English language. He saw his two school works as essential texts in his coherent scheme for systematic instruction in English— one that would culminate in the great quarto dictionary. His political ambitions for his country had been consistently thwarted; but here, in his explication of the language they spoke, would lie his contribution to the American people.

In 1827, the spelling book was being planned, and Webster had not yet had time to devote himself to his dictionary for schools, which would in any case never be as widely used as his spelling book. But he did not dare delay his assaults on behalf of the latter. The threat from spellers compiled on the plan of "Elocution Walker," as the British lexicographer was called, was too pressing.[15] Now almost seventy years old, Webster marshalled his resources to carry war into the enemy camp and rout the spelling books invading his territory. In all respects, it was a reprise of the great battle he had waged in the 1780s.

WEBSTER AND HIS PUBLISHERS

Webster was prepared to leave the compilation of his spelling book to someone else, but not the question of its publisher. In July 1827, before he had even chosen his assistant, Webster sent off the first letter in what was to be a lengthy and rather acrimonious correspondence between himself and Henry Hudson & Co.[16] (Hudson & Co., it will be recalled, had held the entire 1818 copyright of the *American Spelling Book* since purchasing it from Webster in advance in 1816.) In the letter, Webster informed Hudson that he was planning to alter his spelling book and produce a new edition of it.[17]

The problems that this raised for Hudson were considerable. After all, he was the sole holder of the right to assign licenses to printers all over the country. He had paid a large sum for this right, and the income from the licenses for the spelling book must have constituted a major portion of his wealth. He still had no less than five years unexpired on the contract: the copyright for the *American Spelling Book* did not run out until March 1832. What Webster was asking him to do was to introduce a new work which would seriously undermine the commercial value of the old.

Hudson was not slow to realize this. He would consent to the alterations, he told Webster in response to the latter's first feelers, provided that his contract with the publishers of Webster's old spelling book would not be affected. He told Webster that there would be no pecuniary advantage in a new speller: it would be "attacked by Walker, Walker in various shapes and from various quarters." The attacks would only cease, in his opinion, if the name of Walker were made "auxilliary or at least converted into a neutral."[18] (Given Webster's sensitivity on the subject of Walker, Hudson's well-intentioned suggestion was surely the gravest of tactical errors.)

A year later, in 1828, when the possible publication of the new speller seemed more of a reality, Hudson spoke much more forcefully: "It appears to me that there would be insuperable objections to the publication during the term of the present Sp. book" of a work intended to replace it. The publishers of the *American Spelling Book* paid in advance for the right to print a specified number, whether they printed that number or not. ". . . they would therefore be opposed to the introduction of any new work that would in any degree diminish the sales of the old," especially if the sales of the new work should prove to be extensive.[19]

Hudson warned Webster that, if any of the publishers refused to agree with Webster's plan, the new work could not be printed without breach of contract.[20] In point of fact, it was by no means clear that this was so. Webster clearly did not think so, as in October Hudson was writing to him again: "As to *my own* obligation, I know that I am bound by contract as well as by every principle of honor & justice not to assist in the introduction of a new one without the consent of the publishers of the old."[21] It is clear that Hudson was becoming thoroughly alarmed. One does not need to appeal to principle if one's legal standing is secure.

Hudson stood to lose even more financially than it appeared.

He sold all the licenses in advance, and at first glance it would seem that he was in a much better position than the publishers, as he had already secured his income. But in fact, as the deals worked out in practice, every publisher, in negotiating for a license, sought to obtain a license for the fewest number of copies possible, and then paid extra for any copies over that number. As Hudson explained it to Webster, one party to the negotiations (the publisher) was trying "to fix his purchase of a definite annual number *as low* as he can, with the intention to print as many as he can over that, & the other party" (Hudson himself) was "endeavoring to fix the annual number as high as he can persuade the purchaser to consent to."[22] Much of Hudson's income came from these additional copies paid for after they were printed.

Worse was to come for Hudson, however. He made the mistake of telling Webster that if he were to act as his agent for the new work—provided the publishers of the old agreed to its introduction—he must act as agent for the whole right. This passage in Hudson's letter has been marked by Webster with a row of penciled Xs—a notation he reserved for opinions with which he violently disagreed.[23] In March of the following year he wrote loftily to Hudson that it would "not be practicable to carry into effect our project respecting the new Spelling Book, on the plan proposed, so that further proceedings on your part may be discontinued. I must keep the work in my own hands."[24]

The *Elementary Spelling Book* was published in New York and elsewhere that same year. It took Hudson some time for the blow to sink in, and for him to enquire why Webster had not seen fit to give him the agency (for he had no part of it, let alone the whole agency) for the new spelling book.[25] Webster gave, as his reason, the fact that several of the copy-owners had professed themselves dissatisfied with Hudson's management. The market had been overstocked (a familiar complaint on Webster's part), and the price of the book had sunk.[26]

As those who might get the agency in Hudson's stead were not the most impartial judges of his management, Hudson was rightly incensed. "It strikes me as somewhat extraordinary," he wrote to Webster by return mail, "that you should deprive me of an agency, that you had solicited me to accept, on a charge of mismanagement by interested persons and that without even an enquiry of me as to the justice of the charge."[27] Hudson

proceeded to give Webster complete details of the copies
published by each purchaser.[28] He had earlier told Webster that
the sales of the *American Spelling Book* had averaged over 350,000 a
year, for the years 1825 to 1827,[29] and his fuller figures
confirmed the earlier ones. His main point was that the
publishers consistently printed more copies than their original
license had stipulated. He asked, of his figures, "Are they
evidence of mismanagement? Is it I who have overstocked the
market or compelled the publishers to do it? Or do these
complaints arise from the disappointment of those who would
publish 80 or 100 M [thousand] on a right to print 50 M? I have
no doubt," he continued, "that the introduction of the new work
has been prejudicial to my interest."[30]

It was too late. Webster showed no signs of softening his
stand. A full eighteen months later, in September 1831, Webster
wrote to Hudson to tell him that he had ascertained, at least to
his own satisfaction, that "the American Spelling Book has,
during your holding the right, been dismissed from one half or
two thirds of all the schools in the Eastern & Middle States. The
ground lost could never be recovered without the aid of my
dictionary & a *new* spelling book."[31]

If this were indeed the case, it is also true that Webster was
not aiding his old spelling book. In 1831 he published a
pamphlet which publicized his works on the English language,
including his *Elementary Spelling Book*. In it, he took the
opportunity to attack his own earlier work—despite the fact that
Henry Hudson's agency of it still had almost a year to run. "The
American Spelling Book, in consequence of some changes in
pronunciation which have taken place since its first publication,
and of negligence in workmen, is now incorrect, and not
conformable to my dictionaries. In addition to this, spurious or
counterfeit editions are in market, and editions miserably
printed, against which it is proper to caution the public."[32] No
wonder Henry Hudson wrote indignantly to Webster that it had
been their joint agreement that the new spelling book should be
published with the old, and substituted for it as fast as was
proper, but that "it was never agreed that the old one should in
any other way be suspended till my right had expired."[33]

While the early part of this rather bitter correspondence was
being carried on, Webster was looking for a publisher who would
be worthy of his confidence. In April 1829 he went to New York

with the aim of finding a publisher to stereotype the speller and "preparing the way for its reception." This preparation took the form of his initiating a meeting, on May 18, of a score or so of teachers and "literary gentlemen," who formed a small committee to examine the merits of the *American Dictionary*. At a second meeting a week later, the committee presented to about fifty persons a favorable report which was passed with only a few dissenting voices. On May 28 an article appeared in the *New-York Evening Post* (couched in language that was undeniably Webster's), mentioning his forthcoming school dictionary and spelling book as well as the system of diacritical marks he had devised to "complete the scheme for facilitating the acquisition of the language." The article closed with the remark that between forty and fifty of the principal teachers in New York, both male and female, had already "manifested their cordial approbation of this system of elementary instruction."

Controversy had attended the birth of Webster's first spelling book, and laced the air with charges of plagiarism. Controversy would now attend the birth of his last speller, but this time Webster would be accused not of copying from others but of getting someone else to do his work. On June 27, when the speller was still not in print, a letter to the *Evening Post* bearing the unmistakable imprint of Lyman Cobb launched the attack on Webster. Cobb accused Webster of using others to compile the spelling book, naming both the deceased Daniel Barnes and Aaron Ely, and even quoting the actual sum that Webster was paying Ely for his assistance. Cobb displayed particular outrage at the earlier article's closing remarks about the teachers' report: he poined out, with perfect justice, that these teachers had "manifested their *cordial approbation* of a series of books which they have *never seen*." He charged further that Webster's presence at these meetings had precluded any discussion about the propriety of such a report, let alone a discussion of the merits of the dictionary itself.

A sharp exchange of letters ensued in the *Evening Post*. Those for the defence included a response from the committee members, who insisted that Webster had spoken at the meeting only at their insistence, and suggested that those one or two individuals who had voted against the report were those "whose interest... would be in some degree affected" by it. The correspondence for the other side seemed to flow from just one pen. The counsel for the prosecution signed himself "Candour" (with an -*our* spelling that betrayed Cobb's authorship) and headed his statement "Webster's Spelling Book compiled by Aaron Ely." Cobb attacked discrepancies of spelling among Webster's various dictionaries and listed inconsistencies within the now published speller. The final word came, not from Webster, who for once stayed out of the cross-fire, but from Aaron Ely. He thanked "Candour" for his criticisms on the misprints in the spelling book, said that these already had been corrected, and defended the part he had played in the composition of the speller. "A good Spelling Book," he said, "... requires a man of great *literary attainments*, united with a long *experience* in *teaching*, to make such a book. That Dr. Webster is a man of great literary attainments all *candid* critics have admitted." (By implication, Ely took the credit for the teaching experience that the book required.) At this point, an exasperated editor said firmly that his paper could no longer lend its columns to these interminable altercations. Ely himself would never see what became of his work on the speller. He died on September 29, a month after his letter had appeared in the *Evening Post*.[34]

The spelling book which had occasioned all this heat had appeared in print in July. It was published by J. P. Haven & R. Lockwood of New York and was stereotyped by A. Chandler. The phrasing of its title could have done nothing to console Henry Hudson, for it read, *The Elementary Spelling Book: being an Improvement on the American Spelling Book*. The following year White, Gallaher & White, also of New York, published the first edition of Webster's school dictionary.[35]

In assigning the school dictionary to the White firm, Webster ran afoul of another publisher. Sherman Converse of New York, it will be recalled, had been the publisher who had taken on the immense task of printing Webster's *American Dictionary*: an immense task not only because it involved the typesetting of some 70,000 words and their definitions, but because, in order to print some of the languages that Webster included in his etymologies, Converse had had to send to Europe for the typefaces.

In 1828, with the great dictionary barely off the press, Converse learned that he was not to be Webster's publisher for the school dictionary, which was, of course, an abridgement of the original quarto edition of the *American Dictionary*. He did not mince his words to Webster: "but for me your Dictionary would have rested in Manuscript—There seems," he continued sarcastically, "to be peculiar apprehension lest I should make something for my great labour and expense of time and money and I suppose this is the reason why others are preferred." He predicted disaster if Webster attempted to publish the work himself. (This was not an approach likely to please Webster. On the back of Converse's letter, Webster made the annotation "Menacing letter!")[36]

In 1831, no doubt impressed by the production of his school dictionary, Webster made his decision. The firm of White, Gallaher & White was to have the sole agency—comparable to the agency he had awarded Hudson & Co. in 1816—of the new spelling book, for a term of thirteen years. Anyone who wished to publish the book would have to apply for a license to the White firm. In June 1831, he and the White partners signed a contract.[37]

That same day Webster and the Whites signed a second contract. One of its provisions was reminiscent of the early agreement with Hudson & Co.: Webster was attempting to further his son, William, in a profession. The contract stipulated that if William were to enter into a partnership, he was to be granted a license to print not less than 30,000 spelling books annually. In addition, the Whites undertook to assist him in the sale of books in New York City.[38]

* * *

During the two years that passed between the first publication of the new spelling book in July 1829 and Webster's decision to let White, Gallaher & White have its agency in June 1831, Webster took charge of the work, and with his inimitable energy and concentration, focused on those external aspects of it that he had always considered important.

Price and Uniformity. Two matters that had caused him many problems in the early days, when he was promoting the *American Spelling Book*, were the uniformity of price and the uniformity of all the editions, nation-wide. In 1804 he had taken care of these problems, as far as he could, with a contract designed to tackle these issues.[39] As we have seen, that contract had been a great improvement on what had gone before. The contract he now prepared for his spelling book, in 1830, and the form of it that White, Gallaher & White used, when they were granting licenses, took his 1804 contract one step further.[40] The license gave the prospective publishers of the spelling book the right to print a prescribed number of copies within a set time limit (for example, 90,000 over three years). The fee paid for this license was seven mills a copy (that is, seven dollars per thousand copies)— substantially less than the cent per copy that Webster had received in 1804. (The fee to the Whites for 90,000 copies would therefore be $630.) The number of copies that could be printed annually was limited in the contract.

The built-in accounting system was used again: the publisher was to inform the Whites of the number of copies printed, and (as a check on their truthfulness) enclose a "certificate of the foreman of the office, or of the pressman who shall perform the work, stating the number of quires of perfect paper that have been printed in said book." Twenty-one quires were to be calculated as being used for 1,000 copies. (Webster had calculated twenty-two for the old *American Spelling Book*.)

In addition, as much control over the selling price was set as could be hoped for. The contract stipulated that the license-holder was not to sell at a price less than would give him a net profit (including the cost of the license) of thirteen per cent. A license could be renewed, but only if the conditions had been complied with. And there was a final stipulation, which had not appeared in the 1804 license: "Should said [publisher] at any time during the terms of this license, commence printing or publishing any other spelling book, then our obligation to renew is void."[41] At his peril would a publisher dare to print another speller while publishing Webster's.

This printed license ensured, as far as was humanly possible, uniformity among the terms that were offered potential publishers of the speller, and uniformity—if they abided by its provisions—in the speller's retail price. The internal aspects of the speller itself—its type size, kind and quality—were taken care of by the recent revolution in printing, the invention of the stereotyping process. From now on, the purchaser of the license for the speller would have to buy stereotyped plates from the New York foundry of Adoniram Chandler,[42] or some other foundry.

The stereotyping process had already been used for a great

many editions of the revised *American Spelling Book*.[43] Stereotyping was ideally suited to textbook production, where repeated editions fully justified the initial expense of the plates. By its use, Webster disposed of all the problems of variations between different editions, issued by a variety of publishers, that had so vexed him in his youth. Or almost all: for any error that existed on the plates was reproduced by every publisher. William alerted his father to one such mistake. "I did not know till I read your letter," replied Webster, "that I had left *enthrall* in my Preface uncorrected. It should be *inthrall*. I will have the plate altered."[44]

Copyright Protection. Decades earlier, as a young man, Webster as we know had been a prime mover in the campaign for the copyright protection he correctly saw as essential to his work. It is almost with awe, now, that we see him, at this second period in his life when he was launching a new spelling book, once again involving himself in a fight for improved copyright legislation.

Webster had been in touch with Daniel Webster in 1826, hoping to persuade him to promote legislation that would assign the benefits to an author from his work for perpetuity.[45] Daniel Webster saw disadvantages to that but had been hopeful of obtaining an improved law.[46] Now, in the fall of 1830, when Noah Webster's son-in-law, William W. Ellsworth, failed to get a copyright bill through the Judiciary Committee of the House of Representatives, Webster decided to bolster the cause by the weight of his personal presence. In December, he traveled to Washington and stayed there near his daughter Emily Ellsworth and her family.

Here at Washington, at long last, Webster's unremitting labors met with accolades. It seemed as if every elected official knew and admired him. Members of Congress greeted him most cordially. "They had learned in my books," Webster wrote to another daughter, "—they were glad to see me, and ready to do me any kindness in their power. They all seemed to think also that my great labors deserve some uncommon reward. Indeed," Webster added, "I know of nothing that has given me more pleasure in my journeys, the last summer and this winter, than the respect and kindness manifested towards me in consequence of the use of my books. It convinces me that my fellow citizens consider me as their benefactor and the benefactor of my country."[47]

Webster's warm reception did not end at the congressional level. He was invited to dine with President Jackson, sat at his right hand, and was able to grumble about the foreign cast of the food in his letters home.[48] On New Year's Day, 1831, he and the Ellsworths "all attended the President's Levee. It was *jam, jam* ... the Ladies were dressed—I don't know how—Emily can tell. But our family looked as well as any of them."[49]

Two days later, Webster gave an hour's discourse on the English language in the Hall of the House of Representatives, who had given him this privilege by a resolution. His audience listened "with profound attention."[50] Emily, who had of course been among his audience, reported that her father had said nothing of his own labors, but that, "should the bill for extending the copyright law be carried successfully, he should rejoice for himself, his family, for his country."[51]

Three days later, Webster and Emily were present in the gallery of the House of Representatives to witness the passing of the copyright bill, without a division. "I have reason to think my presence here has been useful in this affair;" was Webster's simple comment, "& I rejoice very much in the result." He took less pleasure in his sudden popularity on the Washington social scene. "I begin to be invited to parties, but shall avoid them as much as possible, except those which are given by N[ew] England people."[52]

In February the copyright bill became law. It gave authors exclusive rights to their own works for twenty-eight years, and renewal rights to their widows and children for another fourteen. Webster was able to write home to Rebecca, "My great object is now accomplished."[53]

There had only been one dark cloud in the sunny Washington sky: the arrival of Sherman Converse on the scene to aid the passage of the bill. Webster's relationship with Converse, after he had denied him the publication of the school dictionary, can readily be imagined. He was not happy to see Converse now, in Washington. "Fortunately the bill had passed the House of Representatives before he arrived. A more unpopular man could not be selected; & if any opposer of the bill had stated to the house how Mr C. has used or abused his monopoly, (as it is called,) of my dictionary, he probably would have defeated the bill."[54] While Webster was perfectly correct in believing that sponsorship by the wrong person can do as much harm as that by the right person can do good, one is permitted a little skepticism about Converse's supposed villainy, under the circumstances.

PROMOTION OF THE SPELLING BOOK

Webster had not rested content with securing for his work the protection of the law in 1785, but had sought to promote it actively with all the means at his disposal. Now in 1831 he once again set in train a host of activities designed to bring his speller and other works to the favorable attention of the public. "Since the passing of the copyright Bill, I have been taking measures to obtain the patronage of the men who are at the head of our national affairs, to aid me in my purposes," he wrote home. "I had at first intended to give another lecture & after that, to invite the attention of gentlemen to a proposition for a vote to encourage the use of my books as standards of spelling."[55]

Recommendations and Advertisements. Whether Congress would actually have voted for Webster's orthography to be the national standard, we shall never know. As it was, the wintry weather defeated his plan, which he had to abandon for fear of not drawing an audience. He therefore fell back on his first and oldest standby: recommendations. With a skill that one cannot but admire, he used his Washington fame as America's leading lexicographer to obtain recommendations from scores of the elected representatives of the American people. He knew what he was about: "the signatures of such a respectable number of gentlemen from every state in the Union, will be of no inconsiderable use to me."[56]

When Webster later printed up the recommendations on a flyer for promotional purposes, they filled one enormous page, half of which ran as follows: "The subscribers highly appreciate Dr. Webster's purpose and attempt to improve the English language, by rendering its orthography more simple, regular and uniform." The subscribers found it desirable that "one standard dictionary should be used by the numerous millions of people who are to inhabit the vast extent of territory belonging to the United States; as the use of such a standard may prevent the formation of dialects in states remote from each other, and impress upon the language *uniformity* and *stability* . . . we rejoice that the *American Dictionary* bids fair to become such a standard, and" (a cunning addition slipped in by Webster which touched on his other works without actually being an outright recommendation) "we sincerely hope that the author's elementary books for primary schools and academies will commend themselves to the general use of our fellow citizens." The text was dated Washington, February 1831.

This impressive document in favor of Webster's dictionary was signed by thirty-one senators, including Daniel Webster from the State of Massachusetts, and no fewer than seventy-three Congressmen. Among them was, of course, William Ellsworth of Connecticut.[57]

Not content with the signatures of the majority of congress, Webster sought recommendations also from those whom he always called "men of literature" or "literary men." From these, he was able to obtain a notice that was more specific about his spelling book. On his flyer, following after the long list of names of members of congress who had supported his dictionary as a standard work, there follows a rider: "The value and success of that work" (that is, the *American Dictionary of the English Language*) "will no doubt contribute towards securing for the *Elementary Spelling Book*, by the same author, a currency with the public, corresponding to that which its predecessor, the *American Spelling Book*, so long possessed." The subscribers trusted that Dr. Webster's series of books would "find their way into all our schools."[58] The faculty of Yale appeared in full force among the names of the subscribers: President Jeremiah Day was there, as was Benjamin Silliman, Professor of Chemistry at Yale. Also there—but causing no surprise to anyone—were the names of Chauncey A. Goodrich, Professor of Rhetoric and Oratory at Yale, and the Rev. William Fowler, Professor of Chemistry and Natural History at Middlebury College. Both were sons-in-law to Webster.

Altogether it was a list that must have warmed Webster's heart. With one single exception, every type of person whom one could possibly call upon to recommend his speller was there: university professors, Webster's personal friends and relations, the nation's famous men—only the recommendation from the satisfied schoolmaster was missing. In any case, it was hard to see how even one more name could have been fitted onto the page.

Recommendations were always useful for advertising purposes, and Webster of course encouraged his publishers to use them when they inserted any advertisements in the public press.[59] But, as we have seen, Webster had never remained content to rely on advertising alone to promote his books. Once again, just as he had in those early years when he was smoothing the path to success for his *American Spelling Book*, Webster undertook all kinds of activities that would today be grouped under the rubric of public relations. There was one difference on this occasion: he hired someone else to do much of the promotional work for him.

Agents. It should not be thought that Webster employed another man because he believed that he himself was too old to go on tour, or perhaps considered that it was beneath his dignity—for he traveled around the New England territory for months at a time to promote his books. In the spring of 1831, for example, he went on a six month tour, leaving Washington to travel all the way to Portland, Maine, to see what had happened to his old speller in the common schools and to pave the way for the introduction of his new one.[60]

It was not so much that Webster had less strength to go touring the country for publicity purposes. It was rather that there was now much more country to tour. Thirteen coastal states had comprised the American confederation when Webster set out on his first promotional tour in 1785. Since that time, the relentless expansion westward had shifted the focus of America from the coast to the interior. Nine states west of the Appalachian Mountains had been incorporated into the Union and invited the attention of the merchant.

So the great West of America beckoned to Webster for its commercial possibilities and for the chance to spread his scheme of education across the whole country. In 1830 both his speller and his school dictionary were in print. Webster had denied the agency for either book to Hudson & Co., but had not yet determined who should have it. Looking for a man who would conduct an agency on his behalf in the western states, Webster found such a man in the person of Walter Bidwell. On April 20, 1830 (eight months before Webster's trip to Washington), Bidwell signed a contract with Webster, in which his responsibilities were outlined clearly. His "principal business will be to converse with literary men, wherever he may travel[,] in regard to my views in introducing a set of school books into use, which shall be uniform in orthography & pronunciation; to distribute

my pamphlet containing recommendations; & to make contracts
for the sale of copy right of my Elementary Spelling Book."
Bidwell was "particularly to visit some of the clergy & the
principal teachers of schools in Philadelphia & Baltimore, &
obtain their names & influence, if practicable."

Webster had planned out the type of territory that a license
should cover. Bidwell was to give one license for the speller in
northern Ohio; another in Detroit for the whole of Michigan;
and another, if possible, for the state of Indiana. Legally, there
was no way to restrict any one publisher from selling wherever
he wanted, but in this private contract with Bidwell Webster at
least could state what he would like. Sales of the speller were to
be restricted to the state or district in which a publisher had
exclusive printing rights. Publishers "are not to send great
quantities into the districts of other proprietors, so as to
overstock the market & reduce the price."[61]

Two days later Bidwell set off from New Haven. He kept a
log of his activities in a little book, which he also used for
collecting endorsements from the "literary men" whom he
encountered on his trip.[62] These were the recommendations that
Webster would later incorporate into his large flyer, which also
contained the congressional subscribers.

Bidwell's journal shows that there was no modern method of
publicizing a textbook and soliciting its adoption by a school
system that was unknown in 1830. Contact with leading citizens;
the solicitation of reviews; the distribution of informative
leaflets; donations of examination copies of the textbook—the
importance of all these approaches was well understood by
Bidwell. While one of the main purposes of his trip was to obtain
direct recommendations, he did not neglect less direct sponsorship: he was well aware of the value of the "old boy" network,
where a man will look favorably upon a book simply because it is
recommended to him by someone he was at school with. In
addition, Bidwell was alert to the importance of any and every
meeting of teachers, as a forum for his promotional efforts. As
far as the opposition went, he was also prepared: he fully
appreciated the influence that a local author of a rival work
could exert in favor of his textbooks, if he were either a teacher
or, better still, in a position of prominence on a school board.

Armed as well as any modern promoter for both offensive
and defensive action, Bidwell entered the fray. He gives us

glimpses of his tactics in the pages of his diary. He initially followed the route that Webster himself had pursued in 1785. From New Haven he traveled west, then south, obtaining a recommendation from Dr. Samuel Miller, the president of Princeton. In Philadelphia, he left circulars at the Athenaeum, the Franklin Institute, at libraries and at reading rooms. Proceeding to Baltimore, then Washington, he called on the President of the College at Georgetown, and even a nunnery, where ninety-two girls were being instructed. He was able to take advantage of the free congressional mail, and of the sponsorship it suggested, by having a large number of circulars sent off to the southern and western states, to presidents of various colleges, and to the members of boards of trustees.

In Fredericktown, Maryland, Bidwell spoke to local personalities, as well as to the principal teachers, showed them the *Elementary Spelling Book* and the school dictionary, and gave them a copy of the speller. He did not omit to send a circular to the principal of the Catholic school.

Now Bidwell changed his course and started for the west. In Pittsburgh he "called on the President & Prof.[s] of the Western University, clergymen, judges, Teachers, Booksellers," and warned Webster of the strong Cobb interest there, with the consolation "but still a warm & friendly feeling in favor of Dr. W.[s] series of Books." He traveled to Kentucky, reaching Lexington, which Webster had told him was an important location. There he found that there was about to be a meeting of teachers. He left circulars with an ally, "who would call the attention of the meeting to the subject & distribute circulars."

Finally, he reached Cincinnati. Cincinnati at that time was the gateway to the new western states and the center of commercial activity.[63] Bidwell fully appreciated its importance. "Here is & will be much competition[.] Mr Picket Author of a spelling Book from N. York & teacher, exerts his personal influence to introduce his book & Mr Guilford a Trustee is publisher of it." Better news was that the principal of a school for 200 boys, Mr. N. Holley—happily a roommate and classmate of Yale's President Day, who had signed up as a recommender—had long wanted to see a copy of the *Elementary* and promised to show his free copy to other teachers "& exert his personal influence in its favor."

Still in Cincinnati, Bidwell called on the President of the

College of Teachers. The society was the leading organization of teachers in the west, which met annually to discuss matters of educational interest. The president—who fortunately happened to be a graduate of Yale—undertook to introduce the subject of Webster's works to the society at its next meeting. Leaving no stone unturned, Bidwell sent off a circular to every trustee of every school in Cincinnati. As a result of a long conversation with Bidwell, the "celebrated Judge Hall of Illinois" said he would exert his influence in his home state. A clergyman promised he would give Webster's *American Dictionary* an "elaborate notice" in one of the local newspapers.

Bidwell then continued his publicity campaign in Ohio, visiting Hamilton, Dayton and Columbus. In Mansfield, he managed to assemble the lawyers who had gathered there for the session of the county court and gave them a lecture on Webster's views. He also spoke to a local judge, who had originally come from Connecticut. The lawyers, according to Bidwell, promised to use their influence.

In addition to obtaining recommendations, making all these personal contacts, and publicizing Webster's works by circulars and free copies, Bidwell was also visiting and contacting publishers and booksellers to see if he could come up with some contracts for publishing Webster's spelling book. In Cincinnati, he visited the Rev. Mr. Eastman, whom Webster had mentioned in their original agreement as being authorized to make contracts for Tennessee, Mississippi and Alabama. Eastman appears to have become slightly alarmed by what was expected of a Webster agent, but undertook to represent Webster's interest "as far as his other duties & circumstances would allow." Despite Eastman's lack of enthusiasm, Bidwell gave him a power of attorney, and a copy of the instructions and form of assignment to be followed in allocating licenses.

The firm of Morgan & Sanxay, in Cincinnati, was at this time the sole western proprietor of the *American Spelling Book*. They told Bidwell that the rumor all over Cincinnati was that Webster was not the author of the *Elementary Spelling Book*. The report was based on a letter from New York, which had been sent to a local teacher. (Lyman Cobb, as we shall see, was no doubt the villain.) "I contradicted the report in every shape," said Bidwell stoutly. "... Morgan & Sanxay were satisfied & ordered a set of the plates." The firm insisted, however, on retaining their hold on the places where the *American Spelling Book* had been used, "for the sake of keeping out others until they could introduce the Elementary."[64]

It is not at all clear whether Bidwell made any money from the trip, as his only salary seems to have been the seven mills that would be obtained as a commission from any contract he made out for the spelling book: nowhere does he record actually making out a contract. From Webster's point of view, however, Bidwell's agency must have been most helpful. Bidwell had made contacts with the leading citizens in the middle and western states, and had at least taken the first steps towards getting the *Elementary* published in the west. Webster must have come to the conclusion, however, that the licensing should be centralized, just as it had been since 1818, under the management of Hudson & Co.; for in June 1831, as we have seen, he assigned the entire agency of the spelling book to White, Gallaher & White of New York. For richer or poorer, Bidwell does not reappear in Webster's documents.

If Webster used paid agents as a prime means of promoting his works, at a time when there was too much ground to cover for him to work the area singlehandedly, we should not suppose that he, in 1830, failed to avail himself of the assistance of his friends and relations any more than he had in his youth. Virtually every person with whom Webster had cordial relations was pressed into service one way or another—even if only at the simple level of reporting back on how the *Elementary* was faring.

Webster used his friends, if they were professional educators, as the prime source for his long list of recommendations. But his prop and stay for assistance was, of course, his own family. Webster took it for granted that William, as his only son, should perform chores for him of all sorts. He expected William to contact printers when William was in Virginia, only just married,[65] and to report on what spelling was adopted by the local newspaper.[66] Webster's daughters were asked to enquire of local booksellers (or have their husbands enquire) about how the speller and school dictionary were faring in local schools.[67] Webster's sons-in-law, to a man, worked for the cause. William Fowler, Harriet's husband, put letters in the local newspapers on behalf of Webster's books.[68] William Ellsworth, a U.S. Representative for the state of Connecticut, had prepared the new copyright bill. Chauncey Goodrich, Julia's husband, who as a

Yale professor lived in the same town as his parents-in-law, consistently took the greatest interest in Webster's works.[69] Even Horatio Southgate made his contribution. Because of the scandal over his housekeeper after his wife Mary died, he had not been considered fit to bring up a Webster grandchild, but he was still worth something as an unpaid agent. At Webster's request, Southgate made the rounds of the Portland booksellers to see if the old *American Spelling Book* was holding its own against its competitors and to seek out a publisher worthy of the new speller.[70]

ATTACKS ON COMPETITORS

Webster's persistent queries about the sales of his spelling books, both old and new, were based, as we have seen, on the very real threat posed to his works by the rival spelling books flooding the market in the early 1830s. Those reviewed by the *American Journal of Education* in the early years of its publication by no means exhausted the list of competitors. Horatio Southgate, when he looked at the competition in Portland, had found twenty different spelling books on the market.[71] Webster's New Hampshire publisher reported that *Marshall's, Cumming's, Emerson's, Boston National, Lee's* and *Picket's* books had generally replaced the old speller in most schools.[72] The *Emerson, Hawes* and *Picket* spellers were mentioned as the chief competitors in Maine.[73]

Not all of these, of course, sold extensively enough to warrant Webster's attention. It is significant that Webster himself pinpointed, as threats, those spelling books that were being promoted most vigorously by their publishers or authors. "The great exertion in favor of Emerson's, Cobbs, Sears &c have lessened the sales of my book—" he wrote Henry Hudson in 1830, "but something will be done to recover the ground, & I believe with some success."[74]

It is noteworthy that the spelling book which Webster attacked most fiercely was that of Lyman Cobb, who regarded the promotion of his book in exactly the same light as Webster did his.[75] The rivalry between the two men dated from well before the publication of Webster's new speller. In March 1826, Webster's notice "To the Public" had appeared in New Haven. In this notice, it will be recalled, Webster had denounced the attachment of Americans to all things British as a "species of slavery," and had attacked Samuel Johnson as a lexicographer and John Walker as an orthoepist. In the attempts to rival his book, said Webster, "it has been found expedient to depreciate my work and to charge me with *innovation*," and with introducing a scheme of orthography and pronunciation that was vague and pedantic. "Surely, if this is true, if my book is really a bad one, I have been very much deceived . . . . But I have examined some of the books which are sent into the world to correct the evil I have done. One of them is little less than a copy of mine—it contains *almost all my tables*, with no alteration except the transposition of a few words . . . the *pronunciation is mine*," added Webster.[76]

The spelling book Webster referred to was that of Elihu Marshall,[77] but it was Lyman Cobb who felt called upon to take up the cudgels. Cobb used the Walker *Dictionary* for his orthography, and so was heavy-handed with his *publicks* and *honours*. His *A Just Standard for Pronouncing the English Language* first appeared in 1821, and by 1826 was in a revised and stereotyped edition. Cobb took it upon himself to offer a prize for the best essay on spelling books, and when none was forthcoming, obligingly wrote one himself.[78] Under the pseudonym Examinator, he authored a series of thirteen articles in the *Albany Argus* over the winter and spring of 1827 and 1828. The paper must have been short on news, for it is hard to imagine a discussion that held less interest for the general public.

Cobb opened his salvo with an estimation of the importance of the spelling book. "It is the first elementary work placed in the hands of the scholar. From this he derives his earliest impressions of the nature and utility of the language in which he is to speak and write . . . from this he is to acquire the practice of spelling and pronouncing correctly."[79] He then turned to Webster's spelling book—the *American Spelling Book*, of course, as the *Elementary* was not yet compiled. It was, according to Cobb, "in most general use, and the oldest work" of any that he planned to review, given that "the pioneer performance of Mr. Dilworth" had become "almost obsolete . . . Mr. Webster's spelling book was founded upon and succeeded Dilworth's. It was so superiour to its predecessor, in many respects, as to acquire an immediate and unparalleled popularity, which it has sustained with little interruption for more than *forty years*."[80] It was only within the last few years that other authors had attempted to improve upon it.

Cobb then proceeded to give a content analysis of the speller and his criticisms of its defects. It had, for example, only 5,800 words for spelling (if one excluded plurals and derivatives) and it omitted words of six or seven syllables, such as *illegitimacy, indefatigable*, and *impracticability*.[81] Cobb gave credit where credit was due, however, granting that Webster's classification of words was "unquestionably, far superiour to Dilworth's." Webster's classification of words according to their accentuation and sound was much better than Dilworth's classification by the number of letters in a word. (As we have seen, past opinion, Webster's own characterization, and modern evaluation agree with this judgment.) When Cobb criticized the spelling book for mixing up, in one table, words with various terminations: *-sion*, with *-tion*, and *-cial* with *-sial*, he was voicing a criticism that was pertinent to a speller that was the incarnation of spelling-for-spelling; but not to one that was, as Webster's had been and still was, an embodiment of spelling-for-reading.

In later numbers, Cobb criticized Webster on every conceivable score: on the defects in his words "of the same sound, but different in spelling" (Webster had omitted *brake:break* and *fore:four*); on the discrepancies in orthography between the speller and Webster's 1817 reissue of his 1807 dictionary for schools; on omissions in Webster's analysis of sounds, such as not informing the pupil that *-ed* had the sound of *t* in *attached*. Cobb also pointed out internal inconsistencies in the speller, contrasted Webster's orthography with Walker's, argued the impropriety of using both in the same school, and so on. The most convincing part of his attack lay in his citing the discrepancies in spelling between Webster's dictionaries of 1806 and 1817. In short, said Cobb, quoting Webster's earlier article, the spelling book really was a "bad one."[82]

In the last of his thirteen articles, Cobb became more personal. He suggested that while Webster had absolved Samuel Johnson from blame for the errors in his dictionary on the grounds that he was constantly depressed by disease and poverty, Webster could not invoke the same excuse for himself for permitting errors to remain in his speller year after year. Insinuating that Webster was both healthy and wealthy, Cobb claimed that Webster had admitted to the sale of over 7,000,000 spellers, which had enabled him to complete a dictionary on which he had worked for twenty years, and on which he had spent $30,000.[83]

Webster's response to this low blow was lofty. Ignoring Cobb's minute criticisms, he said it was not to be wondered at that there were errors, defects and inconsistencies in his dictionaries—there were in all dictionaries. He also renewed his attack on the Johnson and Walker dictionaries and said that his own dictionary, now in the press, would, he hoped, correct some of these deficiencies.[84]

Examinator's reply to this bordered on the apoplectic. Webster had "not attempted to justify or defend any one principle or example which I have pointed out in his Spelling-book as *defective, contradictory*, or *inconsistent*." He was particularly upset by Webster's suggestion that the pronunciation in his works agreed with that of the "well-bred" people in England (a claim Webster was fond of making). These "pretensions of Mr. Webster, indicate a greater share of pedantry and egotism than I am pleased to find in a countryman who has hitherto enjoyed so great a share of publick confidence and patronage." Cobb challenged Webster to prove his assertion that Walker's dictionary was the most incorrect, promising that he would then "meet his remarks on my numbers frankly and with pleasure . . . but until he shall pursue this course, I shall pass them in silence."[85] This was too good an offer to be refused, and Webster wisely refrained from a reply.

The battle was far from over, however. Cobb, armed with long lists of recommendations for his own work, took to the road and showed exhibits of parallel pages from his own and Webster's speller at teachers' meetings. Webster, meanwhile, toured the whole of New York state in the summer of 1827, repeated the tour in 1828, and took a trip through New England. It was an excursion that he would make every summer until his death. Everywhere he could, he lectured at teachers' meetings, and spoke to college students.[86]

All of Cobb's criticisms, of course, had appeared before the publication of the *American Dictionary*, the *Elementary Spelling Book*, or the new dictionary for schools, which were published between 1828 and 1830. (Cobb's criticisms must have been most helpful to Aaron Ely as he worked on the compilation of the revised spelling book.) When all his works on language were in print, Webster issued a pamphlet titled a *Series of Books for Systematic Instruction in the English Language*. The four books concerned were, of course, his great *American Dictionary*, in quarto; the Worcester abridgement of the quarto, in octavo form; his dictionary for schools; and his *Elementary Spelling Book.*[87]

Cobb had seen the pamphlet listing congressional support for Webster's books. It had not pleased him. The publication of this small volume enraged him further. He launched into a fifty-six page diatribe, which would have been much lengthier had the print not been so small. In it, he reproduced his earlier publications and reviews of Webster's dictionaries. He attacked Webster for the inconsistencies in spelling within the *American Dictionary* and among other dictionaries and the speller. His last ten pages were devoted to a listing of words which had been spelled differently in the several works. Cobb found Webster's preface to his school dictionary particularly unacceptable. In it, Webster had admitted his errors and said that it was unlikely that he would ever again read the whole of the quarto or octavo editions, as repose after his labors was essential during the short period of life which remained for him. "And yet," said Cobb, "Mr. Webster, after this appeal to the *sympathies* of the community, relative to the errours which had been discovered in his works, instead of seeking *'repose,'* has traveled almost without cessation, making speeches in the different cities and large villages, *puffing* his new system of spelling, and, at the same time, *condemning* Johnson, Walker, and others."[88]

Webster was not slow in formulating his reply. He pointed out that Cobb, writing pseudonymously, had earlier urged the "publick" to compare the *American Spelling Book* to his own spelling book in which the defects had supposedly been remedied. "Here Cobb's motives are disclosed in all their extent," Webster suggested. Then he turned to Cobb's latest attack: "In this pamphlet he takes up the old spelling book and dictionaries, which Dr. Webster had discarded, and two of which are out of print, and compares them with his new series of books, showing that they do not agree in spelling." Webster noted that Cobb had sent this pamphlet to all the members of Congress, judges and professors who had recommended Webster's books, asking them "to do me the justice to compare the following strictures with the publications to which they refer." Webster made short shrift of this suggestion: *"Dear Sir!—pray do me the justice—*to do what?—why, only to undertake the labor of six months!—for the task could not be performed in a less time. And to what purpose?—only to satisfy yourselves that Dr. Webster does not spell every word now as he did forty years ago; and then they may determine whether or not, they will use Cobb's books instead of Webster's."[89]

While Cobb was the most vocal of all of Webster's competitors, there were other threats to Webster's hold on the market besides rival spelling books and their vociferous authors. His old work was being plagiarized. Nathan Guilford, whom Bidwell had mentioned in his report on Cincinnati as a publisher, had put out, in 1831, a frank imitation of the *American Spelling Book*, actually declaring in the title that it was "Revised and Improved by Nathan Guilford." As Hudson & Co. had the full rights to the speller, it was that firm and not Webster himself which had to resort to the law, as Hudson did that same summer.[90]

Other Books. Although the *Series of Books for Systematic Instruction in the English Language* represented Webster's final words on the teaching of English (as he viewed it), the books did not exhaust Webster's contributions to education. He planned a range of books which would instruct the child in every aspect of knowledge. With his astonishing energy, he began to write yet more textbooks for schools. In 1830 he saw *A Biography for the Use of Schools* off the press.[91] It was a work of clearly written, brief biographies of figures from Homer to Jesus Christ, and it included lives of George Washington and Benjamin Franklin. The following year the *Elementary Primer* appeared. Its title declared that it was an introduction to the *Elementary Spelling Book*. It is a charming little work, lavishly illustrated, which has as its first lesson, after the *ab*'s and *ba*'s, "I am to be up. Is he to be on us?" The diacritical marks conformed to those of the *Elementary* and the dictionary for schools.[92] In addition, to provide the *Elementary* with a supporting grammar, just as he had his original speller, Webster put out a revision titled *An Improved Grammar*.[93]

One year later, in 1832, Webster's *History of the United States* was published. Over 350 pages in size, it took the United States from the origin of the human race to recent events.[94] He offered the book to Durrie and Peck, telling them that if they printed a 2,000 copy edition for him, they need pay him no premium but a 100 copies, which he would use "chiefly for donation, to make it better known." If the work succeeded, Durrie and Peck would be the exclusive publishers, paying Webster three cents a copy.[95]

With these four additional schoolbooks added to his long

list of credits, Webster turned back to his work on language, this time to bowdlerize it. He undertook a task that today seems wholly inappropriate: an emendation of the common version of the Bible. Its purpose was to strip the Bible free of what Webster considered to be offensive expressions (such as *breast*), and ungrammatical usage (such as *unloose*), and to improve its intelligibility.[96] Webster once said that he considered it the most important enterprise of his life.[97]

* * *

While he was working to clean up the Bible, Webster kept his fingers on the pulse of his school texts. A report early in 1833, from his publishers in Canadaigua, New York, said that the *Elementary Spelling Book* was fast taking the place of other spelling books, and that they, as well as the publishers at Rochester and Buffalo, had not been able to keep up with the demand. "We wish as much could be said of the School Dictionary; but the fact is, very few dictionaries are used in our Schools, of *any* kind." They had sold fewer than 200 copies since its publication. The Canadaigua publishers blamed the high price of the dictionary— they had to charge eighty-seven cents for it—for its lack of success. It was competing with Walker's dictionary, which retailed for fifty cents or less: "for *prices* have more to do in the matter, than the *merit* or *quality* of the book."[98]

As we have seen, the *Elementary Spelling Book* had been in the hands of White, Gallaher & White since June 1831. Sometime early in 1832 the firm reorganized, and the agency was thereafter handled by the successor firm, N. & J. White of New York.[99] Although Webster had been relieved, since June 1831, of the necessity of sending out his own agents, he still kept the usefulness of agents very much in mind. "I think the coming summer & autumn very important to our interests," he wrote to the Whites in March 1832. "Efforts should be extensively made by agents to let my new books be known in parts of the interior country, where people have not much knowledge of the subject, & in the western states."[100]

As Webster was already thinking in terms of the western market and its huge potential, a letter he received from Corey & Fairbank, the Cincinnati publishing firm, was of particular interest to him. In May 1833, Corey wrote to Webster to urge him not to republish the old speller, the *American Spelling Book*, as it would be detrimental to the sales of the new. (One is surprised to find that Webster was even contemplating such a step.)[101] Corey & Fairbank had in only the past year printed between 30,000 and 40,000 copies of the new speller and anticipated annual editions of 100,000 copies.[102]

Webster and the Cincinnati firm kept in touch,[103] and in November 1834, Corey & Fairbank asked for the stereotype plates for Webster's school dictionary and United States history. They believed that they could introduce the works much more effectively into the western market if they were published locally than if they were only available from eastern publishers. The reasons they gave were twofold: first, "There is a general disposition with the Western people to patronize such works as are published among them to the exclusion of others." Second, the publisher had a greater interest in circulating publications that were his own, and was able to do it more easily "as he can manufacture his books without paying out but a small proportion of cash." In contrast, if he had books shipped in, he had to pay entirely in cash. (This willingness to exist on credit would not, it would turn out, prove to be the advantage it appeared.)

Corey continued his letter by saying that he anticipated success with the dictionary and history, because he had done so well with the speller, even though "when we commenced the Speller we were laughed at by all other publishers." He claimed that the spelling books put out by Morgan & Sanxay and the Guilfords (who held licenses for the old *American Spelling Book*), were now "hardly worth publishing."[104]

This letter seems to have motivated Webster to reevaluate the course he should pursue for encouraging the adoption of his books. He was well aware, as we have seen, of the vital role Cincinnati played for the western market, situated as the city was at the center of the river transportation system. Now Corey had pointed out another factor to him: the provincialism of the west. So strong was the antipathy felt by west for east, that there were those who likened the rivalry to that which had existed between the American colonies and England.[105] This regional feeling—a result, perhaps, as it has been suggested, of the immense transportation and currency difficulties faced by western firms who had to do business with the east—[106] meant that a western publisher would do far better for Webster's books in the west than any eastern publisher.

It appeared to Webster that here was a chance to kill two

birds with one stone. On the one hand, he needed a representative of his own, preferably actually engaged in the printing business in a western firm, to exploit the almost untapped resources of the rapidly expanding west. On the other, he wished to place William in a profession. Since his marriage in 1831, William had been only briefly employed in a firm that promptly went bankrupt; his father had had to come to his rescue and pay off his creditors.[107] Both of these concerns would be taken care of at the same time: Webster would send William west to Cincinnati, where he would sound out the feasibility of joining a publishing firm—probably Corey & Fairbank—that would dedicate itself almost exclusively to publishing Webster's books.

VIII

William Webster and the West
"He Was Certainly Born
Under an Unlucky Planet"

In May 1835 William Webster set off west to scout out the western market on behalf of his father's books. He sent home his first report: Webster's publishers in Pittsburgh, he wrote to his father, had warned him that "Cobb's agents are scouring the country & are successful: that so long as there is no house in Pittsburg [sic] sufficiently interested in your book to counteract the operation of Cobb's publishers, your books must suffer." The news of the sales of the octavo dictionary (Worcester's abridgment) was better—but the school dictionary and Webster's *History* were almost unknown. "I feel more and more the necessity of having a House this side of the mountains extensively engaged in the manufacture & sale of your books," was William's verdict.[1] Rather than set up on his own, William felt he should associate himself with some already established firm.

WILLIAM WEBSTER AS PUBLISHER

When William reached Cincinnati, he found the firm of Corey & Fairbank ready for his offer of partnership. On May 12, the firm became Corey, Fairbank & Webster.[2] William was to contribute $6,000 for the partnership—$530 of this represented the sole rights to the publication of the *History*, the remainder was his rights to print the speller. William returned east to make arrangements for his wife, Rosalie, and their two little boys, Eugene and Stuart, to stay in New Haven. He was back in

Cincinnati, ready for the cutthroat world of book-publishing in the west, on July 1.

Anybody who knew William would not have been overly sanguine about his success. It was true that no one knew his father's work better than he: it was William, after all, who had made a fair copy of tens of thousands of his father's words for the printer of the great dictionary. And he was certainly loyal to everything his father had sought to achieve, and in sympathy with all of his aims. If anything, he was loyal to a fault. "My sensibility to everything that affects your authority or popularity as an author is so extreme," he told his father when a New York newspaper abandoned Webster's orthography, "that every change of this kind against you makes me wretched."[3] But it is extremely doubtful that he had the temperament for business, however hard he tried to make a success of it. His introduction to the publishing world had not been auspicious. At fourteen, he had been apprenticed, one recalls, to the Hartford firm of Hudson and Co., and with a view to one day becoming a partner. That arrangement had not lasted a year: "Hudson says that I take no interest in the business of the store, & that I am taken up with pleasure more than in business," William had confessed at the time.[4] Three years after that fiasco, William spent time at Amherst College, which his father had been instrumental in founding.[5] While there, he contracted debts. As he was then still a minor, his irate father had had to find some way of paying them, at a time when he needed all the money he could find for his trip to Europe. ("I hardly know which should excite most indignation, in my breast, the conduct of the debtor or of the creditors," Webster had fumed.)[6] Nor had William's recent experience with a firm been encouraging. Thus far in his life, the best thing that had happened to William was his marrying the charming southerner, Rosalie Stuart.[7]

Now in Cincinnati, through the hot summer of 1835, William found his new position difficult socially, missed his wife and children keenly, and soon plunged into such financial difficulties with his business partners that his father had to give him $200, and loan him an additional $1,000, to offset what the partners insisted was owed them.[8] William's plight was partly due to the fact that his father had prevailed upon him to give him back the printing rights to the *History* in the east. This had annoyed Corey and Fairbank, who not unnaturally claimed that

William was not contributing to the firm the capital he had promised.[9] (The entire Cincinnati episode, indeed, is one of Webster's intervening, often with most unfortunate results, in William's business affairs.)

There was no sign of trouble at first, even though Fairbank, the firm's senior partner, died in July. (Webster's reaction to this news was classic: "I regret to hear that one of the partners is dead. I hope this event will not disturb the operations of the house.")[10] Throughout the summer and early fall, business was booming. "We make no exertion with our books now—We sell faster than we can possibly furnish books." The firm was determined to get rid of all its miscellaneous stock and concentrate solely on school books. William listed the editions that had been published and sold since the first of July. They included 7,250 copies of the *Elementary Reader*, 6,000 copies of the *Western Reader*, 5,500 copies of the *Primary Reader*, a thousand copy edition of Webster's *History*, and 50,000 spellers. William reckoned that the firm made from 65 to 85 per cent profit on all the books except the spelling books, and perhaps the history.[11]

The first glimmer of trouble appeared early in November. William enclosed a list of the firm's new publications and boasted that it was by far the largest their side of the mountains. But when he talked of publishing his father's *Lessons for Youth* in the spring, he added: "It is too late for the fall sales—even if we could hazard the extra capital necessary—but this we cannot do without danger."[12]

In February 1836 William wrote that he was not able to answer all his father's letters, because he had so much to do and so many cares to occupy his mind.[13] Early in March, he reported that business was pretty fair. But his father's old reader, now called *Lessons for Youth*, was a failure: it was "too large a book & does not sell."[14] On March 14, William stated, in no uncertain terms, that he wanted to leave the concern, even at a loss. He outlined the difficulties: it was true that the firm did a large business, but gave a long credit line, and the "Character of the country merchants for prompt & certain payment is not good." The firm required a large capital to sustain itself and was obliged to rely on the banks. To meet the interest exacted by the banks, they often had to draw on their own customers—and then rely on these drafts being honored. Often they were not, "& we are compelled to rain money suddenly to take them up. Often we are

obliged to forward money to the customer to meet our own dft."
It had been like that for two years—borrow, borrow. The old
firm of Corey & Fairbank had been paying a tremendously high
interest, which Mr. Corey had contrived to shift to the new firm,
"so that we may do a very large business & yet be compelled to
pay so much interest as to consume the principal profit."[15]

The moment of truth was upon them. The firm was on the
verge of bankruptcy. Webster senior responded with strong
words, but not with money. (After all, William already owed him
$1,000 in cash, not to mention the rights to the spellers.) "I
know the importance of the West to me & my agents & probably
to my heirs. Whatever I can do shall be done." William should
find some wealthy friends in Cincinnati to make some advances.
Whatever arrangements had to be made, he hoped William
would try to reserve the right to his best publications. "I feel
distressed for you & Mr. Corey & his family—but sympathy is all
that I can give at present for relief."[16]

The firm struggled on, while Webster senior dispatched his
son-in-law Chauncey Goodrich to Cincinnati to investigate the
business. William blamed his own and his partner's disaster on
the loss of confidence in them by the banking community, and
the state of the roads that winter, which had prevented their
agents from traveling for three months. In addition, he was very
bitter with Corey. He had good reason to believe that the old
firm would not have lasted a month but for the capital his father
had poured into it.[17]

A look at the firm's list of assets and liabilities, when it was
finally drawn up a year later, shows a sorry story. A sad little note
on "stock on hand" says, "have omitted copying the assets as the
whole avail. of them will not pay the first class of creditors or the
Amount due for Bank debts." The debts labeled as due to the
banks totaled over $7,000. William proved to be correct in one
respect: of the minor debts, by far the largest was the sum owed
Corey & Fairbank, who claimed $2,201.35. Only one of the other
minor debts was larger than $1,000.[18]

Noah Webster went to Cincinnati himself in June to see
what could be done.[19] All of his suggestions, however, proved
more of a hindrance than a help. But he was determined that
business should continue. He urged his son-in-law, William
Fowler, to run to the rescue and take over the business.[20] Fowler
was planning on leaving Middlebury College, where he had been

for four years, to look for a change of climate for Harriet, who was ill. He was far too prudent, however, to involve himself with William,[21] and the suggestion simply complicated matters for poor William.

One lifeline did surface from the shipwreck, as July progressed: the *Elementary Spelling Book*. Noah urged William to continue to publish the spelling book until they could devise a plan to keep on an establishment of bookselling in Cincinnati.[22] Despite virtual bankruptcy, the firm continued to do this.[23] When it became clear, even to Noah, that there was no solution but to dispose of all available assets in order to satisfy the firm's creditors, William was insistent that he should retain control of the spelling book: "all my plans have failed & I have not much faith in any of them now—But the Spelling Book may be the means of my getting reinstated by & by."[24]

Early in August a settlement was finally reached. William retained the rights to the speller by giving Corey a note for $1,000.[25] A lawyer took charge of the firm, while Corey continued as a salaried agent.[26] (The new arrangement did not work out very happily for William: "Corey, now he is made agent, treats me like a dog.")[27] At one point it looked as if William would be able to form a new firm, in partnership with Burgess & Morgan. The latter was a son of Ephraim Morgan, whose standing in the community was beyond reproach. It turned out, however, that William was not able to deliver to this firm, as he had promised, a license for Kentucky—because his father, without informing him, had already given another firm the right to print in Kentucky.[28] Burgess & Morgan used this as a pretext to divest themselves of any connection with William, other than to give him a note for $2,500, in exchange for the right to print as many spelling books as they wished.[29] William, as did his father, toyed with the idea of his entering into a business relationship with the Cincinnati firm of Truman & Smith. This was an unrealistic expectation, for as William himself said, "Truman & Smith have already gone as far into publishing as their means will justify."[30]

WILLIAM WEBSTER AS AGENT

As William's financial woes deepened during the course of the year 1836, another anxiety was added to his load. A little daughter (named Rebecca for her paternal grandmother) had been born that July, after his family had rejoined him. She had a strawberry mark on her arm, hot to the touch, which the local doctors considered highly dangerous.[31]

Yet not once, as William grappled with his professional and personal problems, did he slacken his efforts on behalf of his father's books. His letters east kept his father fully informed, not only of how the printing was progressing, but also of William's own promotional activities. William was useful in many ways. For one thing, he was able to counteract the widespread impression that his father had not compiled the *Elementary Spelling Book* himself.[32] (Given that this was at least partially true, as we have seen, one is a little surprised by the vehemence with which this was castigated by both father and son as an arrant falsehood.) William also enjoyed sending his father an account of a visitor to the firm's offices. The old man—74 years old, William said—"sat down on one of our boxes to 'see if Noah Webster had not injured the Spelling book by his alterations.' After examining it for some time, he said 'Well put up a dozen.' 'I used this book 40 years ago, & my sons have used it, & now my grandchildren shall have it.' "[33]

William was particularly valuable in carrying on the war against the *Elementary Spelling Book*'s rivals—chief among which was Cobb's speller. The activities of Cobb's agents had, of course, been one of the reasons for William's venturing into the publishing business in the west.[34] One of the first pieces to come off William's press, on his joining Corey & Fairbank, was a run of 5,000 pamphlets attacking Cobb.[35] The pamphlets had come in handy when one of Cobb's agents had been in the area, preparing to give a lecture on "discrepancies in Dr. Webster's books." The Whites (who were, it will be recalled, Webster's sole agent in the east at this time) had their own agent in the Cincinnati area. To "prepare him better," the Whites' agent had given the Cobb agent one of Webster's pamphlets. The latter waited uneasily for half an hour, then announced that he would not give his lecture after all: the audience, he said, was too small. The next morning he left town early for Detroit.[36] William was even able to take advantage of Cobb's relentless faultfinding. He hoped that a friend would obtain for him, from one of Cobb's own agents, a list of the errors Cobb had found in Webster's spelling book.[37]

William's letters home show him to have a keen appreciation

of the parts that were played by different segments of the community in the selection of textbooks. Teachers were, as they had always been, a group to cultivate: William planned to show local schoolmasters a copy of Webster's revised grammar.[38] He was quick to understand the importance of the recently formed College of Teachers, an organization that met every October in Cincinnati to discuss education. Among its members were men of local, and occasionally national, reputation such as Lyman Beecher, Calvin Stowe, and William Holmes McGuffey (then professor of ancient languages at Miami University, Ohio, and soon to be President of Cincinnati College).[39] Another of its members was the textbook author, Albert Picket. Picket was in the process of getting out a revised version of his spelling book (coauthored with his brother John), and "will doubtless do somewhat toward interesting other teachers in his book," said William.[40]

In addition to being known personally to so many eminent citizens, Picket had the advantage of being a westerner. His book was "rec^d very favorably by teachers here, who know Mr Picket, & who think the labors of a man who has lived in the West all his life, should be remunerated."[41] Webster senior's answer to this parochialism in schoolbooks was predictably unsympathetic: "Your Western people begin to think they must make their own School books. This is well enough; but one exception should be urged in every part of the country; this is, that books for teaching to spell & pronounce English words ought *not to be multiplied*. It is important that all the people of this country should follow one dictionary & Spelling book, that all may speak & write alike. This is a matter of national importance."[42]

William was more realistic than his father about the chances of promoting the latter's plan of having only one dictionary and one spelling book in just one city, let alone the whole country. "Every large House in Cincinnati publishes a Spelling book," he replied, "*Webster's, Pickets, Ruter's, Guilford's, & Cobbs* [sic]—& others have been enlisted in favor of Emerson, or Comby—All these Houses have their agents & their friends, & we have still to struggle against great competition." He had been proved correct in his assessment of Picket's popularity: the Trustees of the Cincinnati public schools had decided to adopt Picket's spelling book. The only consolation was that they had also adopted Webster's *History*.[43]

William had some interesting insights to offer his father on the relationship between newspaper editors, authors, and booksellers. Noah had, as was his wont, been sending a stream of news releases across the mountains for William to place: a favorable notice of the Bible;[44] a puff of his sales in the east called a "Statement of Facts;"[45] a certificate signed by members of the Yale faculty, endorsing his books;[46] various papers containing notices of his books (which he had placed in newspapers in the east and middle states "at a considerable expense;")[47] and even a discussion of the relationship between himself and Daniel Webster.[48] Now he had a critique of Picket for William to place. William wrote that his firm found it difficult to get editors to insert anything in the papers. "If they puff your works, they are sure to offend a half dozen authors or booksellers on whom they depend for patronage, & who are already jealous of the extent our books have obtained in circulation—"[49] It would be particularly difficult to get any criticism of Picket into the papers. "He is personally very popular in the city, & Mr Brainerds [sic] office, is over Barnes' Book-Store, & they are very intimate."[50] (Brainerd was the editor of the Cincinnati *Journal*;[51] Barnes was Picket's publisher.)[52] A more succinct expression of the potentially incestuous relationship that exists between a newspaper editor and his advertisers, or the difficulty of honorably combining newspaper work with publishing, would be hard to find.

Despite all his misgivings, William did place Webster's attack on Picket in the local newspapers. His cousin Edward Cranch sent it in for him, and William omitted expressions of his father's that might have aroused suspicion as to the authorship.[53] But William would have done better to stick to his own convictions: the letter called forth such a virulent counterattack from Picket that the editors refused to insert any more copy on the subject. William was accused of being the author of the original article, and the writer of the counterattack was "rather severe on me," said William ruefully.[54]

Albert Picket was not the only textbook author to take advantage of his position as a local notable. By October 1836 the first two books of a new series of reading textbooks had appeared on the scene, published by Truman & Smith. They were titled *The Eclectic First* and *Second Reader* and were authored by William Holmes McGuffey. "There has been recently a convention of the College of Teachers," reported William, "& there is a great rivalry between Picket's publisher & Truman & Smith, the publishers of Prof. McGuffey's series of books. There is a determined effort to use only Western Books . . . We are doing what we can for you, but having Mr. Pickett [sic] & Prof. McGuffey (who by the way) [sic] is very much your friend) residing here in the very midst of our Teachers, we have powerful obstacles to contend with."[55] William was witnessing, in fact, the birth of a publishing miracle whose sales volume would eventually exceed even that of his father's spelling book. Truman & Smith, he told his father that December, "are making money now, & Mr Chester [William's lawyer in the dissolution of the publishing house] says it will be a rich House."[56]

William's own relationship with the firm of Truman & Smith, even after it became clear that the possibilities of a business alliance with it were slim, continued to be cordial. He forwarded to his father a copy of the first number of Truman & Smith's news sheet, the *School Advocate*, which was edited by President McGuffey and other leading lights in Cincinnati. William had no illusions as to why the paper was coming out: "The Pickets were getting up one [a newspaper] under the auspices of the College of Teachers, & intending to make it the medium of circulating a knowlege of their books—Truman & Smith published theirs to counteract this effect in some degree & to extend the influence of their own house—The Eclectic Series by Pres' McGuffey is getting an immense run, & their little paper, circulated gratuitously, will be a powerful instrument in promoting their sales—" The *Eclectic* series used, William added, his father's orthography, and he wished there could be a union of his interests and theirs.[57]

Webster was all in favor of promoting an attack on the Pickets' spelling book and sent William ten copies of his printed circular titled "To Messrs. A. Picket and J. W. Picket." (In this circular, Webster accused the Pickets of plagiarism: in particular, of copying from his pronunciation key seven of his "points"— diacritical marks—for marking vowels.)[58] Smith advised sending out a hundred of these pamphlets, and his firm distributed what they had on hand.[59] Continuing this little exchange of publications, Truman & Smith gave William copies of the *Eclectic* series for his father, together with a copy of Picket's Grammar. They asked Webster senior if he would review the latter for their newspaper.[60] (They no doubt anticipated an unfavorable review.)

WILLIAM WEBSTER IN LAFAYETTE

With the hope of a business alliance with Truman & Smith gone, as it was by February 1837, there remained the pressing problem of what William was to do for a living.[61] Back east, there were others in his family besides his father who had something to say on the subject. William's sister Emily was all sympathy: "He was certainly born under an unlucky planet," was her comment. " 'Tis pity he ever left N[ew] H[aven] where he lived so sweetly."[62] But Harriet Fowler was not so softhearted. She may have been alarmed by her husband's having even contemplated the idea of running to William's rescue. "William," she wrote, in one of the strongest letters that Noah ever received from his dutiful children, "has already had quite too much of Fathers [sic] patrimony and in saying this I speak the opinion of each of my sisters, and when I look about and see how other young men labor to support themselves independently of their friends, I confess I feel ashamed of my brother, who is *willing* that continual sums should be advanced for him by his father who has already advanced so much.—He ought to go and find employment." Had William been left to his own resources earlier, she continued, he might now be able to support his family.[63]

Perhaps it was this letter, coupled with William's final admission that a business connection with Truman & Smith was out of the question,[64] that led Noah to urge his son to pursue his plan of getting a clerkship at Lafayette, Indiana,[65] instead of continuing to press him to start up a newspaper, which was his earlier fancy.[66] (Even William had had the sense to balk at that idea.)[67] So in March William set off west from Cincinnati to spy out the possibilities for employment. By the end of March he was in Lafayette, and in April he bought farmland there from his relative Edward Ellsworth. He then escorted his family to Virginia; Rosalie and the children were to wait there until he could be settled in his new venture, a dairy farm.[68] Fortunately— given that William was even less likely to succeed as a dairy farmer than as a publisher—the deal fell through,[69] and in May

William obtained a position in the Lafayette bank.[70] For once in his life, he did rather well: in July he was promoted to teller.[71]

Not once, during the continuing crisis that William seemed to transport with him wherever he went, did either he or his father falter in their joint determination to promote the latter's books. Webster senior even capitalized on his son's misfortunes by seizing the opportunity of William's progression west to have William check out possible sites for the publication of the speller. That same April he obtained for William, from N. & J. White, the right to license publishers west of the Allegheny Mountains. "I think it important, in this crisis," he wrote William, "to strengthen my interest, by extending the privilege of publishing that book [the *Elementary*] to at least *one* person, perhaps to *two*, in Indiana, & Illinois, & perhaps to one in Detroit & one in St. Louis." William could make a judgment as to whether Indianapolis, Lafayette, Terre Haute, Springfield, Alton, and St. Louis were well situated as far as paper, binding and so on were concerned. If William were to sell licenses for 100,000 copies of the speller a year, he would receive $200 in commissions.[72]

True to form, William faithfully tried to carry out his father's instructions. And slowly but surely the *Elementary Spelling Book* gained ground in the west. By October even Webster was pleased: "the sales of my old Speller are declining, & my Elementary is going very well, notwithstanding competition."[73] A month later, William told his father that he should expand the number of license holders for the west, as Burgess & Crane, successors to Corey & Webster, were not supplying the market.[74]

By June 1838 William was "embarrassed" by the demand for licenses to print for the speller.[75] In January 1839 he reported that, from May 1, 1837 to January 1, 1839, he had issued licenses for no fewer than 200,000 copies of the speller. Burgess & Crane of Cincinnati had taken up five separate licenses for a total of 150,000 copies.[76] (Despite their huge sales, Burgess & Crane did no better than Corey & Webster had done. The firm collapsed in April and sold its plates to Ephraim Morgan's firm, Morgan & Co.)[77]

The improvement in William's financial fortunes was not matched in his personal life. Rosalie and his children had rejoined him the previous May, having been separated from him for just over a year. As he watched for his children on the approaching steamboat, he "could distinctly hear their little voices above the roar of steam & noise of wheels crying 'father, father.' "[78] There was no little girl in Rosalie's arms, however, as she and the boys stood on the deck scanning the bank for their first glimpse of William: Rebecca had died of whooping cough during their separation.[79] Luckily, they disembarked at Louisville. Had Rosalie and the boys remained on the steamship until Cincinnati, William would have been left with no family at all: the *Moselle*, on which they had travelled, continued its voyage, only to explode a few hours later in one of the most ghastly, if spectacular, steamship disasters of the century.[80]

William did well in the bank despite a fright or two because of the inevitable bank politics,[81] and had a salary raise. In addition to his salary, he had the income from the licenses of the speller and, most lucrative of all, an extra income from the fees he charged as a notary public.[82] But the climate was brutal: being right on the river, the whole family suffered from "the chills"— constant bouts of malaria. To add to William's own discomfort, the bank was designed without windows: all the light came from a dome, which allowed the sun to beat mercilessly down on the staff from above, while the only ventilation was from the bank doors when they were open.[83] Nonetheless, the young Websters seemed to be putting down roots, and in April William wrote to his father that they were thinking of buying a lot and putting up a house on it.[84]

Webster had found it hard to part with his only son, when William had left New Haven four years earlier. "The separation," he had told William then, "was as severe to me as any that I have ever experienced, except that of your leaving the church to which you belonged."[85] Now he was over eighty years of age, and William's news was more than he could bear. He approached the head of the White firm in New York and asked him to relinquish the agency of the entire speller. "The commission I now pay on his agency & yours would support your family," Noah wrote to his son. He was determined to put the large dictionary to the press once again, "& I have one or two other books that must be pushed into the market. I want your aid, & if my speller should continue in use, I can maintain your family, till you can find business." He ended his letter with a greater display of emotion than one can read in any other of his letters, "I am becoming old & infirm & I want your aid. I hope you will not buy, till you hear further from your affectionate father."[86]

IX

"Here I Close My Literary Labors"

When, in May 1839, Webster told his son that he was old and infirm and wanted his aid, William was not slow to respond.[1] He resigned from the bank in Lafayette at the end of June and made preparations for his return home to New England.[2] Webster was anxious for his son's return because he had decided, at the age of eighty, to publish a new, unabridged edition, in octavo form, of the *American Dictionary*. In this enormous undertaking, William would be needed to keep the accounts and correct the proof sheets.[3]

In order to support William, Webster would take back the agency of the spelling book from N. & J. White, who had been its sole proprietors since at least February 1832.[4] For every copy of the spelling book that they had licensed, the Whites had been receiving seven mills; two of these they had kept as their commission, passing on the other five to Webster. Webster now reckoned that he would charge six mills a copy to a publisher, provided the publisher paid him in advance; this would give him an income of one mill more than he received under the current arrangement. He was tired, he said, of the losses he had incurred by giving credit.[5]

There was a certain amount of family resistance to the idea of William's coming home. After all, he had lost $6,000 of someone else's money, and owed his father $1,000 on top of that. Chauncey Goodrich had undertaken to pay the interest on half the amount; Webster himself presumably planned to underwrite the bill for the rest. Julia Goodrich had a few words to say on the subject of William's return. "Notwithstanding Sister

Julia's discouraging letter," wrote William petulantly from Lafayette to his father, "I do feel that we might as well die of starvation in a healthy country as of chills & perhaps starvation here."[6] Harriet Fowler, who had never been William's favorite, wrote of him that they would "all *be glad* to see him, if he can find employment without depending upon you for his future support."[7] (Her letter to William himself by no means conveyed even this much enthusiasm. William said it caused him great unhappiness.)[8]

Had Webster not needed the agency of the spelling book for himself and William, there is no reason to suppose that he would have altered the existing arrangement with the Whites. The firm had had the prudence to do everything that could be expected of them: they were meticulous in their accounts, and in addition had kept Webster up to date on all the aspects of the spelling book that he considered important. They had warned him, for example, that he must take legal steps to stop a Concord publisher from flooding the market with tens of thousands of unauthorized copies of the old spelling book.[9] They had pounced on publishers for printing poor editions.[10] They had themselves spent $2,000 for their own agent, whom William had met and regarded highly, to go west to publicize the book.[11] They had kept Webster up to date on the inroads or retrenchments being made by his competitors. They were particularly sensitive to Webster's need to hear that Cobb, in spite of his exertions against Webster, was doing poorly.[12]

Nonetheless, Webster determined to take the whole business back into his own hands, and the Whites surrendered the agency in the fall of 1839, after William and his family had returned to New Haven.[13] The Websters assigned responsibility for granting licenses "west of the mountains" to Ephraim Morgan in Cincinnati the following May.[14] (Morgan was well known to William, of course, from the latter's dealings with him in Cincinnati.)

BOOKS BY WEBSTER

Webster had not been idle while his son was so unsuccessfully engaged in the printing and publishing business in Cincinnati. He had written three more books in the last few years and republished two others. Both *The Teacher* and *The Little Franklin* appeared in 1836.[15] The former in fact represented a descendant of the portion of the old-fashioned spelling book that was devoted to "words of the same sound, but different signification," for its first section was "words pronounced alike, but different in meaning and orthography." Sure enough, one can find, in the pages of *The Teacher*,

> *bare*, naked
> *bear*, to produce, sustain
> *bear*, a wild animal

Its other content included such matters as a listing of the names of tools, trees and so forth, without definitions; a proof of the Creator's intelligence, omnipotence and benevolence ("Order, regularity, harmony, and uniformity in the works of creation, prove *design* in the Creator; and *design* implies *intelligence*. Hence we infer with certainty that God is an *intelligent* being"); an alphabetical list of 718 Latin words from which English words are derived; and a moral catechism:

> Q. *Is labor a curse or a blessing?*
> A. Hard labor or drudgery is often a curse, by making life toilsome and painful. But constant moderate labor is the greatest of blessings.[16]

The Little Franklin was the last version of the early reader that Webster would ever produce. Webster claimed in his preface that it was designed to "amuse and please pupils, while they are learning to read.... These lessons are also intended to impress upon young minds, some truths which may be useful in the common affairs of life." The lessons begin with words of one and two syllables.

> Children go to school to learn to spell, and read, and write, and cipher. Some children learn fast, and some do not; some are very good children; others are not. We all love good children; such as behave well and mind their parents and teachers.

The little work is a storehouse of Webster's ethical and religious value system. His strictures on stealing apples are reminiscent of his earliest fable. "Boys should not climb over fences to get fruit which is not their own." Girls "may very early learn to sew or knit.... Girls should also do house work, and learn to do it well. They should use the broom and the brush, for exercise, as well as for cleanliness." The slip-shod girl is censured. "And how she looks! What an odious sight! She must be cured of her sluttishness, or she will never get a good husband." Rules for behavior are followed by rules for spelling and a note on the spelling book. "The Spelling Book," wrote the author of the *Elementary*, "is the poor man's library for learning his own language, and his children may learn to read at home without any teacher."[17]

In addition to *The Teacher* and *The Little Franklin*, both designed to support his *Elementary Spelling Book*, Webster wrote *A Manual of Useful Studies*, which was published in 1839. Its contents ranged from the "Solar System" to the "Laws Respecting Females" and the "Rules of Orthography."[18] That same year he published the New Testament separately from his Bible, and republished his *Improved Grammar*, which had first appeared in 1831. All these works were destined to be thoroughly unsuccessful. With but three exceptions, they appeared only in a few New Haven editions.[19]

With these textbooks out of the way, Webster once again turned to his lexicographical interests. To the united horror of his family, he now, in the fall of 1839, set about mortgaging his house in order to raise the huge sums he needed to make the new edition of the *American Dictionary of the English Language*.[20] Worse still, despite the fact that every time he had ever dabbled in publishing his own books himself—in New York in 1796, or during the previous few years vicariously through William—he had met with financial disaster, Webster set his mind upon publishing his mammoth dictionary himself.

Back in New Haven only a week, William wrote to his sister Emily Ellsworth for help. He had done, he said, all that he could to persuade his father "to yield his opinions *for once in his life* to the wishes & anxious apprehension of every member of his family." Emily should enlist the aid of her husband. "You know that father has more respect for his opinions than for the opinions of all the rest of us."[21] Not even William Ellsworth was able to prevail, however, for when the first unabridged octavo edition was finally completed, in January 1841, after being over fifteen months in the press, the title page bore the rubric "New Haven: Published by the author." With difficulty was Webster's family able to persuade him to reduce his plan of printing 4,000 or even 5,000 copies, and instead to print 3,000. Even so, over 1,400 of these would remain unsold at the time of Webster's death.[22]

Promotion. Just as he had always done throughout the entire course of his life, Webster pursued the publishing aspects of his books with undiminished energy. As far as the speller was concerned, he had already settled matters of its uniformity among publishers in both content and price: his licenses insisted upon stereotype plates and a minimum price. Webster's keen business sense also alerted him to the disastrous effect that trade sales and auctions had on the price of his books, which could be bought there for a pittance, and then retailed at a price which undercut his entire market: by 1841, the printed license included a clause prohibiting the purchaser of the license both from sending copies of the speller to trade sales and from selling them at auctions.[23]

With unrelenting attention to detail, Webster fretted over the various book production matters in his other works. He discussed the binding, the font, and stereotyping of a new edition of his Bible, and made minor corrections for it.[24] He asked his booksellers all across the country how his books were selling.[25] In addition, he made use of those tried-and-true ways of promoting his books that had served him so well in the past. He procured recommendations for his Bible (the Yale faculty was once again his standby);[26] he advertised directly and indirectly; and he inserted letters in the newspapers.[27] Nothing had changed.

Agents. Webster's relations were still acting as unpaid agents. His sons-in-law, as usual, were worth their weight in gold. It had been Chauncey Goodrich who had been despatched across the mountains to aid the floundering William. William Fowler, up in Middlebury College, Vermont, wrote reviews of his father-in-law's books,[28] and used his position in college to influence the faculty in their choice of textbooks: "As I was on the committee this year for publishing the catalogue the faculty agreed that Websters Grammar shall take the place of Murrays."[29] He also informed Webster of any change in spelling book adoption that came within his ken.[30] William Ellsworth in Washington was not considered too busy with the affairs of his constituents to escape being asked to insert an article in the newspaper on the errors in the common version of the Bible.[31] Eliza's husband, Henry Jones, was a valuable aid: as a schoolmaster, he was able to introduce his father-in-law's books into his classes, and report back that it was with difficulty that he could keep his boys from reading *Lessons for Youth* until all hours.[32]

Even more distant relations were pressed into service. The Rev. Samuel Parker, husband of Webster's niece in Ithaca, New York, distributed pamphlets and copies of the *Manual* for Webster among teachers of academies and clergymen, and left copies for sale at local booksellers. Parker's wife kept Webster abreast of the latest schoolbook adoption: unfortunately, it was of Cobb's works in their entirety, which from his speller to his dictionary were published by the only large publishing house in the region. She suspected collusion among the publishers, teachers and school trustees in the choice. "I can hardly repress my indignation at the seeming self-interest of men who are the guardians of education, and from whom we ought to expect better things."[33] As it turns out, there was an explanation for Parker's energetic distribution of Webster's books. He had written a book on tours and had asked Webster to subscribe his name to a recommendation of it. Webster, with the *quid pro quo* none too disguised, had responded, why not "take a tour of a month in your state, to show some of my books to those who are interested in education."[34]

For those services that Webster could not extract as filial duty or as an exchange for favors rendered, he was prepared to pay. Or so, at least, it appeared. Another Webster relative, young J. W. Webster of Waterbury, set off with high hopes of turning an honest penny by selling the new edition of the giant Webster dictionary on a commission basis. He was out of work, he wrote in an elegant script, and could start just as soon as Webster sent him the particulars. Could Webster kindly advance him a small amount to start him off?[35] That was on April 10, 1841. By April 30, now in Northampton, Massachusetts, young Webster had only sold two copies of the dictionary, which was about as attractive, and expensive, a purchase as the modern encyclopedia. Unknown to his uncle, reported young Webster, there had already been an agent in the area before he arrived. He thought that he had not had a fair trial, however, and was going up the river. He still hoped to sell enough to pay at least for his expenses.[36]

His letter from Providence, Rhode Island, three weeks later, written in rather desperate handwriting and disfigured by despairing ink blotches, told its own story. "Thus far I have not been able to dispose of a *single copy*, & I have seen 60, or 70, Gentlemen who were thought to be most literary." His insertions of the "Commendations" of the dictionary into the local newspaper had cost him five dollars. Instead of meeting his expenses, he had disposed of all his funds. He wanted to return home, "for I am entirely disheartened from my continuation of ill luck." His letter closed with an urgent plea for funds to enable him to pay his hotel bill and leave town. "Please write me immediately for my expences [sic] are accumulating rapidly, board being very high at the Hotels in the City—"[37]

We do not know whether Webster rescued his unfortunate young relative or not. He certainly did not employ him again. But he by no means abandoned the idea of having agents working for him on commission. From September 1841 until the spring of 1842, Webster had no fewer than three agents working for him at different times. William Goodwin only lasted a month,[38] but Constantine McMahon was a man after Webster's own heart. McMahon was on the road in horse and carriage almost continuously in the fall of 1841, when he combed the small towns of Connecticut in order to promote the circulation of Webster's Bible, New Testament, *Improved Grammar*, and *Manual of Useful Studies*. As he zigzagged over Fairfield and Litchfield counties, McMahon distributed pamphlets, left free copies of the New Testament and Bible, and sold the *Manual* and grammar to anyone who would purchase them. He kept a "Daily Memorandum" of his tour, with a scrupulous account of his expenses.

Everywhere McMahon went, he exacted promises of personal promotion from the recipients of the gifts. In Waterbury, for example, McMahon recorded his progress for October 6, 1841:

1 Testament P[resent] to Mr Fuller, Teacher of the Academy. will use his endeavors to get all Dr W. Schol Books into use in—will use the Bible & Testament in his School + 1 Manuel [sic] pd 37½

In Woodbury the next day, McMahon tracked down a Rev. Andrew, who accepted the free Bible and Testament, and purchased the *Manual*.

Mr. A. and rest of the Com.[mittee] will use their

influence in Introducing Dr W. Book in preference to
any others—Dinner & Horse 37½

In Washington, McMahon recorded that the Rev. Mr. Hayes
was "in favor of excluding all other Authors in futur [sic] by a
Vote of the Lawful Committee." In Litchfield, a T. Smith Esq.
advised the members of his committee to "Coincide and unite
for the Good of the County" in introducing all Webster's books
at the same time. Only now and then were a few sour notes
struck: in the village of Kent, the Rev. Andrews accepted the free
Bible and Testament but refrained from buying the *Manual*: he
"has no *change*." He would form his opinion of the books after
examining them. This leg of McMahon's tour ended two weeks
later on a positive note: at Cheshire the Rev. Mr. Colton bought
the grammar—he was the only person on the tour to do so—and
the *Manual*, and expressed himself "in favor of all Dr W. School
Books, & hopes they will all come into use."[39]
     It is clear that Webster was so well known in Connecticut,
his home state, that many of McMahon's contacts felt almost a
sense of obligation to Webster for his herculean labors of the
past. In Norwalk, during McMahon's tour of Fairfield County,
one purchaser of the *Manual* told McMahon that he would "do all
he can to Recommend in Gratitude for past favors Rec^d from
Dr W.— Books." Some of the men approached by McMahon
knew Webster personally. Rev. Mr. Smith of Stamford "joyfully
received the Bible, as coming from his most Honored and
Venerable friend," and said that he would gladly take the
dictionary at the price but could only see to read a little. Like
Milton, he would "get his Daughter to Read the new School
Book to him, being anxious to know if it is an improvement on
D^r W— former works." Lieutenant Governor Hawley, also of
Stamford, was a committee man, and promised to "examine the
Books & attend the Meetings of Town & County for the benefits
Rec^d from D^r W— past labors."[40]
     All of this must have been music to Webster's ears, and after
Christmas 1841 he sent McMahon off again, this time to track
down "literary gentlemen" in New Jersey, Pennsylvania, Delaware,
Maryland and Washington, D.C. Besides continuing his meticu-
lous accounts, McMahon kept Webster informed of his progress
by mail. One of his earliest ports of call was Elizabeth, New
Jersey, where he visited some sixteen families to see if he could

sell them copies of the fourteen-dollar dictionary. He met with no better luck than young J. W. Webster had: "they plead poverty. The Mayor Wm Chetwood setting the example."[41]

As he continued his journey, McMahon took advantage of all the bookselling lore that Webster had amassed over the decades. At Harrisburg, the Pennsylvania capital, he obtained introductions to "leading members of both Houses" and was invited by the Speaker himself to leave samples of the books and distribute pamphlets. At Newark, Delaware, he visited the local college, buttonholed the college president and professors, looked in on the principal of the academy and talked with the principals of the Female Seminary and the district schools. On each visit he displayed a copy of the dictionary and left examination copies of Webster's Bible, grammar, *Manual* and *Teacher* overnight. "Tomorrow I shall cal [sic] on them all again for answers and sell them as many of the Books as I can. Taking back those not Sold—" The only fly in the ointment was that money was so scarce.[42]

McMahon had pleasant news from Baltimore. Webster's grammar and *Manual* had been welcomed everywhere,

> from the known reputation of their author, & bid fair to come into general use. The way the Teachers propose to do it, is to take the Books into their Schools, giving each pupil the opportunity of Reading in turn, & get them in favor of it & then, their Parents will be disposed to Purchase for them.—For I can assure you, the People are tired of buying new Books at the call of every new instructor.[43]

(This seems to be the only instance, in the Webster papers, of children being considered a pressure group worthy of cultivation because of their potential influence on their parents.) After Baltimore McMahon went as far south as Washington, D.C. and then headed for home. He was back in New Haven by the end of March. Even for the experienced McMahon, being a Webster agent was hardly a lucrative job: after fully three months on the road, at wages of $2.00 a day, his income and expenditures of $400 virtually balanced each other out, and he netted exactly $6.78![44]

The last of Webster's three agents in these years was a Mr. Dayton. In March 1842 Webster received unwelcome news from his niece, Jerusha Parker, in Ithaca, New York. "I am sorry the books do not sell better here," she wrote, ". . . but between Salem Town, Cobb and Sanders, . . . the authors of better books have been treated rather unkindly." She and her husband had only sold six Bibles, four copies of the *Teacher*, two of the *Manual*, and a mere four dozen spellers.[45] Two weeks later, Webster was issuing instructions of a military precision to Mr. Dayton, for an assault on recalcitrant New York State:

Instructions

Mr Dayton will go to Stamford, & thence about fourteen Miles to Bedford, where there is an Academy. Call on Judge Jay, & present to him my respects—offer my books & take his advice, as to the best mode of proceeding.

Pass through Putnam county to Fish Kill & Poughkeepsie—thence to Hudson—Cross the river to Katskill—thence to Delhi, in Delaware County, & thence through Broome or Chenango, to Ithaca. There call first on the Rev Samuel Parker, who married my niece, & consult with him. He has of mine in possession, Bibles, Testaments, Manuals, Teacher and Spelling Books—If you want any of these or think you can sell them, he is requested to let you have what you want.

From Ithaca, pass on to Cazenovia, where you may call on Henry, Hitchcock & Co my publishers, & consult with them, leaving with them a few copies of my books, & the advertisement. It may be as well also to leave a few with Mr Parker in Ithaca & advertise them there—

From Cazenovia, you may proceed to Albany, through Rome or Saratoga, as you think best.

In Albany, call first on Mr Garfield & consult with him—Try to induce the teachers in Albany to use my Manual & History—& sell what Bibles you can. Give a copy of the handbill to Mr Young Secretary of State—& a copy of the Testament, which I hope may be introduced into schools. Go to the Mess[rs] Skinners, & leave a few copies of my books & insert the advertisement in their paper.

From Albany proceed homeward, by the best route.

In all places, call on the clergymen of the place, & three or four of the principal inhabitants only, as you will not have time to do more— Try to sell the Bible, Testament, History, Manual & Grammar to the teachers of all Academies & High Schools.

Keep an exact account of all expenditures. Leave a copy of the Pamphlet containing recommendations with teachers & literary men, or such others, as may choose to take it. also [sic] leave two or three dozen of them with Mr Parker, & as many with Henry, Hitchcock & Co in Caznovia. [sic]

Let the advertisement which you carry be inserted in a Newspaper in Poughkeepsie, in Hudson, in Cazenovia, and in Albany, at as little expense as may be.

N. Webster

April 7, 1842[46]

Dayton was still on the road that July.[47]

Attacks on Rival Spelling Books. None of the three agents used by Webster during 1841 and 1842 mentions promoting the spelling book. This, presumably, was because the book was already well entrenched and had its own publishers to promote it. It should not be thought, however, that Webster slackened his grip on the affairs of this, his most successful work. As he had always done, he kept up to date on the *Elementary Spelling Book's* competitors. In his manuscripts, we find one attack after another on rival works. Webster's onslaughts range from a general and broad critique of current dictionaries and schoolbooks, such as that prepared for a lecture before the New York Lyceum in 1839,[48] to the most detailed criticisms of individual spelling books.

No contemporary author of any importance was spared by Webster's pen. On language in general, Lyman Cobb was attacked for the words spelled incorrectly in his dictionary; Albert Picket for the errors in his grammar; Joseph Worcester for giving too many alternate pronunciations in his small dictionary: "How is the teacher or pupil to know what authority to prefer? What sort of guide is such a book?" Spelling book authors were criticized for using antiquated and inconsistent orthography—as did, according to Webster, B. D. Emerson; for considering *w* to be a consonant (according to Webster, it was the vowel *oo*), which was Sanders' crime; or for differing from Webster in his analysis of derivatives, as did Salem Town.[49]

In an essay titled a "brief sketch of the errors contained in certain elementary books" (which was not brief at all) Webster attacked the spellers of Cobb, Emerson, Bentley, Sanders, and that of Gallaudet and Hooker for incorporating Walker's "most mischievous error" of regarding the *n* in *thank* as equivalent to *ng*: "But *bank, brink, uncle*, pronounced *bangk, bringk, ungle*, would be absolutely barbarous." He remonstrated with Sanders, Salem Town and Bentley for including so-called synonyms in their spelling books.[50] The spelling books that had appeared in 1825 and later, modeled after Walker's dictionary, were dismissed as a group. Their only virtue was that they had adopted Webster's syllable division and classification scheme.[51]

All of Webster's criticisms had the same thrust. Where the other spelling books had any merit, it was because they were— depending on his frame of mind at the time of writing—inspired by, modeled upon, copied from, or frank plagiarisms of his own work. Where they were deficient, it was because they were pursuing orthography and pronunciation that differed from his own. His only real reference to content in a rival speller was his onslaught upon the few recent spelling books (such as Salem Town's) that attempted to teach definition at the same time as they taught spelling. Webster considered this a grave mistake.

Where Webster's pen failed him, William's took over. Under the pseudonym "Americanus" in January 1842, William attacked a spelling book that had given particular provocation, in that it had been introduced into the very town in which the Websters lived: the *English Spelling Book* of Alonzo B. Chapin.[52] Chapin, according to William, "who is *chairman* of the *school committee* of New Haven, had, by *individual* application to *some* of the members of that committee, prevailed upon a majority of them to sanction its introduction into the Lancastrian school in that city." (It was naturally one thing for Webster to use his personal influence in any and every way to secure the introduction of his works into a school—and quite another for someone else to do so.) A lively correspondence ensued in the columns of the New Haven *Daily Herald* until the editor put a stop to it. In this case, perhaps even Webster became embarassed by the controversy, for William eventually said that he had begun the correspondence without his father's knowledge.[53]

So the war against rival spelling books continued unabated, the contest being fought as keenly by father and son in the last years of Webster's life as it had been when Noah Webster was in his twenties. Any publisher who was under the impression that he could print a rival speller with impunity was rapidly disabused of this delusion. Not only did Webster write into his licenses that the contract was renewable on condition that his was the only speller published; it was even considered intolerable for a publisher to have published other spellers *before* taking on Webster's, particularly if it were authored by that bête noire, Lyman Cobb. When a Watertown publishing company asked Webster, early in 1840, if they might publish the *Elementary*, they received a sharp reply.

> You print Cobb's Sp. Book, and I see by the Report of the Superintendent of Schools, that his book is chiefly used in Jefferson County. It is not improbable that this work is profitable to you, but it is proper that I should protect myself from the efforts of that man to check the sales of my book. His Spelling Book is a *trespass on my rights*. The best part of the book is taken from mine, & his orthography is wholly obsolete in England [which happened to be quite untrue], & chiefly so in this country. If under these circumstances, I should grant a license to another publisher in the vicinity of the lake, you ought not, & I think you would not complain.[54]

Webster was prepared to give a license to some other firm, apparently, as a form of retribution.

SALES OF THE ELEMENTARY SPELLING BOOK

In spite of its by now substantial field of rivals, the *Elementary Spelling Book* seemed to have a sales life of its own. Webster's own account books tell the story. In 1832, when the firm of N. & J. White was still handling the book, they had sold licenses for 503,000 copies of the speller. In 1835 the Whites sold 506,700; in 1839, 821,640. After Webster took back the agency for William, in November of that year, he recorded the sale of licenses for a grand total of 998,000 copies of the *Elementary* for the period January 1840 to October 1842.[55] These last figures include licenses sold west of Pennsylvania and the Allegheny mountains: for in May 1840, as we have seen, Webster made Ephraim Morgan of Cincinnati sole agent for his speller in those areas.[56]

No fewer than twenty different publishers were noted by Webster as the purchasers of licenses in 1839. They represented states over most of the country: Maine, Vermont, New Hampshire, Connecticut, New York, New Jersey, Pennsylvania, Maryland, Virginia, Ohio and Indiana.[57] Missing from Webster's 1839 list is the Massachusetts' firm of E. & L. Merriam, which also put out an edition of the speller that year.[58] Other publishers from 1839 to 1843 that do not appear in Webster's accounts were an unidentified firm in Tennessee, which published one or more editions in 1841, and a Montreal firm, which produced an edition in 1842.[59]

But perhaps not even a complete list of publishers and the numbers of copies licensed could give us a full picture of the extent to which the *Elementary Spelling Book* was coming into use across the United States. Mere figures can hardly convey how universally it was now accepted. We do know that it enjoyed an enviable position in the state of Michigan: it had been officially adopted there as a school text, state-wide.[60] While the eastern states resisted the idea of having one book or series adopted by law into an entire school system, this would become a common practice in the newer states in the west. So the stage was set for further conquests by the *Elementary*.

CURTAIN

In March 1843 a letter to the editor appeared in the *New York Tribune*, attacking the paper for using the spellings of *hight* and *traveler*. The writer suggested that the *Tribune* was following Webster in "all his nonsense"—and signed himself "Old Dilworth." The editor rose to the defence of his paper's orthography. Did "Old Dilworth" really wish them to go back to *critick* and *critical*; or *labourer* and *laborious*? "We endeavor to spell *consistently*—to follow the analogies of the Language, and of course we generally spell according to NOAH WEBSTER."[61]

Webster could not resist entering into a newspaper argument with anyone, let alone someone who signed himself "Dilworth." It would prove to be the last of his newspaper appearances. "'Old Dilworth' should learn not to write about what he does not fully comprehend," he responded. Men "*should read my rules* before they *condemn my practice.*"[62] Two days later, Old Dilworth slipped in a parting shot: he had learned all his spelling, he said, from a book called "WEBSTER'S *Spelling*-Book. Perhaps you may have heard of such a work." He was unwilling, said Old Dilworth, to "unlearn what was acquired with so much painstaking, and occasional applications of the ferule, the more especially as he is supported in his 'old jargon' by an authority so unquestionable as 'NOAH WEBSTER, JUNIOR.' "[63]

There is a feeling of reprise infusing the spring of 1843, and yet a sense of finality. Webster had finished yet another book. It was a collection of articles that he had written over the years, and it included a discussion of how children should be taught to read.[64] The essay stands as one of the last defences of spelling-for-reading. Early in May, Webster wrote to the Parkers in Ithaca about his new edition of the Bible. In his letter, he summed up a lifetime of work on the English language. "In this edition I have still further improved the language, & completed my design. . . . I have published a small volume of papers, containing my own writings, & accounts of transactions in which I had an agency. The last article contains a brief account of the errors in our language & in school books. And here I close my literary labors."[65]

As usual, Webster was concerned about the publication of his new work. William had been working with him all along, ever since his return from the west, and had proved invaluable. For these past four years, the Websters had been licensing spellers in the middle and eastern United States. Now Webster wished to alter the arrangements once more. He and William had considered the possibility of entering a partnership with a Simeon Ide, who was connected with a Claremont publishing firm, but had abandoned the idea by December of the previous year.[66] Instead, Webster now offered the firm of Cooledge, in New York, the sole rights to the speller for fourteen years, to begin in May.[67] (The firm already printed more of his books than did any other, according to Webster, and he considered that they made "good books.")[68]

If we were to suppose, however, that Webster was finally losing interest in the circulation of his works, and wished to spend the last years of his life free from the anxieties and annoyances of the publishing business, we would be sadly mistaken. On May 5, 1843 we see a letter to Webster from his son. William is in Brooklyn, New York, where he has just settled into his new house, and is exhausted. "The parcels you sent to us of your new work were rec^d," William informed his father. He hoped to publish the book in a few days.[69]

The sense of *déjà vu* deepens. Despite the complete failure of every printing and selling venture that either Webster, Noah or William, had ever personally engaged in, and despite the warning of William Ellsworth, who had told Webster crisply that William should not be established in business with another capital,[70] Noah Webster was once again attempting to engage in publishing himself, through his son. William was heading the publishing firm of Webster & Clark, in Fulton Street, Brooklyn. Nothing had been learned, it seemed, from the earlier fiasco in the west.

"We like our new house exceedingly," reported William. "Rosalie thinks it by far the most convenient house we have ever occupied, & the broad pavement in front, in a comparatively quiet street, proves a great comfort to the boys." He found the long walk to and from Fulton Street, however, hard on the feet.[71]

A couple of days later, William received a letter from his father, addressed to Messrs Webster & Clark. For the first time, there is a perceptible shakiness in the handwriting. At the age of eighty-five, Webster was at last starting to seem old. "I inclose three two dollar bills to pay for advertising the Collection of papers in Philadelphia, Baltimore & Washington," he wrote, specifying precisely which newspapers he intended; "be cautious of not suffering your advertisements to be continued long in the newspapers—the expense will be great & it is needless."[72] He was vexed to find a mistake in the new plate of the speller, which of course was reproduced on every page of the spelling books that he would be sending William from New Haven: *fierce* was misprinted as *fiene*. "I regret this, & in my own copies I shall draw a line across the word with a red pencil. I think Eugene & Stuart may do the same in all your copies."[73] (One doubts if William's sons would have forsaken their Brooklyn sidewalk to carry out this chore with a good grace.)

That same day, on May 8, William was able to tell his father that the firm of Webster & Clark had completed the arrangement of the store as far as shelves, counter, desks, painting and so forth were concerned. But they were running low on money. They still had to finance a painted sign and pay for the binding and advertising. It was "uphill business," said William, "to go on without credit & without cash." Insurance was proving expensive, too, at two per cent, and hard to obtain even at that price. William was waiting for his father to hear from Ephraim Morgan, as he needed his credit in order to print the speller. Nonetheless, the following day he was able to inform his father that the *Collection of Papers* was out and looked very well. William's letter crossed with one from Webster suggesting that William draw on him for $100; "the spellers I sent you are a present to the firm."[74]

By May 18 Webster was sorry to hear that William was desponding. He told his son not to be concerned about his latest book; Cooledge should continue to publish the speller, as William did not have the capital for it, and William could receive the two mills commission.[75]

Four days later, Webster wrote William another letter. The firm of Sanford, in Cleveland, had been a subject of discussion earlier in their correspondence. Sanford was printing illegally—if they had books with Cooledge's imprints on them, they were forgeries, and Sanford, said Webster, should be prosecuted.[76]

On this letter there is a sorrowful annotation, in William's flawless script: "the last letter ever written by my father, the day he was seized with pleurisy." Webster had gone on a three mile walk that day, calling on friends in New Haven. The day was chilly, and he felt faint on his return home and had difficulty breathing. Four or five days later, his condition deteriorated sharply. "It soon became necessary," his son-in-law Chauncey Goodrich recalled, "to inform him that he was in imminent danger. He received the communication with surprise, but with entire composure."[77]

Webster was finally to go beyond the reach of worldly matters. His children were summoned to his side. William was called for urgently. By one of those coincidences that the Websters liked to call "providential," Webster's old pastor from New Haven, the Rev. Stuart, who had so joyfully welcomed Webster into the church when Webster surrendered himself once and for all to his God thirty-five years earlier, was visiting New Haven. Chauncey Goodrich described the scene: the Rev. Stuart

> called immediately; and the interview brought into
> affecting comparison the beginning and the end of that

long period of consecration to the service of Christ. The same hopes which had cheered the vigor of manhood, were now shedding a softened light over the decay and sufferings of age. 'I know in whom I have believed,'— such was the solemn and affecting testimony which he [Webster] gave to his friend, while the hand of death was upon him,—'I *know* in whom I have believed, and that he is able to keep that which I have committed to him against that day.' Thus, without one doubt, one fear, he resigned his soul into the hands of his Maker, and died on the 28th day of May, 1843, in the eighty-fifth year of his age.[78]

Those who knew Webster well would have felt that something was omitted from this account. We are indebted to Webster's children for filling in the gap. There is a letter in the Webster files from Ephraim Morgan—the letter that both father and son had been waiting for ("you know how slow he is," Webster had said).[79] It arrived in time for Webster to see it. "Recd by my father who urged me a short time before he died to read it—but two or three hours," is William's annotation.[80]

But it is Webster's fifth daughter, Eliza Jones, who gives us the details so palpably missing from Goodrich's version of her father's death. The last book Webster ever took in his hands was his spelling book, which he intended should be a gift to her son Henry Webster Jones, the youngest of his grandchildren. And Eliza recorded how William had reached his father's deathbed in time: "the meeting between the dying man and his only son was deeply affecting. Father could then converse with ease and had a long conversation with him on business."[81]

X

Epilogue
"That All May Speak and Write Alike"

The story was ended for Webster, but not for his spelling book. His family was not tempted to allow William to publish it, and by August made arrangements for the *Elementary Spelling Book* to be solely in the hands of George F. Cooledge & Brother of New York. (Provision was made for honoring certain rights already held by the firm of Sanborn & Carter, in Portland, Maine.)[1] On a press specially built for the *Elementary*, the Cooledge firm devoted "the whole capacity of the fastest steam press in the United States to the printing of it," according to H. L. Mencken. "The press turned out 525 copies an hour, or 5,250 a day."[2]

In 1857 Cooledge sold the rights to the speller to G. & C. Merriam of Springfield, Massachusetts, who subcontracted with D. Appleton to print it.[3] By 1859 Appleton & Co. claimed that they were printing 4,480 copies a day—over 1,500,000 copies a year. The company said that the aggregate sales of the book equalled the entire population of the United States.[4]

The Civil War disrupted the distribution of the work, of course, and the South had to do without Webster spellers. According to one post-bellum report, the South "found its need of Webster's Spelling-Book so sore that a surreptitious edition was published in Macon, Ga." The same account claims that the post-war production of Webster spellers was about a million annually, except for a jump in sales to 1,596,708 copies, for the one year after the war ended.[5]

In the Webster papers of the New York Public Library is a dateless newspaper clipping (probably to be dated about 1870) from the Brooklyn *Eagle*. The article is titled "Book Making," and discusses the Appleton publishing firm and the press that put out the Webster speller.

> That press ... had been in daily operation for a dozen years or more, printing the "Speller," as Webster's old fashioned spelling book is called. The demand for this work is very large. Appleton & Co. hold the copyright, and print upward of a million and a quarter of them in a year. The demand for them comes mainly from the South and West. It is still issued in the dark colored covers familiar to childhood, and the sight thereof brought to the mind of the writer vivid pictures of "spelling down" and "keeping in," associated with the life and hum of a district school. Some of the employees of the establishment do nothing but work upon the "speller" the year round.[6]

In 1880 William H. Appleton was asked which of his firm's books sold the best. " 'Webster's Speller,' " replied Appleton, "and it has the largest sale of any book in the world except the Bible. We sell a million copies a year ... Yes, and we have been selling it at that rate for forty years. ... We sell them in cases of seventy-two dozen, and they are bought by all the large dry-goods houses and supply stores, and furnished by them to every cross-roads store in the country."[7]

The year 1883 marked the hundredth anniversary of the birth of Webster's spelling book. Joel Benton wrote a commemorative article (in the *Magazine of American History*) on the book he remembered so well from his youth.

> But what pleasant memories remain with those who long ago studied Webster's Spelling-Book! The very pages in their precise form are pictured for us on indelible tablets. It was a great triumph when the young student got to "Baker," for it was the first step away from monosyllables. But it seemed like a long road to him before he would get to "immateriality" and "incomprehensibility." How or when he was to do it seemed incomprehensible enough then. Those who, in beginning to read, discovered that "She fed the old hen," "Ann can hem my cap," "Fire will burn wood and

coal," "A tiger will kill and eat a man," and other similar facts, little thought that in all their after life nothing they might learn would ever seem so touching and significant.[8]

In the early decades of the twentieth century, there were still many Americans who remembered the book as an inseparable part of their childhood. Mark Sullivan reminisced of the blue-back speller:

Everyone was familiar with its vivid blue covers, and had a curious affection for it. In 1912 a speaker before the Oklahoma Legislative, to prove a point he was making, held up a book, and heard from the older men in the room an audible whisper of pleased recognition: "My God, it's an old blue-back speller."[9]

* * *

In the decades after Webster died, the role of the spelling book changed. No longer was it the first instructional text in reading. It was superseded in that honorable position by the new style of readers, of which the *McGuffey Readers* were the most conspicuous and popular examples. Now it was being sold as a spelling book in the modern sense. One of its functions was to act as arbiter in the "spelling-schools," or spelling bees, that were so popular in the nineteenth century.[10]

One of the unanswered questions of the history of American reading instruction is how long spelling books served any role in the teaching of reading. My own hunch is that they were used for this purpose, in conjunction with the new style of readers, for longer than one might suppose. Certainly we have indications that the *Elementary Spelling Book* was used as late as 1866 as a book to teach reading. The evidence comes from the southern United States, and is provided unwittingly by the same Appleton who, in 1880, said that his firm had been selling 1,000,000 copies of Webster's speller for forty years. The only time this figure had changed, remarked Appleton, was for the one year following the end of the Civil War, when sales jumped by an astounding 500,000 copies. The increase was due to the newly emancipated slaves, "who thought it only necessary to have a 'Webster's Speller' to read," sneered Appleton. "After that year it fell back to the original million, and has never varied."[11]

Convinced that liberation and literacy went hand in hand, and forbidden for so long to aspire to the freedom that the written word bestows, the freedmen and freedwomen of the south turned to Webster's spelling book for their instruction in the art of reading. What more eloquent and moving tribute could there be to the mythic dimensions that the blue-back speller had assumed in American culture as a heritage common to all?

CONCLUSION

This book was written with several purposes in mind: to discover why Webster's spelling book was such a tremendous success even in his own lifetime; to set the work, in its various forms, in the context of its own times; and to see if light would be shed, along the way, on the character of its author.

There were surely two moments in the long life of the spelling book when its fate hung in the balance. The first was when it had just arrived on the scene in 1783, and was faced with the task of wresting the public's loyalty and affection from its model and rival, Thomas Dilworth's *New Guide to the English Tongue*. The second was when Webster, resurfacing from his total immersion in his great dictionary, realized that his share of the textbook market had seriously eroded. His response was the creation of a dramatically different version of his spelling book, now to be called the *Elementary Spelling Book*; and it indicated that he himself considered this another time of crisis in the life of the speller.

If we look at the 1783 *Grammatical Institute of the English Language, Part I* from the perspective of those who were seeing it for the first time, it is clear that Webster had no easy task ahead of him in persuading the public to accept it. All the discussions of the work that remain to us focus, interestingly, not on the fact that this was a book written by an American in the new American Republic (which was the approach that Webster himself would stress), but on its relationship to Dilworth's book. The controversies that surround it are not those of nationalism; instead, they center on two themes: the book's technical aspects (both content and methodology) and its unfamiliarity to the public. For the former, Webster defended the originality of his syllabic division and pointed to the merits of his arrangement of words. He deferred to public sentiment by reorganizing the work in later editions, so that the lessons appeared earlier. He also introduced the fables and illustrations that had been characteristic of Dilworth's book, and missed in Webster's. At the same time he excised any material that smacked of the frivolous. In terms of the work's unfamiliarity, Webster had to contend both with members of the public who were loyal to Dilworth as "the nurse of us all," and with school trustees who were "fearful of injuring the school" by introducing an unknown spelling book. In addition, he had to overcome the material disadvantage of being obliged to offer his book to the public at a much higher price than Dilworth's. For Dilworth's book was produced in huge editions by publishers all over the country who, not having to pay any royalties, "afford it very cheap."[1]

Webster's frontal attack on these twin roadblocks to success was multifaceted. First, he had taken pains to produce a better product than Dilworth. This was an age which firmly believed that the function of an elementary reading book (which is precisely what the spelling book was) was to introduce children to the correspondences between letters and sounds. There was universal agreement among Webster's contemporaries that his key for indicating letter-sound correspondences was greatly superior to anything in Dilworth.[2] In fact, anyone who tried to popularize a spelling book after Webster's also had to produce a work which was adequate in this respect. William Perry's speller, for example, which Isaiah Thomas marketed in response to the challenge of Webster's, had a most complex and sophisticated method of indicating pronunciation.[3] Second, Webster went to unusual lengths to overcome the disadvantage his book labored under as a newcomer, by mounting a publicity and public relations campaign that made his name, his books, and even his person, well known all over the country.[4]

Webster had a third arrow in his quiver. With a plan for American education that was far more ambitious than just marketing a little spelling book, he placed his first work squarely in the mainstream of the American Revolution. In later life, he could never refer to it without somehow tying it to the end of the Revolutionary War.[5] At the time, he introduced it as an exemplar of American independence: he called for cultural independence as the indispensable accompaniment of political independence. For the book was designed not merely to teach children to read, but to purify and unify the very language they spoke. Webster purposed to introduce a "federal language," and to "diffuse a uniformity and purity of *language*" throughout the new republic.[6] (Here we must note, once again, that whatever the objective likelihood was of a spelling book doing any such thing, the claim was considered not merely plausible, but axiomatic, by Webster's contemporaries.)[7]

One of the most intriguing questions that arises from the birth and rapid rise to fame of the *Institute* (soon to be retitled, in 1787, the *American Spelling Book*, a much better name for the times) is how much each of these three factors—Webster's improvements in the technical aspects of the work, his publicizing it, and his insistence that it was an instrument for fostering a truly American language—contributed to the success of the book.

The length of time in which the speller's fate hung in the balance, it should be noted, was remarkably short. We may dub the speller an unequivocal success from the moment when Isaiah Thomas procured the rights to publish it in 1789.[8] Given that Thomas already had two other spellers on the market, his purchase of the Webster license is undeniable testimony to the fact that the speller had already become part and parcel of the American consciousness, and a textbook publisher would do without it at his peril. (In fact, virtually every nationally known American publisher, including Mathew Carey, tried to get his hands on it.)[9] This view is supported by comparing how the Webster speller fared in relation to Dilworth's: from 1792 on, Webster's sales increased in inverse proportion to Dilworth's, which underwent a steep decline.[10] In all, the *American Spelling Book* reigned supreme for a total of some forty years, as even Lyman Cobb, its bitterest critic and author of a rival speller, had to admit.[11] So the period for which we have to explain the meteoric rise of the speller is relatively brief—a time span of only six years or so, from 1783 to 1789.

When the spelling book first appeared, its success, it will be recalled, was "better than he [Webster] had expected."[12] And indeed its growth in sales was remarkable. The first edition of 5,000 copies was sold out in a few months; Webster was working on a second, revised edition in June of 1784, and he was able to claim that over 12,000 copies in all had been sold by January 1785, while the speller was then in its third edition.[13] It would be a mistake, however, to assume that only at this point did Webster see that he had a money-spinner on his hands, and seek to exploit it by starting on his eighteen-month tour that May. Recall that "Dilworth's Ghost" had accused Webster of hawking his speller in towns where he had once taught. Webster's innocent response that he happened to be visiting a sister and had just carried a few books with him at the entreaty of his friends, should not deceive us.[14] Everything points to his having brought the book to the attention of the public from the very first. The advertisements for the book date from October 1783, and it was extensively advertised after January 1785.[15] The nationwide tour, from May 1785 on, was not so much the start of a publicity campaign, as some have thought, as the climax to it.

Given the enthusiasm with which Webster promoted the work and the months of touring in which he used his lectures to bring himself and his books to the public eye, the cynic might be tempted to attribute the success of the spelling book to Webster's promotional efforts alone, and argue that its improvements over Dilworth or its claim to foster an American language were really immaterial to its success. This is not a proposition that can be accepted, however, for there is a "control group" in the form of Webster's other parts of the *Institute*, namely, his grammar and his reader. It should be borne in mind that Webster promoted all parts of his *Institute* at the same time, both during his tour of May 1785 and subsequently. Yet neither the grammar nor the reader succeeded, either in comparison to the speller, or more to the point, when compared with other grammars and readers. Webster's grammar was soon superseded by Lindley Murray's, and his reader was ousted by two main rivals, Caleb Bingham's *American Preceptor*, and Lindley Murray's *English Reader*.[16]

The fate of Webster's *American Selection* is particularly pertinent to this discussion. Unlike his spelling book, which had to wrestle with Dilworth, Webster's reader had the field entirely to itself at the time of its first publication in 1785. Readers as a type subsequently became a key text in every school system. (In fact, records of books in the New York State schools for the years 1827, 1830 and 1831 show that Lindley Murray's *English*

Reader was the single most widely used book in the entire school system. No one spelling book was so popular.)[17] So, if Webster's publicity efforts had been the only key to a book's success, the *American Selection* would surely have cornered the market, and we know it did not. It is therefore only reasonable to conclude that the Webster speller did not succeed solely because of its dextrous promotion.

The fate of *The Little Reader's Assistant* (1790) is also relevant. Although it was a book which was valuable in theory, because it was to bridge the gap between speller and reader, in practice it only ran to a few editions. Admittedly, Webster does not seem to have publicized it much, other than by advertising. But the real reason for its failure was surely not that he failed to promote it, but that it was too unconventional in both orthography and content. Respellings like *hed* and *nabor* were not acceptable, as later controversies over Webster's more unconventional spellings indicate[18]; and its openly antislavery sentiments were undoubtedly considered unsuitable for a textbook.[19] Webster's lack of success with *The Little Reader's Assistant* suggests that one of the reasons for his considerable success with his speller was that it was *not* unconventional: it resembled Dilworth's enough to be recognizable as an improved Dilworth, rather than a totally unfamiliar work. The changes that Webster made to his *New England Primer*, which restored the book to a version much closer to the original classic, also indicate that the public had conservative tastes in textbooks to which he was responding.[20] Not for nothing have textbooks been dubbed "guardians of tradition."[21]

The critical elements in the speller's initial success, then, were essentially three. First, there were the merits of the speller itself, which while adhering faithfully to the alphabet method, illuminated the relationship between letters and sounds with a clarity never achieved before in a work for children. Moreover, Webster improved and refined the work as time went on: he returned the lessons to their time-honored place after the tables; he created new tables and added additional words to existing ones; he excised any material that might be considered even faintly frivolous; and he kept an eagle's eye on the accuracy of the work, correcting misprints and misspellings.

The second element in the speller's success was Webster's skill in making it known to the public. He produced a work that was recognizable as an improved Dilworth (previously the most popular speller), and he went to extraordinary pains to publicize it. Third, in his introduction to his first edition, he linked his little book to the great experiment in American independence. Surely this was more of a factor than perhaps even his readers were aware of at the time. He spoke for a national language at a critical moment in American history when the public was predisposed to hear him.

The one aspect that we cannot credit for the success of the 1783 speller and its early revisions is Webster's own personal prestige. His early commercial success with his speller was not matched by a corresponding rise in his own popularity. In those early years he had been accused of plagiarism and sanctimony, and called pedantic, dull and arrogant; even his own friends urged "diffidence" upon him.[22] If it seems that this view is based upon too great a reliance on stray comments issuing from prejudiced sources (such as Webster's enemy Samuel Campbell of New York), it is well to look at Webster's view of the matter. When his speller or other books were criticized, his immediate reaction was to attribute such attacks to his personal unpopularity, which he believed stemmed from his outspokenness on political matters and his spirited defense of the republic. So sure was he that "any doctrines I might advance, under the signature of my name, would not meet the consideration they might deserve," that he issued two books anonymously, and often withheld his name from his essays in the public press.[23]

SUCCESS OF THE ELEMENTARY SPELLING BOOK (1829)

By the time Webster published his dictionary in 1828, however, almost a half-century had passed since his first appearance in print. And the public regard for him had undergone a substantial change. The brash young author had become the beloved patriot-intellectual, whose literary labors on behalf of his country were known to all. The fruits of his last quarter-century of labor, his *American Dictionary of the English Language*, were scorned by none. His *American Spelling Book* had become the most widely sold book in the nation, and most of those who admired the former had learned to read from the latter. In addition, Webster had buttressed his position as a leading figure in American education by producing a series of other textbooks.

It was well for Webster that he had an edge in this respect; for while he had been laboring over his dictionary, time had not stood still. By the time he was able, once again, to focus on his elementary book, he found to his dismay that it faced not one Dilworth as its rival, but literally dozens of other spelling books, most of them published after 1825.[24]

As we know, Webster accused his publisher, Henry Hudson, of allowing the textbook market to slip from his grasp, and took the unprecedented step of introducing a brand new work to the public before the copyright to the old one had expired. In one sense, his criticisms of Hudson's guardianship were just. The growth of the sales of the speller was not what could be reasonably anticipated from its previous exploits.[25] In addition, all the evidence Webster could gather from his sources also indicated that many school systems had forsaken his speller and adopted another in its place.[26] In another sense, however, his accusations of Hudson were unjust. For the fact that Webster saw it necessary to produce a wholly revised book, so different from its predecessor that many thought (reasonably enough, as we know) that he had not written it himself, indicates that no matter what anyone had done to promote the old *American Spelling Book*, it would not have retained its hold on the public. Truth to tell, it looked thoroughly old-fashioned. The work that Webster produced to replace it, written (under Webster's close supervision) by a New York educator who was more in touch with contemporary taste than the septuagenarian Webster, was much more modern in flavor. Its overt religious content (but not its covert message) plummeted from forty-seven to ten per cent, and was a precursor of a general shift in the direction of secularity.[27]

Not all the alterations Webster made to his old book, however, were to its advantage. The new book's initial lack of pictures, and its substitution of isolated sentences for any kind of connected prose, let alone a story or fable, alarmed even some of Webster's publishers.[28] What is more, the book's typography looked strikingly different, not just from Webster's old book, but from anything else on the market. To appreciate how novel Webster's diacritical markings and new alphabetical characters appeared, it should be recalled that the American public was used to seeing a numerical marking system (whether in Webster's speller or another's); it had no experience with a modified alphabet; and, in all works which used the orthography of John Walker of England, it was accustomed to reading spellings like *centre, honour,* and *musick.*[29]

By no means all of Webster's innovations proved acceptable. His new forms of the letters *c, s, t,* and *u* were doomed to extinction, and he was forced to retreat somewhat on his more extreme respellings, introduced into this edition for the first time. He also found it necessary to reintroduce some of the illustrated fables.[30] On the credit side, Webster's major classes of orthographic reform survive to this day, and a diacritical marking system would become the standard way of indicating pronunciation in later school texts. Indeed, a true measure of their success, his orthography was copied and his "points" rapidly plagiarized by other authors.[31] And Webster's classification of spelling words was now pretty well perfect. The great octosyllabic *incomprehensibility* would be the pinnacle of accomplishment in the rugged art of spelling.[32] In addition, in this version Webster solved all those technical aspects of uniformity that had plagued him in his youth, for the new speller was now always printed from stereotyped plates.[33]

The internal features of the 1829 speller, then, were less unequivocally in its favor than those of its 1783 predecessor. And, paradoxically, Webster was faced once again with the difficulty of introducing an unfamiliar work to the public. For he was competing not only against the many rivals that had appeared since 1825, but against his own *American Spelling Book.* Men looked very carefully at this new edition to "see if Noah Webster had not injured the Spelling book by his alterations."[34] In addition, Webster had to counter the parochialism of the west, where westerners favored western books.[35] No wonder Webster turned to his tried-and-true methods of pushing his new book into the public eye, in order to win for it the affection and esteem enjoyed by his old.

If the *Elementary* was at a disadvantage in some respects, it was certainly not so in terms of Webster's promotional efforts. Indeed, nothing is better documented in this book than the zeal with which this septuagenarian plunged, once again, into the icy waters of textbook competition, in a mirror image of the efforts of his youth.[36]

Nonetheless, it would again be unjust to ascribe the success of the *Elementary* to Webster's remarkable skill in promotion.

For there were other books that he had written or edited and was "pushing." His Bible, for example, and his revised grammar and *Manual of Useful Studies*—these were all works that Webster promoted vigorously.[37] Yet only his spelling book soared away in its sales until it seemed to have a life of its own, and William, out in the west, was "embarrassed" by the demand for licenses to it.[38]

It seems reasonable, then, to identify the reasons for the success of the 1829 spelling book as follows. If it was not considered undeniably superior to its rivals on all counts, its virtues outweighed its defects. Its key aspects—its system of points to indicate pronunciation and its major orthographical reforms—were generally adopted by later writers. It had as full a listing of polysyllabic words as could be found. It also had the advantage of Webster's skilled promotional efforts, which he expanded beyond the circle of his own friends and relatives, employing for the first time paid agents to promote and sell the work. Finally, it had the advantage of its author's reputation. Nothing, said Webster in 1830, had given him more pleasure, "than the respect and kindness manifested towards me in consequence of the use of my books. It convinces me that my fellow citizens consider me as their benefactor and the benefactor of my country."[39] "Gratitude for past favors Rec[d]. from D[r] W— Books" was the refrain that rang in Webster's ears.[40] The name of Webster had reached mythic proportions. The new Webster speller, once it had passed inspection, was able to inherit all the affection and respect of the old. "I used this book 40 years ago," said the same old man who was afraid that Webster had injured his book by altering it, "& my sons have used it, & now my grandchildren shall have it."[41] The Webster speller was a part of America itself.

It is ironic, of course, that this last Webster speller was not entirely Webster's own work. As we know, he had employed Aaron Ely to write for him.[42] How much each man contributed to the book is not at all clear. Aaron Ely provided a small clue to the part he had played in its compilation when Lyman Cobb criticized the omission of words such as *bailiff* and *caitiff* from the *Elementary*. Ely's response was that these and other words ending in *-ff* "were in the manuscript which I wrote, and they must be inserted in the next edition" of the speller. Webster said that he had "employed a person to write for me," but that every part of the *Elementary* and the 1830 school dictionary was "corrected, arranged, and the words marked for pronunciation, by my own hand."[43] We realize that Webster cared not at all about content; in his view, the value of a spelling book rested on the twin rocks of orthography and pronunciation.[44] Significantly, he took issue with other spelling books on these grounds alone.[45] It seems therefore probable that he gave Ely general directions about the lists of spelling words and that Ely wrote the sentences. Webster certainly divided the words into syllables himself and added the diacritical marks for pronunciation.

It should not be thought that Webster was therefore dishonest in claiming the book as his own. As far as he was concerned, he had been responsible for the only elements in the book that really mattered—the form of the written language. In his cavalier disregard for meaning, he was in fact forever distancing himself from those who, even before the publication of the *Elementary Spelling Book*, were attacking the very foundations upon which every speller rested.

A spirit of reform was in the air in the 1820s; it held that the child's nature was not inherently sinful (as had been believed for so long), and could be trained to virtue. This new view of the child was ushering in new aims in education. A child should understand, even enjoy, his schooling, claimed the reformers. So the spelling book's use of the alphabet method, its long lists of words (all too many of which children had never heard before), and its inherent lack of interest were already under siege. When William Holmes McGuffey's carefully sequenced *Eclectic First* and *Second Readers* were published in 1836, they took the country by storm as the prototype of the reading text of the future. For the first time in the history of American reading instruction, children would have the chance to learn to read from simple stories about other children, lavishly illustrated, instead of from long lists of often meaningless words, which rarely reappeared in a context.[46]

* * *

The man who emerges at the end of the saga of his spelling book is closer to Warfel's celebrationist portrait than to Rollins' revisionist depiction. But the patriarch is perhaps more human, and less perfect, than Warfel saw him. Webster's relationship with his son, for example, is revealing. Webster seems to have overcompensated for the feelings of intense anxiety that he experienced when his father in effect turned him out into the world at the age of twenty. He went so much to the other extreme with his own son that he kept William (for whom he cared perhaps more than for anyone else in his life[47]) in a state of prolonged emotional and financial dependence. It was a favoritism, incidentally, that was as deeply resented by William's sisters as Noah's preferential treatment had once been by his own brothers. If Noah overplayed his hand as a father, he underplayed it as a son. His father went bankrupt as a result of mortgaging his farm for Noah's Yale education and was once reduced to asking his son for $10. Yet Noah apparently gave him little emotional or financial support in his final years.[48]

Webster's relationships with his publishers, too, leave something to be desired. The reward for publishing a Webster work seemed all too often to have been the loss of future contracts. Henry Hudson's firm had published the *American Spelling Book* in all its versions since 1783. Yet Hudson's stewardship was repaid by the publication of a rival work, in which he was forbidden any share, three years before his rights to the old work expired.[49] (Professional concerns may well not have been the only ones behind Webster's decision, in this instance: the fact that Hudson had dismissed William from his apprenticeship with the firm cannot have furthered his cause.)[50] Sherman Converse went bankrupt soon after publishing the first edition of the *American Dictionary*, and there was truth in his jibe that "there seems to be peculiar apprehension lest I should make something for my great labour and expense of time and money."[51]

On the other hand, Webster emerges from the tale with his integrity unstained. He was high-handed with his publishers, but he was never dishonest. Nor did he sacrifice his principles to expediency. He might retreat on some of his more extreme spelling reforms, but he never betrayed them altogether, even when they threatened the welfare of his speller.[52] His life was replete with instances where he parlayed future profits into present losses, for the sake of yet another work which had little widespread appeal.[53] Even his astounding publicity efforts were not primarily aimed at making himself rich, but at marketing works in whose value he deeply believed.

Certainly, it is not possible to accept Rollins' vision of

Webster in his last years as a tired old man who, after 1840, retreated into a private world, ending his long journey in disillusionment, bitterness and despair.[54] On the contrary, Webster's interest in the business aspects of his books (one, by the way, entirely overlooked in the "official" version of Webster's life offered us by his son-in-law Chauncey Goodrich[55]) was a lifelong companion to his interest in language. We see Webster as the vigorous, determined and optimistic businessman until the very end.[56]

Nor does Webster emerge as a man who wholly lost his faith either in the American people or in his ability to make a contribution to the Republic. At the end of his days, as at the beginning, Webster promoted, defined, respelled and cared deeply about the American language. "It is important that all the people of this country should follow one dictionary & Spelling book, that all may speak & write alike. This is a matter of national importance," he told William late in his life.[57]

If the spelling book failed to achieve the uniformity in the language spoken by Americans that Webster hoped for, it was not his personal failure, but the failure of a hope impossible of fulfilment, linguistically speaking. Nonetheless, whatever slight influence Webster did have on the spoken language must have been in the direction of "uniformity." With the written language he was on safer ground. His major spelling reforms, adopted by the McGuffey *Eclectic Readers* destined to replace his own book as America's most popular reading instructional text, became the standard American orthography and distinguish American from British spelling to this day.[58]

In assessing Webster's contribution to education, we should note that many of his textbooks were in essence ahead of their time. His *History*, for example, prefigured a work that would, much later, be a standard feature of the school curriculum. In contrast, his spelling book eventually fell behind the times. Webster had engaged in a vigorous dialectic on the subject of reading education all his life. As so often happens, however, when the moment for reassessment came Webster hardly knew what the discussion was about. A man of an earlier age, he was not intellectually prepared to entertain the argument that children should understand what they read. He confronted the issue of meaning in children's texts, and denied its importance. As a result, the success of the McGuffey *Eclectic Readers* was one of the few events within his lifetime whose significance he failed to grasp.

Had the spelling book not had a second string to its bow—which was, of course, that it could and did teach children to spell as well as to read—it might have fallen on hard times once the new McGuffey-style reading textbooks established themselves after 1836. As it was, the *Elementary Spelling Book* went soaring into the stratosphere, becoming the most widely published work written by one person (two, if you wish to give Aaron Ely his due) that the world has ever known. So this, indeed, was Webster's extraordinary contribution: for its first half-century, his spelling book taught America's children to read; for its second half-century, it taught them to spell. Moreover, there were half a million men and women who turned gratefully to the blue-back speller for reading instruction three-quarters of a century after Webster first compiled it.[59]

* * *

There is another side to the story of Noah Webster and his spelling book. As the tale has unfolded it has provided us, willy-nilly, with a window seat on the American publishing scene. Webster was so intimately involved with the printing aspects of his book that each change he made to successive editions faithfully mirrored the evolution of the American publishing industry. His earliest speller was hand-set and displayed the old-fashioned *f*-like *s*; his last speller was stereotyped and its typeface could be that of the twentieth century.

If Webster's spellers may be said to reflect the course of American publishing, they may also be claimed to have altered its face. Webster's diacritical marking scheme was as genuinely innovative in 1829 as his numbering system had been forty-six years earlier. Both became standard in reading instruction texts. Moreover, because Webster was so quick to appreciate technical improvements in printing (such as the use of standing type or stereotyping), he set high standards of textbook production that ensured that his rivals would sooner or later follow his lead.

Ironically, there is one facet of publishing where Webster's role seems to have been overstated (not least by Webster himself): he is less entitled to the appellation "father of copyright" than we once thought.[60] He might, however, with greater justice be termed the "father of royalties." His 1804 contract, which tied his income for the first time directly to the number of books printed, may well have been the earliest of its kind. The checks and balances that Webster built into the system seem not to have appeared elsewhere.[61] He was undoubtedly the first American author to profit from a royalty system on so large a scale. Even today, few authors have been able to devote twenty years of their life to their writing, as Webster did while he worked on his *American Dictionary*, supported by the income from a single book.

Important as was Webster's constant presence on the publishing scene of the early American Republic, there is another significant aspect to his involvement with his own textbooks. Webster's lifelong enthusiasm for book promotion will bear further scrutiny. The promotional practices of Webster's time, all of which he understood so well—the use of recommendations, advertisements, press releases and lectures to draw the public's attention to a book, the handout of free and examination copies, the employment of agents—these were not initiated by Webster, although he certainly honed them to a fine edge. The ethical questions that these practices raise surely prove crucial to an understanding of the later history of the American textbook industry.

The adoption of textbooks by a school system is an extremely important decision that should be made, ideally, on educational grounds alone. Given the financial considerations at stake, however, those entrusted with making the decisions are likely to be exposed to pressure from those who stand to gain from the adoption of a particular textbook. Four groups emerge from Webster's manuscripts who were (and still are) potentially involved with decisions on textbook adoption. In order of importance, these were the school trustees (or school committee), teachers, parents and children. The group most directly involved was the school committee, which was therefore the prime target for pressure, but other groups were vulnerable too. We encountered many instances of publicity aimed at teachers, and even one aimed at children.[62]

Where is the line to be drawn between legitimate marketing practices and illegitimate ones? Or between the proper and improper use of personal influence in textbook adoption? The story of Webster provides us with several insights into these issues, and demonstrates that they are by no means always clear cut. It has shown the difficulty of honorably combining advertising and newspaper publishing, particularly in a close-knit community such as William observed in Cincinnati.[63] It has suggested the conflict of interest inherent in any situation where a textbook author is directly involved in textbook selection, as Alonzo Chapin was as chair of a school committee.[64] It has revealed the potential for exploitation that exists if an author is in a position of leadership in an educational organization. He may use his reputation for self-advertisement or use the sponsorship of the organization to publicize his work, as the Picket brothers apparently did.[65] We have observed the temptation for a publisher to pass off a publicity venture as an educational publication.[66] Finally, we have seen in Webster himself the questionable use of his giant personal prestige outside the educational arena to secure, on several occasions, recommendations of his textbooks.[67]

When do we sanction these and related practices? And when do we become indignant, like Webster's niece, at the "collusion" and "self-interest of men who are the guardians of education, and from whom we ought to expect better things"?[68] These questions often have relevance today.

Note on the Sources

That so much Webster material is extant is not a freak of historical preservation. In part it is due to the contemporary habit of keeping letters, which accounts for the large number of Webster's own letters that remain to us. But it is also thanks to Webster himself, who early in life took to preserving not only his incoming correspondence (at first just his personal letters, later his business correspondence as well), but also newspaper clippings of anything he had written or any controversy in which he had involved himself. It is not pure happenstance, for example, that The New York Public Library has a copy of the very issue of the Hartford *Connecticut Courant* of 1783 that published Webster's first advertisement for the spelling book. It is because Webster himself kept that issue, as we know from his notations upon it. Similarly, he saved copies of the first editions of his books, often jotting the wisdom of hindsight in their margins. It is a consequence of Webster's own sense of history and of the role he played in it (one, I may say, that he was the last to minimize) that we still have so many of his papers.

There are Webster letters to be found all over the country, but the major collection of Websteriana is housed in the manuscript division of The New York Public Library, where the researcher will find ten boxes of Webster's papers, as well as his account books and diaries. These manuscripts range from the earliest business correspondence with his publishers, Hudson & Goodwin of Hartford, Connecticut, to his final letter, penned only a few days before he died. A most valuable source for this book proved to be the letters *to* Webster, a collection that seems to be virtually complete, although the business correspondence of his last years is to be found in The Connecticut Historical Society, which has the second largest holdings of Websteriana.

Besides this important material, significant collections of Webster manuscripts are located in The Pierpont Morgan Library of New York, The New-York Historical Society, the Sterling Memorial Library of Yale University and The Jones Society, Inc. of Amherst, Massachusetts. Other libraries holding letters that proved relevant to this book were The Library of Congress, The Historical Society of Pennsylvania in Philadelphia, and the American Antiquarian Society of Worcester.

Webster's precision and historical sense seem to have been bequeathed to his descendants. His favorite granddaughter, Emily Ellsworth Fowler Ford, wrote *Notes on the Life of Noah Webster* (1912), incorporating in it both primary source material and glimpses of Webster's family life. Her daughter and Webster's great granddaughter, Emily Ellsworth Ford Skeel, undertook the herculean task of compiling a complete bibliography of Webster's published works. Her *Bibliography of the Writings of Noah Webster* (1958), brilliantly edited by Edwin H. Carpenter Jr., is a prime source for any Webster student, and was invaluable for this particular study. Skeel's meticulous amassing of Webster's numerous editions of his different works is the basis for my assertions about the "popularity" or "success" of a given Webster book. For I have everywhere assumed that the more often a book was printed, the greater was its popularity and appeal to the public. The *American Bibliography* of Charles Evans (1903–1959), with its supplement by Roger Bristol (1970), provided corresponding evidence for the popularity of non-Webster textbooks up to 1800, the Shaw-Shoemaker *American Bibliography, A Preliminary Checklist* (1958–1965) for textbooks after 1800.

No one working on Webster can fail to use the standard biography by Harry Warfel, *Noah Webster: Schoolmaster to America* (1936). Though scrupulously based on primary sources, it is not documented, and this lack is only to some extent filled by Warfel's edition of *Letters of Noah Webster* (1953). Warfel's biography is unabashedly in the celebrationist vein, and it is salutary to have a revisionist, and very recent, biography by Richard M. Rollins, *The Long Journey of Noah Webster* (1980).

Other books on Webster include Ervin C. Shoemaker's *Noah*

Webster, Pioneer of Learning (1936), which discusses Webster's educational works, and Horace E. Scudder's *Noah Webster* (1881), which has been outdated ever since the Warfel biography. Homer D. Babbidge Jr. has a useful commentary on each of the extracts selected for his edition of a few of Webster's more patriotic writings in *Noah Webster: On Being American* (1967).

There are several fairly recent dissertations on Webster, but none addressed the themes of the present book. William A. Rosenberg's thesis on Webster's "Influence . . . Upon Language Arts' Teaching" (1967) devotes only a few pages to the spelling book. Dissertations by Gary R. Coll, "Noah Webster, Journalist: 1783–1803" (1971) and Vincent P. Bynack, on Noah Webster, language and the idea of an American culture (1978) are only marginally relevant to my own approach.

As an important textbook in the new American Republic, Webster's spelling book has been included in general studies of old textbooks, such as Charles Carpenter's *History of American Schoolbooks* (1963) and John Nietz's *Old Textbooks* (1961). Few authors, however, have fully appreciated its status as a reading instructional text. Nila Banton Smith in her *American Reading Instruction* (1965) is a notable exception to this stricture.

Abbreviations

AAS	American Antiquarian Society, Worcester, Mass.
CHS	Noah Webster Papers, The Connecticut Historical Society, Hartford, Conn.
HSP	The Historical Society of Pennsylvania, Philadelphia, Pa.
Jones	Noah Webster Collection, The Jones Library, Inc., Amherst, Mass.
LC	Noah Webster, The Library of Congress Manuscript Division, Washington, D.C.
NN	Noah Webster Papers, The New York Public Library Astor, Lenox and Tilden Foundations, New York, N.Y. (Numerals following the NN designation indicate the box number in which the manuscript is to be found.)
NYHS	Miscellaneous Manuscripts, Noah Webster, The New-York Historical Society, New York, N.Y.
PM	Noah Webster Collection, The Pierpont Morgan Library, New York, N.Y.
Yale	Webster Family Papers, Yale University Library, New Haven, Conn.

Note: Unless another collection is identified, the particular manuscript collection within a given library's archives is the Webster collection specified above.

NW	Noah Webster, Jr.
WW	William Webster

Appendixes

The following appendixes represent a synopsis of information on Noah Webster's spelling books that is derived from two main sources: Webster's own accounts and Emily Skeel's *Bibliography of the Writings of Noah Webster*, edited by Edwin Carpenter. The spellers may be grouped into four time periods, corresponding to the length of their copyrights. The first extends from 1783 to 1804 and represents the six editions of the speller from 1783 to 1787, when it was titled *A Grammatical Institute, Part I*, together with its early years as the *American Spelling Book*. It also includes Webster's initial fourteen-year copyright from 1790, the year the United States copyright law was passed, to 1804 (Appendix II). The second time period covers the version titled the *American Spelling Book, revised impression* (or *copy*), which ran from 1804 to 1818 (Appendix V). The third reflects the renewed copyright of 1818 to 1832: that is, the version of the *American* which usually had the additional words "with the latest corrections" (also Appendix V). Last, there is the time period of 1829 to 1843, when Webster copyrighted the *Elementary Spelling Book* (Appendix VI).[1]

The most obvious gap in our data occurs in those early years when Webster's income was not tied to the number of books printed and he did not keep accounts. We know that the earliest editions of Webster spellers (the term "edition" often being used in those days for what we would today call a "printing") were 5,000 or 6,000 copies in size.[2] Even Samuel Campbell's notorious spree of 90,000 copies, in the early 1790s, can be accounted for by positing printings of 6,000 for each of his 15 documented editions.[3] On the other hand, if Patten was correct in saying, in 1790, that Hudson & Goodwin was supplying Connecticut with 20,000 copies annually, it seems that an edition could be as high as 20,000 copies, even then.[4]

In 1796 Webster himself was able to purchase 10,000 copies of his own speller from Hudson & Goodwin and resell half of them to booksellers in Philadelphia alone:[5] this presupposes a much larger number of copies originally printed by Hudson & Goodwin that year. We also know that a license to publish 150,000 copies was advertised for sale by public auction that same year.[6] Firms would increase their output when their licenses were due to expire, as was the case for all licenses in the spring of 1804. Dishonest publishers could be quite unscrupulous: the firm of Bonsal & Niles, which so far as we know printed only two editions between 1797 and 1804, was accused of printing "an extraordinary number" of spellers in all, and of selling 50,000 copies during the year that followed the expiration of its license.[7]

Another perspective on the size of these early editions can be gleaned from the known size of editions in 1804 and thereafter. Licenses awarded to four different firms by Webster for the first year after his reorganization of licenses in 1804 range from 11,800 to 30,000 in size. In 1810, one publisher was granted a license to print 107,700 copies, but still had to renew it the following year for another 67,000 copies.[8] It seems fair, therefore, to assume a constantly increasing rate in the size of editions (printings). Thanks to Skeel's *Bibliography*, we know of 88 separate editions of the speller between 1783 and 1804. Combining what we know about some editions with educated guesses about the size of the other editions, I estimate a total of at least 1,000,000 spellers printed between 1783 and 1804—a total which averages out at under 12,000 copies per edition. (I have not included the 150,000 copies advertised in 1796, a number which seems inconsistent with the other data.)

For the second time period, 1804 to 1818, Webster's income was now related to the numbers of the speller that he licensed, and he kept scrupulous acounts. In theory, the number of copies licensed could differ from those actually printed, in that a licensee might not have printed all the copies to which he was entitled. In practice, however, given that virtually all licenses were renewed (and so implied that the earlier license was exhausted), this difference may be considered immaterial, as may the theoretical difference between spellers printed and spellers actually sold.

The ephemerality of children's textbooks is famous; even so, it is astonishing to see how many editions of Webster's spellers have completely disappeared. Skeel was unable to locate so much as one surviving copy from almost thirty editions which we know of only through Webster's accounts for these years. On the basis of Webster's own figures, the total copies licensed for the period 1804 to 1818 were over 3,223,000. This number should be raised by perhaps 113,000: in an 1815 letter to his publisher, Webster said that he had given a license to a Boston firm to print up to 100,000 in the south, and mentioned a 7,000 edition in Kentucky and two others in Ohio and New Orleans totaling 6,000.[9] We can therefore assume a minimum of 3,336,000 copies for this period.

When Webster handed over the stewardship of his speller to Henry Hudson in 1816 for the copyright renewal that began in 1818, he sold the rights to the speller, as we know, for one large prepayment. The only figures that we have from this period come from the exchange of letters between a beleaguered Hudson and an irate Webster. Hudson gave exact totals for the years 1825 to 1827 only (Appendix V), although he did give some idea of the range of editions by different publishers. Webster himself calculated the totals, by publisher, for these years, and could only have used Hudson's figures to do so. Adding Webster's figures per publisher for the years 1818 to 1832 yields a total of 3,167,000 copies. To these we must add another 400,000 for two firms which Webster mentions without calculating their total output.[10] His total is more trustworthy for this period (when he was in a sense trying to prove to himself how *few* copies had been printed) than in the earlier letter to his publishers in 1815, when he was bent on calculating as many copies as possible with a view to selling his rights. In fact, it is quite likely that he underestimated his totals. He certainly did so in the case of Boston, for which he estimated a fourteen-year total of only 350,000; in contrast, Hudson in 1830 reported a figure of 105,000 for one year alone, and said that the annual figure had sunk below 63,000 for only one year, when it was 57,000.[11] These add up to a minimum of 792,000 Boston spellers by 1830. We must therefore increase Webster's figure for

Boston by some 450,000. In addition, Webster excluded
Hudson's own Connecticut copies from his calculations. These
must have been at least 40,000 annually, given the difference
between the known totals for the years 1825 to 1827 and
Hudson's estimate of annual 350,000, which included his own
copies. This yields, conservatively, another 500,000. These
additions result in a total of some 4,517,000 copies of the
American Spelling Book, "revised edition, with the latest corrections," printed between 1818 and 1832.

If our estimate for the early years is correct, then some
8,850,000 copies of the *American Spelling Book* had been sold by
1832. Webster himself claimed that the number had reached
almost ten million three years before that time.[12] He may have
been exaggerating, but not by much: as he pointed out himself,
the calculation of the number of books allowed to a licensee was
made by assuming that (to take the *American Spelling Book* as an
example) twenty-two quires of paper made a thousand books. In
fact, there would be paper left over: Webster reckoned the
surplus to be five per cent.[13] A publisher could therefore print
more than a thousand books legitimately without having to
account for the extra copies in his premiums to Webster.

For the final period during Webster's lifetime, the reign of
the *Elementary Spelling Book* from 1829 to 1843, we once again
have access to Webster's accounts. Some of these are preserved
in his account book "No. I" in the New York Public Library, but
there is also a "journal" in William's handwriting, housed in the
Connecticut Historical Society, which records premiums paid
for licenses from 1839 on. In addition, we have several lists that
Webster compiled when he himself was trying to figure out
annual totals.[14]

Despite all this information, one gets the impression that
even Webster could no longer keep perfect track of his own
work. As Skeel has pointed out, for example, he has two lists that
both cover the years 1840 to 1842 but which do not wholly tally
with each other.[15] Skeel has reproduced figures both from
Webster's accounts and from various business letters: the total
of *Elementary* spellers documented through these sources
amounts to about 3,868,000 copies (Appendix VII). To these we
would need to add at least another 100,000 copies of the old
American, reprinted after 1832 when the rights, instead of
returning to Webster, became public domain, thanks to an error
in the 1831 copyright law.[16]

If we add all the figures suggested so far, the grand total of Webster spellers between 1783 and 1843 is some 12,700,000. When we take into account the additional copies printed with the surplus paper, not to mention the spellers that never found their way into Webster's accounts or letters, we may justifiably say that this number is an absolute minimum.

Noah Webster would have said that there were many more spellers printed and sold by this time. Chauncey Goodrich, five years after Webster's death, claimed that a figure of about 24 million had been reached by 1847.[17] This does seem to me to be an overstatement, as Webster's accounts show the highest annual total to have been just over 820,000, in 1839. Even reckoning a million copies a year after 1843—the figure suggested by Goodrich—we would reach only 17 million by 1847.

* * *

My book only claims to cover the fate of Webster's speller during his lifetime. Nonetheless, it is tempting to try to render some account of its subsequent sales. The figures from the publishers of the blue-back speller after 1843 seem inconsistent. Mencken does not reveal his source for the statement that Cooledge was printing 5,250 copies a day.[18] This would mean an annual total of 1,600,000; yet when the Appletons took over the printing in 1857 they claimed 1,500,000 copies a year.[19] Another report in the 1870s suggests an annual publication of a million and a quarter copies.[20] If we calculate a million copies annually after 1843, then reckon a million and a half from 1857 to 1860, the outbreak of the Civil War, and a million thereafter except for the well-documented increase of half a million in 1866,[21] we reach an ultra-conservative estimate of over fifty-five million spellers printed by the time of the blue-back's centenary in 1883. Another fifteen million for the next hundred years seems by no means out of line. A historian of the Appleton publishing company said that over 35 million copies were printed between 1855 and 1890.[22] This indicates that the blue-back was still being printed at the rate of a million copies a year between 1880 and 1890. I am therefore inclined to agree with another historian of the Appleton house who put the aggregate at 70 million.[23] Note that this is the figure for the total sales of the speller, in all its forms. The version that came to be known as the blue-back speller was of course Webster's final version, the *Elementary* of 1829.

We can never really be sure of the final figure, which is in any case still growing. But we can be certain of this: Webster's blue-back speller has wielded, by any standards, an extraordinary influence upon American education.

SOURCES FOR APPENDIX I

Fenning, *The Universal Spelling Book*; in *The National Union Catalog, Pre-1956 Imprints* (London: Mansell, 1971), 169: 474–475, and Evans, *American Bibliography*, passim.

Perry, *The Only Sure Guide to the English Tongue*; in *The National Union Catalog*, 451: 567–569, and Evans, *American Biblio-* passim.

Webster. The data from 1783–1804 are obtained from Appendix II. From 1805–1810, the data come from Skeel, *Bibliography* (also, of course, the source of Appendix II).

New England Primer. The source for the 1765–1800 data is Evans, *American Bibliography*, passim, supplemented by Bristol, *Supplement to Charles Evans' American Bibliography*, passim. The source for the data 1801–1810 is *The National Union Catalog*, 412: 345–361.

Dilworth, *A New Guide to the English Tongue*. The data from 1765–1800 come from Evans and Bristol; from 1801–1805 from *The National Union Catalog*, 144: 117–118. After 1810, there are only seven extant editions, the last edition being 1838 (ibid.).

The use of Evans where possible yields more data, as Evans cited works no longer extant, but documented through newspaper advertisements, etc. *The National Union Catalog* lists only extant editions.

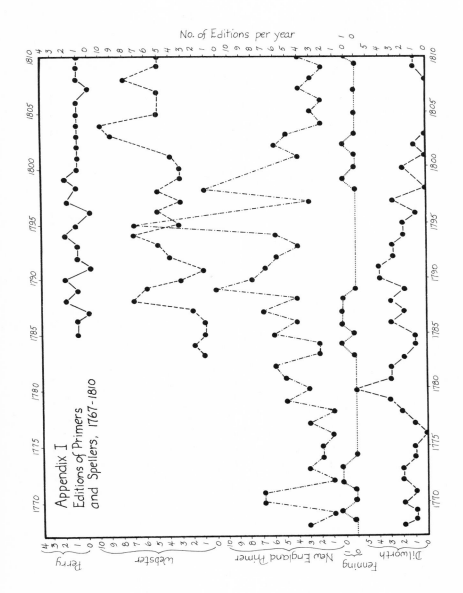

Appendix I
Editions of Primers
and Spellers, 1767-1810

No. of Editions per year

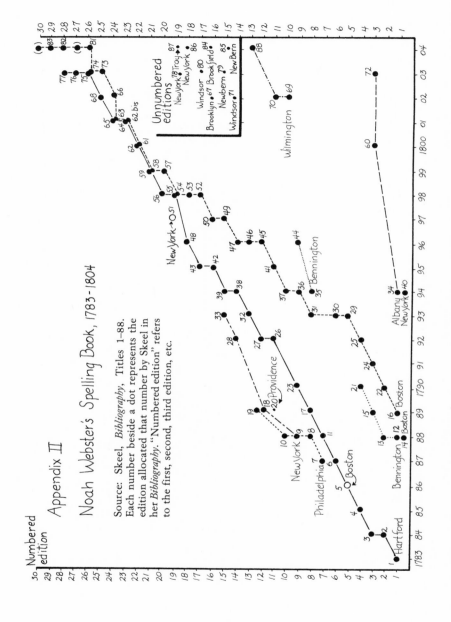

Numbered edition

Appendix II

Noah Webster's Spelling Book, 1783-1804

Source: Skeel, *Bibliography*, Titles 1–88. Each number beside a dot represents the edition allocated that number by Skeel in her *Bibliography*. "Numbered edition" refers to the first, second, third edition, etc.

Unnumbered editions

New York·78·Troy 87
New York· 86
Windsor ·80 ·84
Brooklyn·67 Brookfield·
Newbern 79 85
Windsor 71 NewBern

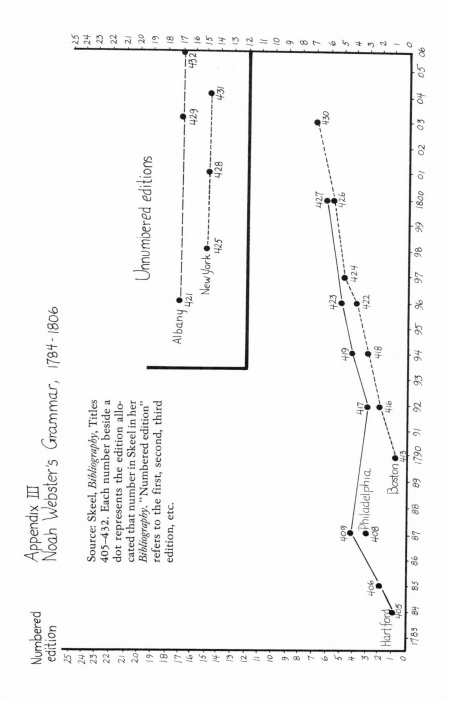

Numbered
edition

Appendix III
Noah Webster's Grammar, 1784-1806

Source: Skeel, *Bibliography*, Titles
405–432. Each number beside a
dot represents the edition allocated that number in Skeel in her
Bibliography. "Numbered edition"
refers to the first, second, third
edition, etc.

Unnumbered editions

Albany 421
New York 425
432
429
431
428
430
427
426
424
423 422
419 418
417 416
Boston 413
Philadelphia
409
408
406
Hartford 405

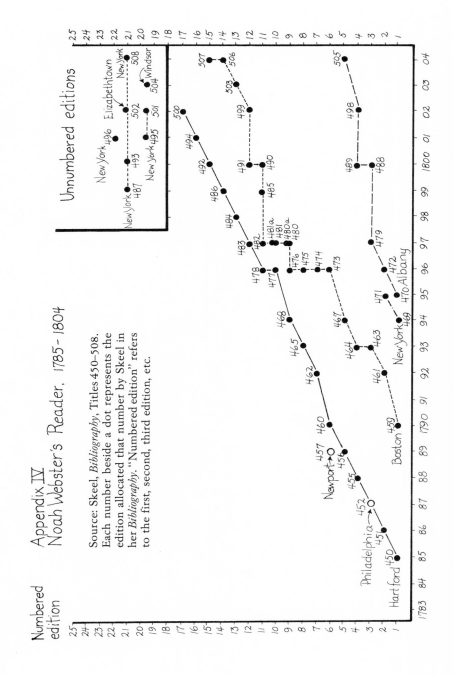

Appendix IV
Noah Webster's Reader, 1785–1804

Source: Skeel, *Bibliography*, Titles 450–508. Each number beside a dot represents the edition allocated that number by Skeel in her *Bibliography*. "Numbered edition" refers to the first, second, third edition, etc.

Numbered edition

Unnumbered editions

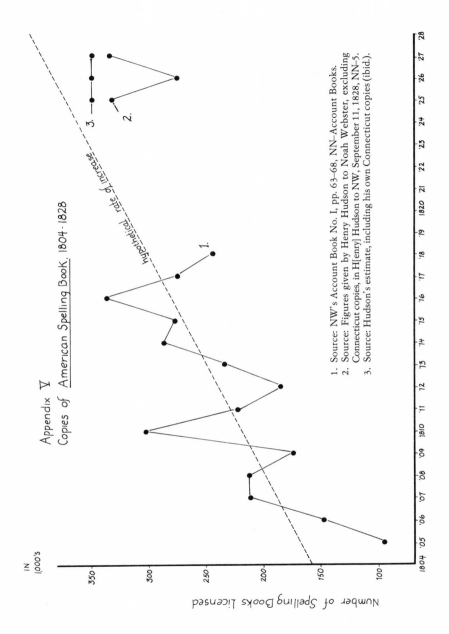

Appendix Ⅴ
Copies of <u>American Spelling Book, 1804-1828</u>

1. Source: NW's Account Book No. I, pp. 63–68, NN–Account Books.
2. Source: Figures given by Henry Hudson to Noah Webster, excluding Connecticut copies, in H[enry] Hudson to NW, September 11, 1828, NN–5.
3. Source: Hudson's estimate, including his own Connecticut copies (ibid.).

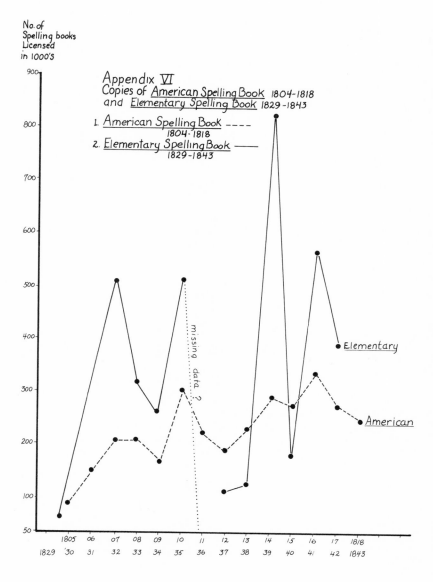

No. of
Spelling books
Licensed
in 1000's

Appendix VI
Copies of American Spelling Book 1804-1818
and Elementary Spelling Book 1829-1843

1. American Spelling Book – – – –
   1804-1818
2. Elementary Spelling Book ———
   1829-1843

missing data ?

Elementary

American

Appendix VII

Annual Totals of

Noah Webster's Spelling Books Licensed

I. Number of copies licensed of *American Spelling Book*, revised copy/impression 1804–1818[1]

1805	95,450
1806	149,050
1807	212,365
1808	213,699
1809	176,500
1810	301,769
1811	222,673
1812	185,067
1813	235,773
1814	288,687
1815	279,075
1816	338,583
1817	277,690
1818	246,878
	3,223,259

Total, 1804–1818

II. Number of copies licensed of *American Spelling Book*, the revised impression, with the latest corrections, 1818–1832[2]

1819–1824	(no annual figures)
1825	321,647 (exclusive of copies printed in Hartford, Conn.)
1826	277,813 (exclusive of copies printed in Hartford, Conn.)
1827	333,329 (exclusive of copies printed in Hartford, Conn.)

(Annual total including copies printed in Hartford, Conn. estimated at 350,000 annually, 1825–1827)

3,167,000 or 3,567,000   Total, 1818–1832[3]

III. Number of copies licensed of *Elementary Spelling Book*, 1829–1843[4]

1829	
1830	70,500
1831	
1832	503,000
1833	309,000
1834	263,848
1835	506,700
1836	12,000
1837	111,000
1838	125,000
1839	821,640
1840	183,430
1841	565,323
1842	396,536
1843	
	3,867,977 Total, 1829–1843

NOTES TO APPENDIX VII

1. Annual totals are calculated from the figures given by Noah Webster for individual publishers in his Account Book No. I, pp. 63–68, NN–Account Book. (These figures are reproduced by Emily Ellsworth Ford Skeel, under individual editions, in her *Bibliography of the Writings of Noah Webster*, Ed. Edwin H. Carpenter, Jr. [1958; rpt. New York: New York Public Library & Arno Press, 1971], pp. 36–57.) The date given is the date of the entry in Webster's account book, even though the entries actually refer to the preceding year. Where there is a gap of a year or more, followed by an entry, the latter has been averaged out over the missing year(s).
2. H[enry] Hudson to NW, September 11, 1828, NN–5. Hudson gave Webster the exact totals for the years 1825–1827, but these did not include the books that he himself published in Hartford, Connecticut. He estimated that, with his own editions, the annual total averaged over 350,000 for those years (ibid.).
3. NW, n.d., NN–10. In this undated letter, Webster estimated totals for individual publishers over the period of Hudson's stewardship of the speller. This total is calculated from Webster's totals. He gave no overall totals for two firms: Ephraim Morgan of Cincinnati, and William H. Niles of Middletown, Connecticut. I have estimated these to be an additional 400,000, making the overall total 3,567,000 for 1818–1832. (See Chapter VII, note 17.)
4. The numbers for the copies licensed of *The Elementary Spelling Book* are variously derived. Those for the years 1829–1831 come from a letter written by Webster to his publishers, NW to Messrs Whites, March 17, 1832, NYHS.

   The figures for 1832–1836 are totals calculated from Webster's figures on individual publishers, in his Account Book No. I, pp. 79–90, NN-Account Book. (The account book records licenses from 1832 to 1835 only, with the exception of Cushing & Sons, Baltimore, for whom figures run from 1832 to 1839. All these figures are reproduced in Skeel, *Bibliography*, pp. 78–98.)

   The figures for 1837–1838 derive from Webster's Account Book No. I (Baltimore only) and also from William's report on the licenses he had sold west of the Allegheny mountains: WW to NW, January 5, 1839, NN–6. (See Chapter VIII, note 76.)

   For the years 1839–1842, the figures derive from Skeel, *Bibliography*, pp. 107–124. The sources used by Skeel are to be found in the Webster papers, NN and CHS. Skeel has also reproduced information on licenses that has appeared in Webster's correspondence (ibid.). These data, too, are included in Appendix VII.

   Note that, as above, the date given is the date entered in Webster's account book. The actual edition is usually that of the preceding year or years. For fuller details of the copies of the spelling books licensed, see Monaghan, "Noah Webster's Speller, 1783–1843," Appendixes.

Appendix VIII

Pronunciation Key to the *American Spelling Book*[1]

INDEX OR KEY

	Long	
1	1	1
a	name	late
e *or* ee	here	feet
i	time	find
o	note	fort
u *or* ew	tune	new
y	dry	defy
	Short	
2	2	2
a	man	hat
e	men	let
i	pit	pin
u	tun	but
y	glory	Egypt
	Broad a or *aw*	
3	3	3
a	bald	tall
o	cost	sought
aw	law	
	Flat a	
4	4	4
a	ask	part
	Short aw	
5	5	5
a	what	was
o	not	from

	Oo proper	
6	6	6
o *or* oo	move	room
	Oo short	
7	7	7
oo	book	stood
u	bush	full
	Short u	
9	9	9
i	fir	bird
o	com*e*	lov*e*
e	her	
	Long a	
10	10	10
e	there	ve*i*n
	Long e	
11	11	11
i	fatig*ue*	pi*que*

oi }
oy } diphthong; voice, joy

ou }
ow } diphthong; loud, now

[1] Noah Webster, *The American Spelling Book* ... 8th Connecticut ed. (Hartford: Hudson & Goodwin, [1789]), p. 23. The only difference between this key and the one being used after 1818 is that there the number 8 (omitted in this edition) replaces the present 9, 9 the 10, and 10 the 11. For that key see Commager, *Noah Webster's American Spelling Book*, p. 25.

Appendix IX

Pronunciation Key to the *Elementary Spelling Book*[1]

KEY

Points and Marks to designate sounds.

Long Vowels

Ā ā – Ē ē – Ī ī – Ō ō – Ū ū – Ȳ ȳ

Ä	ä	as in bär, fäther. [Italian a.]
A̧	a̧	as in fa̧ll. [Broad a, aw, or au.]
A̧	a̧	as in wa̧s, wa̧tch. [Short sound of aw.]
E̱	e̱	as in pre̱y, ve̱in. [a long.]
Ï	ï	as in marïne. [French i; Eng. e long.]
İ	i	as in inch, pin. [i and y short.]
Ĭ	ĭ	as in bĭrd. [u short.]
Ö	ö	as in möve. [French ou; Eng. oo.]
Q	o̧	as in bo̧o̧k, to̧o̧k. [oo short.]
Ŏ	ŏ	as in dŏve, lŏve. [u short.]
U	u	as in fu̱ll, pu̱ll. [Short sound of oo.]
U̧	u̧	as in u̧se, u̧nion. [yu.]
Є	є	as in єap, єope, єup. [k or ke.]
Čh	čh	as in čhaise, mačhine. [sh.]
Ġ	ġ	as in ġem, ġin. [j.]
S̸	s̸	as in mus̸e, his̸. [ez as s.]

th, aspirate as in thin; vocal, as in thou.

---

[1] Noah Webster, *The Elementary Spelling Book; being an Improvement on the American Spelling Book* (Wells River, Vt.: White & Wilcox, 1831), p. 12. (The key was identical in all editions of the *Elementary*.)

Notes

INTRODUCTION

1. Estimates for sales of the speller over its lifetime have varied. Frank L. Mott reckoned 60 or 65 million in his *Golden Multitudes: The Story of Best Sellers in the United States* (New York: Macmillan, 1947), p. 299; Harry R. Warfel suggested a figure of 100 million in *Noah Webster: Schoolmaster to America* (1936; rpt. New York: Octagon Books, 1966), p. 71. Emily Skeel's editor, Edwin H. Carpenter, Jr., considers the lifetime figure of 100 million to be the best estimate: Emily Ellsworth Ford Skeel, *A Bibliography of the Writings of Noah Webster*, ed. Edwin H. Carpenter, Jr. (1958; rpt. New York: New York Public Library & Arno Press, 1971), p. xx. However, a historian of the Appleton publishing company (the firm that printed Webster's speller after 1857) said in 1950 that about 70 million had been sold; Samuel C. Chew, edited with an historical introduction, *Fruit Among the Leaves: An Anniversary Anthology* (New York: Appleton-Century-Crofts, 1950), p. 14. My own estimate inclines to the latter figure; see Appendixes.

2. The first edition of the spelling book has been reproduced by the Noah Webster Foundation & Historical Society of West Hartford, Inc., Connecticut; Skeel, *Bibliography*, Title 1. Henry S. Commager, introd., *Noah Webster's American Spelling Book* (New York: Teachers College, 1962) is a reprint of Noah Webster, *American Spelling Book*, revised impression (Middletown, Conn.: William H. Niles, 1831); Skeel, *Bibliography*, Title 243.

   The entry "Title" after a reference to Skeel's *Bibliography* refers to Skeel's numbered titles of Webster's published works, and is cited for the convenience of the reader. Note, however, that when a page number from Skeel's *Bibliography* is cited, and the numbered title following it appears in parentheses—e.g. Skeel, *Bibliography*, p. 49 (Title 137)—Skeel is the source consulted for the reference, not a copy of the edition itself.

3. Seven million copies of the *McGuffey Readers* had been sold by

1850; about 122 million by 1920: William E. Smith, *About the McGuffeys: William Holmes McGuffey and Alexander H. McGuffey* (Oxford, Ohio: Cullen Print, 1963), p. 21.

4. James A. Scully, "A Biography of William Holmes McGuffey" (Ed. D. Diss., University of Cincinnati, 1967), p. 81.

5. Mott identified *The New England Primer* as the "chief reader and speller for a hundred years in New England and perhaps in the Middle Colonies" and called it the "first school-book best seller"; Mott, *Golden Multitudes*, p. 299. Paul Ford considered that its total sales were, at a conservative estimate, 3 million copies during a period of 150 years; Paul L. Ford, *The New-England Primer: A History of Its Origin and Development with a Reprint of the Unique Copy of the Earliest Known Edition* (New York: Dodd, Mead, 1897), p. 19. See Appendix I.

6. See my comments on Appendix, below. See also Appendix VII for the figures in Webster's account books for the years 1804–1818 and 1829–1843. Webster's estimate of the speller's total sales by 1829 appeared in Noah Webster to Lemuel Shattuck, November 18, 1829, in "History of Elementary School Books," *New-England Magazine*, 2 (1832): 475.

7. Anthony Benezet, *A First Book for Children* (Philadelphia: [Joseph] Crukshank, 1778); Anthony Benezet, *The Pennsylvania Spelling Book*, 2nd ed. (Philadelphia: Joseph Crukshank, 1779).

8. Noah Webster. *A Grammatical Institute, of the English Language...* *Part I* (Hartford, Conn.: Hudson & Goodwin, [1783]), p. 14.

9. To avoid an excess of documentation, material in this introduction will not be documented here if it reappears in the body of the text.

10. The first portion of Webster's essay appeared initially in [Noah Webster], "On Education," *American Magazine*, December 1787, pp. 22–26. The six-part article was continued monthly until May 1788. (It was reproduced, with insignificant changes, in Noah Webster, *A Collection of Essays and Fugitiv* [sic] *Writings* [Boston: for the author, 1790], pp. 1–37.)

    For the consensus on education as a key factor in the preservation of the Republic, see Lawrence A. Cremin, *American Education: The National Experience, 1783–1876* (New York: Harper & Row, 1980), pp. 103–47. Allen O. Hansen, *Liberalism and American Education* (1926; rpt. New York: Octagon Books, 1965), pp. 200–55, discusses Webster's role.

11. Benjamin Rush, "Thoughts upon the Mode of Education Proper in a Republic," (Philadelphia, 1786) in *Essays on Education in the Early Republic*, ed. Frederick Rudolph (Cambridge, Mass.: Belknap Press, 1965), p. 17.

12. [Webster], "On Education," *American Magazine*, December 1787, p. 22.

13. Ibid., p. 23.

14. Ibid., April 1788, p. 312.

15. Ibid., May 1788, p. 374. The phrase "national character" reoccurs in Noah Webster, "To all American Patriots, who value National

Character," NN–8. (Noah Webster is hereafter cited as NW.) On this MS, Webster has noted, "published in the Connecticut Herald May 17 1808." (See Skeel, *Bibliography*, pp. 456–457, no. 163.) See also NW, "Association of American Patriots for the purpose of forming a National Character . . ." NN–8. This was presumably the first draft of the published version.

16. NW to Samuel L. Mitchill, June 29, 1807, Jones.
17. Jefferson regarded Webster as a "mere pedagogue of very limited understanding and very strong prejudices and party passions" (Warfel, *Noah Webster*, p. 272).
18. NW to Lewis Gaylord Clark, November 15, 1838, in Harry R. Warfel, ed., *Letters of Noah Webster* (New York: Library Publishers, 1953), p. 517.
19. Chauncey A. Goodrich, "Memoir of the Author," in Noah Webster, *An American Dictionary of the English Language*, revised and enlarged (Springfield, Mass.: George & Charles Merriam, 1848), p. xix.

CHAPTER I

1. [Noah Webster], "Memoir of Noah Webster, LLD," n.d. (internally dated to 1832, p. 49), Yale. The memoir is unsigned, and written in the third person, but the handwriting is Noah Webster, Jr.'s. See also Emily Ellsworth Fowler Ford, *Notes on the Life of Noah Webster*, 2 vols. (New York: privately printed, 1912), 1:9–12. Emily Ford was NW's granddaughter. In general, for a fuller description of these years see Richard M. Rollins, *The Long Journey of Noah Webster* (Philadelphia: University of Pennsylvania Press, 1980), pp. 7–37; Warfel, *Noah Webster*, pp. 5–50.
2. [NW], "Memoir," p. 3. For Dilworth's speller as the text used in the schools at the time, see NW to Henry Barnard, March 10, 1840, NYHS: "When I was young the books used [in the common schools] were chiefly or wholly Dilworth's spelling Book, the Psalter, Testament & Bible." See also Appendix I.
3. This was Eliza Steele Webster Jones' comment, cited in Ford, *Notes*, 1: 15. Eliza Jones was NW's fifth daughter.
4. NW to James Greenleaf, July 8, 1793, Etting Collection, HSP: "the expenses of my *education* . . . contributed to involve my father & finally to ruin him."
5. [NW], "Memoir," p. 3.
6. Zechariah Swift to NW, December 13, 1776; Icabod Witmore, Jr., to NW, May 24, 1777; Wetmore Meigs to NW, August 20, 1779, all in NN–2. Joel Barlow to NW, January 30, 1779, in Charles B. Todd, *Life and Letters of Joel Barlow, LL.D.* (New York: G. P. Putnam's Sons, 1886), p. 18.
7. "Most of the studies cultivated in our seminaries of learning . . . are not applicable at all to the common occupations of life. This the writer knows by experience." NW, "To the Young of Both Sexes," n.d., PM.

8. Rollins, *The Long Journey*, pp. 14–17.
9. *Noah Webster, on Youth and Old Age: A Sophomore Latin Exercise Given at Yale College, May 4, 1776* (New York: New York Public Library, 1954).
10. Rollins, *The Long Journey*, p. 18.
11. Cited in Warfel, *Noah Webster*, p. 29.
12. Address given by NW at a Sunday School celebration, July 4, 1840; in E[benezer] S. Thomas, *Reminiscences of the Last Sixty-Five Years* (Hartford: printed for the author, 1840), 2: 170–71.
13. Abraham Webster to NW, April 14, 1776, quoted in Ford, *Notes* 1: 19–20.
14. NW, "Autobiographical Notes," n.d., NN–9.
15. [NW], "Memoir," p. 3.
16. Quoted in Ford, *Notes*, 1: 28.
17. NW's own copy of his letter to the Editor of the *Palladium* (New Haven), February 17, 1835, NN–1.
18. [NW], "Memoir," p. 4.
19. NW's own copy of his letter to Thom[as] Dawes, December 20, 1808, NN–1. See also [NW], "Memoir," p. 5. For the sibling jealousy, see Ford, *Notes*, 1: 39.
    Webster's relationship with his parents and siblings deserves more attention than I have given it here. My own evaluation of it is that by his college education and marriage Webster notched himself up a rung on the social ladder, and soon found his family socially beneath him. He seems to have neglected his father in particular. Noah Webster Senior was reduced to asking his son for $10 in 1807. He died in 1813, and it is clear that Webster had not visited him, even though he was aware that his father was ill, nor did he attend his funeral; Noah Webster [Senior] to NW, June 9, 1807, A[braham] Webster to NW, September 4, 1813; William Ellsworth to NW, November 9, 1813.
    Webster's relationship with his elder brother Abraham, who farmed first in Hamilton, N.Y., then in Lebanon, was somewhat better. However, for a man whose published letters alone fill a 500-page volume (Warfel, *Letters*), Noah wrote rarely. Abraham complained of a gap of two years in one letter, and began another, "Dear Brother such in reality you are to me altho we are very negligent in writing to each other"; A[braham] Webster to NW, December 3, 1815, January 12, 1824. Like his father, Abraham once turned to Webster for financial help, which he received; A[braham] Webster to NW, January 3, April 21, 1797. He died in debt at the age of 80, in 1831; Eunice C. Webster to NW, November 14, 1831. (Other letters from Abraham are dated July 27, 1796, October 4, 1825, March 21, 1826—when he asked Noah to get his grandson a job in a store in New Haven—, November 22, 1827, June 8, 1829.) Noah's younger brother Charles died destitute at the age of 55; Emily Ellsworth to NW, March 3, 1817. Noah's sisters no doubt wrote mainly to Rebecca, but Noah did get one letter: Mrs. Ingraham to NW, October 28, 1801. We do

know that he visited one of them around 1784; Chapter II, note 69.

On the credit side, Noah did take some responsibility for his brother Charles' sons. He obtained a midshipman's post for his nephew Nelson by writing to James Madison, and again intervened on Nelson's behalf with the Secretary of War; Nelson Webster to NW, January 6, 1809, July 18, 1811, Eustis to NW, September 28, 1811. Nelson died of "fits" in 1826; Charles Webster to NW, September 26, 1825. Noah also apparently responded helpfully to Nelson's brother Charles, when the latter asked for assistance in getting established in a publishing house. It was a debt that Charles narrowly escaped repaying fourteen years later by taking on William as a partner! Charles Webster to NW, September 29, 1814, October 11, 1828. All these letters are in NN-2 through NN-5.

20. NW's annotation on Wetmore Meigs to NW, August 20, 1779, NN–2; [NW], "Memoir," p. 5.
21. [NW], "Memoir," p. 6.
22. *Gazette of the United States* (Philadelphia), January 13, 1790; ibid., January 9, 16, 1790. In the Yale file, Webster annotated the first article, "written the winter of 1779–1780" (Skeel, *Bibliography*, p. 443).
23. [NW], "Memoir," p. 6.
24. Ibid.
25. *Connecticut Courant and Weekly Intelligencer* (Hartford), June 5, 1781.
26. NW, "Autobiographical Notes."
27. Helen Evertson Smith, *Colonial Days & Ways* (New York: Century, 1900), pp. 269–87.
28. Ibid., p. 280.
29. NW's contribution appeared in the October 1781 issue of the handwritten "The Clio, a Literary Miscellany" (ibid., p. 283).
30. Smith, *Colonial Days & Ways*, pp. 283–84. Juliana's brother Jack was John Cotton Smith, later Governor of Connecticut. He corresponded with NW: John Smith to NW, January 31, 1782, NN–2.
31. Journal of Robert Gilbert Livingston, October 9, 1781, cited in Ford, *Notes*, 1: 46.
32. Joel Benton, "An unwritten chapter in Noah Webster's life. Love and the spelling-book," *Magazine of American History*, 10 (1883): 52–56. This account does not square with Smith, *Colonial Days & Ways*, p. 183, who records that the acting town clerk of Sharon noted in his account book that Webster was paid three dollars a month for teaching in the district school.
33. [NW], "Memoir," p. 6.
34. The three-part series was published in the *New-York Packet* (Fishkill) on January 17, 31 and February 7, 1782; Skeel, *Bibliography*, p. 434, no. 7.
35. Warfel, *Noah Webster*, pp. 49–50.
36. NW, "Autobiographical Notes."
37. [NW], "Memoir," p. 7.

38. Rollins, *The Long Journey*, p. 22.
39. Ibid., pp. 23–24.
40. [NW], "Memoir," p. 7.
41. Quoted in Homer D. Babbidge, Jr., ed., *Noah Webster: On Being American. Selected Writings, 1783–1828* (New York: Praeger, 1967), p. 18. Cf. "In the year 1783, just at the close of the revolution, I published an elementary book" (Noah Webster, *An American Dictionary of the English Language*... 2 vols. [New York: S(herman) Converse, 1828], preface, n.p.).
42. [NW], "Memoir," p. 7.
43. Ibid.; Sam[uel] S. Smith to NW, September 27, 1782, NN–2.
44. Joel Barlow to NW, August 31, 1782; in Todd, *Life and Letters of Joel Barlow, LL.D.*, pp. 41–42.
45. Bruce W. Bugbee, *Genesis of American Patent and Copyright Law* (Washington: Public Affairs Press, 1967), pp. 49–56, 104.
46. John Tebbel, *A History of Book Publishing in the United States* (New York: R. R. Bowker, 1972), 1: 46.
47. NW, "Memorial to the General Assembly of Connecticut," October 24, 1782, NN–8.
48. NW's annotation to the memorial, ibid.
49. "It [*A Grammatical Institute*] was christened by the gentleman who presides over literature in Connecticut" (NW to Dilworth's Ghost [January 19, 1785]; in Warfel, *Letters*, p. 20).
50. NW to John Canfield, January 6, 1783, NN–1; NW, "Memorial to the Legislature of Connecticut," January 6, 1783, NN–8. In an annotation to this memorial, dated September 24, 1783, Webster stated that his memorial had not been read because a general act had been introduced, thanks to a petition by John Ledyard.
51. NW, "Memorial to the Legislature of New York," January 18, 1783, NN–8. For NW's not actually presenting it to the Legislature, see NW's annotation, ibid., and Bugbee, *Genesis of American Patent and Copyright Law*, p. 122.
52. John Ledyard, *A Journal of Captain Cooke's Last Voyage to the Pacific Ocean*... (Hartford: Nathaniel Patten, 1783); Tebbel, *A History of Book Publishing*, 1: 139–40. Ledyard is mentioned by Webster in his annotation of September 24, 1783 (see above, note 50).
53. Bugbee, *Genesis of American Patent and Copyright Law*, p. 108.
54. Tebbel, *A History of Book Publishing*, 1:140; Bugbee, *Genesis of American Patent and Copyright Law*, pp. 114–15.
55. Enoch Perkins to NW, November 4, 1783, NN–2.
56. Noah Webster, *A Collection of Papers on Political, Literary and Moral Subjects* (New York: Webster & Clark, 1843), pp. 173–78. The chapter was a reprint from the *Commercial Advertiser* (New York) of June 21, 1831; Skeel, *Bibliography*, p. 353.
57. [NW], "Memoir," p. 8.
58. Advertisement, *Connecticut Courant*, June 1, 1784.
59. [NW], "Memoir," p. 9.
60. Skeel, *Bibliography*, p. 6. The price was fourteen pence, or ten shillings a dozen; advertisement, *Connecticut Courant*, October 14, 1783.

61. Copies were sent to Elizur Goodrich and Joseph Buckminster, for example; Dr. Elizur Goodrich to NW, September 29, 1783, NN–2; J[oseph] Buckminster to NW, November 17, 1783 (ibid.).

62. Noah Webster, *A Grammatical Institute, of the English Language... Part I* (Hartford: Printed by Hudson & Goodwin for the author, [1783]); Skeel, *Bibliography*, Title 1.

63. [NW], "Memoir," p. 9.

64. NW to Isaiah Thomas, February 23, 1784, Isaiah Thomas Papers, AAS.

65. Noah Webster, *A Grammatical Institute of the English Language ... Part II* (Hartford: Printed by Hudson & Goodwin for the author, 1784); Skeel, *Bibliography*, Title 405.

66. Noah Webster, *A Grammatical Institute of the English Language... Part III* (Hartford: Barlow & Babcock, for the author, 1785); Skeel, *Bibliography*, Title 450.

CHAPTER II

1. See Appendixes II, III and IV.

2. Mott, *Golden Multitudes*, p. 130. See below, note 68, for Webster's claim that 12,000 copies had been sold by January 1785.

3. Appendix II.

4. William Kempe, *The Education of Children in Learning* (1588); in Robert D. Pepper, *Four Tudor Books on Education... Facsimile Reproductions* (Gainesville: Scholars Facsimiles & Reprints, 1966), pp. 223–26.

5. For the alternative approaches, see E. Jennifer Monaghan, "Noah Webster's Speller, 1783–1843: Causes of Its Success as Reading Text" (Ed.D. Diss., Yeshiva University, 1980), pp. 398–416.

6. Ford, *The New-England Primer*; the earliest extant copy is a 1727 edition. For editions of the *New England Primer*, 1767–1810, see Appendix I. See also Charles F. Heartman, *The New-England Primer Issued Prior to 1830* (New York: R. R. Bowker, 1934); Charles F. Heartman, *American Primers, Indian Primers, Royal Primers, and Thirty-Seven Other Types of Non-New England Primers Issued Prior to 1830* (Highland Park, N.J.: H. B. Weiss, 1935).

7. Robert F. Roden, *The Cambridge Press, 1638–1692: A History of the First Printing Press Established in English America, together with a Bibliographical List of the Issues of the Press* (New York: Dodd, Mead, 1905), p. 36.

8. F[ranz] D[aniel] Pastorius, *A New Primmer or Methodical Directions to Attain the True, Spelling, Reading and Writing of English. Whereunto are Added Some Things Necessary and Useful Both for the Young of the Province...* (New York: William Bradford, 1698).

9. The following editions are the earliest documented in Charles Evans, *American Bibliography* (Chicago: privately printed, 1903–1959) Vols. 1–3: Nathaniel Strong, *England's Perfect Schoolmaster, or, Directions for Spelling, Reading...* (Boston: B. Green, 1710); H. Dixon, *The Youth's Instructor in the English Tongue, or the Art of Spelling Improved* (Boston: n.p., 1731); Thomas Dilworth, *A New Guide to the*

English Tongue... (Philadelphia: B. Franklin, 1747); Daniel Fenning, *The Universal Spelling Book; or a New and Easy Guide to the English Language* (Boston: n.p., 1769); *A Child's New Plaything...* 3rd. ed. (Boston: Joseph Edwards, 1744). The most comprehensive index to primers and spelling books before 1800 is that provided by Evans, *American Bibliography*, under the heading "English Language."

10. See preceding note.

11. Evans, *American Bibliography*, Vol. 4, documents editions from the years 1765 to 1773, inclusive, of spelling books other than Dilworth's, as follows: *A Child's New Plaything* (Philadelphia: William Dunlap, 1765); H[enry] Dixon, *The Youth's Instructor in the English Tongue* (Boston: n.p., 1767; Boston: Thomas Leverett, 1768); Daniel Fenning, *The Universal Spelling Book* (Boston: n.p., 1769; Boston: n.p., 1772); George Fox, *Instructions for Right Spelling* (Newport: S. Southwick, 1769); *The Spelling-Book, and Child's Plaything* (New London: Timothy Green, 1769); John Gignoux, *The Child's Best Instructor in Spelling and Reading* (Philadelphia: William Bradford, 1766); and Thomas Watts, *Watt's Complete Spelling Book*, 10th ed. (Philadelphia: W. & T. Bradford, 1771). The nine Dilworth editions published between 1765 and 1771 are documented in Evans as follows: Evans, *Bibliography*, Titles 9951, 10284, 10602, 11240, 11634, and 12027, together with three editions found in Roger P. Bristol, *Supplement to Charles Evans' American Bibliography* (Charlottesville: Bibliographical Society of America, 1970), Titles B2867, B2868, B3714. Five of the editions came from Boston.

12. NW, letter, July 5, 1784, *Freeman's Chronicle*, July 8, 1784; in Warfel, *Letters*, pp. 9–11; Skeel, *Bibliography*, p. 484, A.2; see also Appendix I.

13. The late eighteenth-century view of the relationship between reading and comprehension was that of the British author, James Burgh, whose *Art of Speaking* was a standard text: "For *reading* is nothing but *speaking* what one sees in a book, as if he were expressing his *own* sentiments, as they rise in his mind. And no person reads well, till he comes to speak what he sees in the book before him in the same *natural* manner as he speaks the thoughts, which arise in his *own* mind. And hence it is, that no one can *read* properly what he does not *understand*"; [James Burgh], *The Art of Speaking...*, 4th ed. (Philadelphia: Aitken, 1775), pp. 9–10.

14. Respectively, Dilworth's and Dixon's titles.

15. For the hornbook in the British Isles, see Andrew W. Tuer, *History of the Horn Book* (London, 1896; rpt. New York: B. Blom, 1968); for those imported into the American colonies, see George A. Plimpton, "The Hornbook and Its Use in America," *The Proceedings of the American Antiquarian Society*, new ser., 26 (1916): 264.

16. [Samuel Johnson], *The First Easy Rudiments of Grammar, Applied to the English Tongue* (New York: Holt, 1765), p. 4.

17. R. C. Alston, *A Bibliography of the English Language from the Invention*

of Printing to the Year 1800, Vol. 4, *Spelling Books* (Bradford: for the author, 1967).

18. Thomas Dilworth, *A New Guide to the English Tongue...* (Boston: William McAlpine, 1771), title page, p. viii.
19. Ibid., p. 4.
20. Lydia A. H. Smith, "Three Spelling Books of American Schools, 1740–1800," *Harvard Library Bulletin*, 16 (1968): 72–93. Smith compares the values implicit in the spelling books of Thomas Dilworth, William Perry and Daniel Fenning. She found the most resemblances between Dilworth and Perry: "Both preach endlessly at the child, often in a contradictory way." She considered Fenning a little different, in that he paid some slight attention to children's needs. For Perry's speller, see below, note 26.
21. Webster, *A Grammatical Institute, Part I* [1783], pp. 3–4.
22. Ibid., p. 5.
23. Ibid., p. 6.
24. Dilworth, *A New Guide* (1771), p. ix.
25. Webster, *A Grammatical Institute, Part I* [1783], pp. 8–9.
26. William Perry, *The Only Sure Guide to the English Tongue...* (Worcester: Isaiah Thomas, 1785). This is a copy of the eighth British edition.
27 Webster, *A Grammatical Institute, Part I* [1783], p. 9.
28. NW, MS beginning, "In the year 1782, I compiled a small elementary Book for common schools, in which, by the advice of the late President Smith of Princeton College, I introduced some improvements," PM.
29. Webster, *A Grammatical Institute, Part I* [1783], p. 10.
30. Ibid., pp. 10–11. The Johnson dictionary was probably an earlier edition of Samuel Johnson, *A Dictionary of the English Language... Abstracted from the Folio Edition...* 7th ed., 2 vols. (London: W. Strahan, 1783).
31. Webster, *A Grammatical Institute, Part I* [1783], pp. 12, 14–15.
32. NW to Hudson & Goodwin, September 4, 1788, NYHS. "Federal language" was the phrase used in the advertisement NW asked Hudson & Goodwin to insert in the papers.
33. Timothy Pickering to his wife, October 31, 1783, in Octavius Pickering, *The Life of Timothy Pickering* (Boston: Little, Brown, 1867), 1: 480.
34. Timothy Pickering to NW, October 19, 1785, NN–2. NW has annotated this letter: "the writer... has proved a most valuable friend."
35. NW's Greater Journal, February 25, 1786, NN–Diaries: "Dine with Col Pickering—one of the best of men—."
36. Webster's copy of Tapping Reeve to John Canfield, October 21, 1782, NN–2.
37. NW to John Canfield, January 6, 1783, NN–1.
38. Webster, *An American Dictionary of the English Language* (1828), preface, n.p.
39. Newspaper clipping, *Daily Herald* (New Haven), January 4, 1842, NN–10.

40. Chauncey A. Goodrich, "Memoir of the Author," in *An American Dictionary of the English Language*... revised and enlarged (Springfield, Mass.: Merriam, 1848), p. xvi. See also an undated discussion of spelling books, NN–10; "to the use of this book [the spelling book] has been ascribed that uniformity of pronunciation in this country which is a matter of surprise to foreigners."

41. Dr. Elizur Goodrich to NW, September 29, 1783, NN–2. For a similar opinion—viz., that the change in the division of syllables would be the greatest obstacle to the book's reception, see Sam Baldwin to NW, September 22, 1785 (ibid.).

42. Chauncey A. Goodrich, "Life and Writings of Noah Webster, LL.D.," *American Literary Magazine*, 2 (1848): 9.

43. Webster, *A Grammatical Institute, Part I* [1783], pp. 24, 21–22.

44. See Appendix VIII.

45. Webster, *A Grammatical Institute, Part I* [1783], p. 46.

46. Dr. Elizur Goodrich to NW, September 29, 1783, NN–2.

47. J[oseph] Buckminster to NW, November 17, 1783, NN–2. For other letters by Buckminster, see his to NW, October 30, 1779; October 27, 1784; and July 25, 1785 (ibid.).

48. NW, "In the year 1783 ...," n.d., NN–10. A mention of NW's Quarto Dictionary dates this to post 1828.

49. Webster, *A Grammatical Institute, Part I* [1783], p. 101.

50. Ibid., p. 104.

51. Ibid., p. 110.

52. Ibid., p. 111.

53. Ibid., pp. 113–18; For Daniel Fenning, see above, note 9.

54. It appears as the first lesson of Table XL in Webster, *A Grammatical Institute, Part I* [1783]; of Table XXV in Noah Webster, *The American Spelling Book, Being the First Part of a Grammatical Institute*, 8th Connecticut edition (Hartford: Hudson & Goodwin, [1789]); of Table XXIX in Noah Webster, *The American Spelling Book*... the revised impression, with the latest corrections (Hartford: Hudson & Co., 1823).

55. These are the last lessons of Table XXXVII in Webster, *A Grammatical Institute, Part I* [1783]; of Table XIII in both Webster, *The American Spelling Book*, 8th Conn. ed., [1789], and in Webster, *The American Spelling Book* (1823). The 1783 version omits *the* before "time of school," and misspells "*mend* their ways" as "*mind* their ways." Webster corrected both errors in the later editions.

56. Webster, *A Grammatical Institute, Part I* [1783], mentions Dilworth, pp. 7–10; Fenning, p. 113; Dr. Johnson, p. 11; Sheridan, *Lectures on Elocution*, p. 8, footnote; Lowth, pp. 20, 24, footnotes. For Fenning, see note 9, above. For Johnson, see note 30, above: there was no American publication of Johnson's dictionary in 1783 (Evans, *Bibliography*, lists no American edition). Webster later said he used Entick's pocket dictionary (see note 62, below). Thomas Sheridan, *A Course of Lectures on Elocution*... (London: A. Millar, 1762); *A Rhetorical Grammar of the English Language* (Philadelphia: Bell & Bailey, 1783). Robert Lowth, *A Short Introduction to English Grammar*... (Philadelphia: R. Aitken, 1775).

57. For the whole controversy, see Skeel, *Bibliography*, " 'Dilworth's Ghost' Controversy, 1784–1785," pp. 483–85. The exchange of letters was published in several newspapers. Although the controversy began in the *Freeman's Chronicle* of Hartford, and was then picked up by the New Haven *Connecticut Journal*, most of the subsequent letters appeared first in the Litchfield *Weekly Monitor and American Advertiser*, and were then reprinted a week or so later in the *Connecticut Journal*. The *New York Journal* picked up "Dilworth's Ghost's" first letter, and was treated to a Webster response; Skeel, *Bibliography*, pp. 483–84, A.1, A.4.

58. Ibid., p. 483; Warfel, *Noah Webster*, p. 69.

59. "Dilworth's Ghost," letter, *Freeman's Chronicle* (Hartford), June 24, 1784, rpt. *Connecticut Journal* (New Haven), June 30, 1784. (Note that this is incorrectly cited by Skeel as the *Connecticut Herald*: Skeel, *Bibliography*, p. 483, item A.1.) The items in this controversy are hereafter identified by Skeel's numeration of them in her *Bibliography*, pp. 483–85. For Lowth and Sheridan, see above, note 56. John Ash, *Grammatical Institutes...* (Worcester: Battelle & Green, 1785), first published in New York in 1774, was an introduction to the longer and more difficult work of Bishop Lowth. Dr. William Kenrick published *A New Dictionary* in 1773.

60. See note 12 above.

61. "Thomas Dilworth," letter, *Connecticut Journal*, July 14, 1784; Skeel, *Bibliography*, p. 484, A.3.

62. Noah Webster, letter, July 22, 1784, *New York Journal*, September 23, 1784; in Warfel, *Letters*, pp. 11–19; Skeel, *Bibliography*, p. 484, A.4. "Entick's Pocket Dictionary" was presumably an early version of John Entick, [*Entick's*] *Spelling Dictionary...* a new edition by William Crakelt (Wilmington: Peter Brynberg, 1800), first published in London in 1764. William Perry, the spelling book author (see above, note 26), wrote *The Royal Standard English Dictionary*, which would be reprinted in America by Isaiah Thomas in 1788.

63. "Entity," letter, *Weekly Monitor and American Advertiser* (Litchfield), December 21, 1784; Skeel, *Bibliography*, p. 484, A.6.

64. Skeel, *Bibliography*, p. 484, A.5.

65. "D--- G---," letter, November 10, 1784, *Connecticut Journal*, January 12, 1785; Skeel, *Bibliography*, p. 484, A.9.

66. Noah Webster, letter, n.d., *Connecticut Journal*, February 9, 1785; Skeel, *Bibliography*, p. 484, A.10.

67. "D--- G---," letter, January 6, 1785, *Weekly Monitor*, January 25, 1785; Skeel, *Bibliography*, p. 484, A.11.

68. Noah Webster, letter, [January 19, 1785], *Weekly Monitor*, February 1, 1785, in Warfel, *Letters*, pp. 19–24; Skeel, *Bibliography*, p. 484–85, A.12.

69. Ibid. Webster's copy of the newspaper is in the Rare Book Room, NN.

70. Noah Webster, letter, *Weekly Monitor*, February 15, 1785, in Warfel, *Letters*, pp. 25–31; Skeel, *Bibliography*, p. 485, A.15.

71. Skeel, *Bibliography*, pp. 5, 10–11, 36–37, 58.

72. Ibid., p. 5.
73. Sam Cogswell to NW, May 14, 1788, NN–2.
74. Webster, *The American Spelling Book*, 8th Connecticut edition [1789], Table XXVI. This edition is representative of the 1787 revision.
75. Ibid., Tables XIII, XIV–XV, XLII, XLIV.
76. Noah Webster, *The American Spelling Book* (1823), Table XV. Compare this with Table XV of the 1789 speller.
77. Henry S. Commager, introd., *Noah Webster's American Spelling Book* (New York: Teachers College, 1962), pp. 81, 89–92, 88. These are Tables XXVI and XXXI in this reprint of Noah Webster, *The American Spelling Book . . .* the revised impression, with the latest corrections (Middletown, Conn.: William H. Niles, 1831); Skeel, *Bibliography*, Title 243.
78. A. M. Colton, "Our Old Webster's Spelling Book," *Magazine of American History*, 24 (1890): 465–66.
79. Thomas H. Palmer, "The Teacher's Manual," (Prize Essay), *Common School Journal*, 2 (1840): 301.
80. Webster, *A Grammatical Institute, Part II* (1784), p. 13. The contents of the grammar are discussed in Ervin C. Shoemaker, *Noah Webster, Pioneer of Learning* (New York: Columbia University Press, 1936), pp. 114–43; in Warfel, *Noah Webster*, pp. 80–85; and in William A. Rosenberg, "The Influence and Contribution of Noah Webster upon Language Arts Teaching in the Nineteenth Century" (Ph.D. Diss., University of Connecticut, 1967), pp. 24–36. For editions of this grammar and other Webster grammars, see Skeel, *Bibliography*, pp. 141–60.
81. Webster, *A Grammatical Institute, Part III* (1785), pp. 3–4.
82. Ibid., p. 183. The contents of the reader are discussed in Shoemaker, pp. 144–208; in Warfel, *Noah Webster*, pp. 85–90; and in Rosenberg, "Influence and Contribution," pp. 37–85. For editions of this reader and derivative readers, see Skeel, *Bibliography*, pp. 161–95.
83. NW to Joel Barlow, October 19, 1807, quoted in Skeel, *Bibliography*, p. 152. Webster's rival was Lindley Murray's *English Grammar . . .* 3rd ed. (New York: Isaac Collins, 1800), first published in the U.S. in 1798. Another competitor was *The Young Lady's Accidence* by Caleb Bingham, first published in 1785. The latter ran to twenty editions, according to the "History of Elementary Schoolbooks," *New-England Magazine* 2 (1832): 477.
84. Caleb Bingham, *The American Preceptor . . .* 4th ed. (Boston: Manning & Loring, for the author, 1797) is first documented in Evans, *American Bibliography*, for 1794. It reached sixty-four editions (640,000 copies), according to the "History of Elementary School Books," p. 477.
85. Lindley Murray, *The English Reader, or, Pieces in Prose and Poetry, selected from the Best Writers* (New York: Isaac Collins, 1800) is first documented in Evans, *American Bibliography*, for the year 1799. Its popularity may be gauged from the fact that, in statistics on

schoolbooks in use in New York State in 1827, 1830 and 1831, *The English Reader* is the single most widely used book in the entire state for those years; "School Books in the United States," *American Annals of Education and Instruction* 2 (1832): 378. See also Nila Banton Smith, *American Reading Instruction* (Newark, Del.: International Reading Assoc., 1965), pp. 58–60.

86. Rosenberg, "Influence and Contribution," pp. 41, 43.

CHAPTER III

1. Skeel, *Bibliography*, p. 435, no. 10. The series of eight articles, all but the first signed "Honorius," ran in the *Connecticut Courant* from August 26, 1783 to January 27, 1784.

2. Skeel, *Bibliography*, p. 436, no. 13. These appeared in the *Freeman's Chronicle* from September to November 1783. See above, Chapter I, note 34, for Webster's first "Observations."

3. See Skeel, *Bibliography*, "Webster's Contributions to Other Periodicals," pp. 433–82.

4. Noah Webster, *Sketches of American Policy* (Hartford: Hudson & Goodwin, 1785); Skeel, *Bibliography*, Title 717.

5. Skeel, *Bibliography*, p. 161.

6. The journals are in the MSS Division of the New York Public Library, filed under Webster's papers as "Diaries." They are reproduced in Ford, *Notes*, Vol. 1. Ford calls them the *Greater* and *Lesser Journal*.

7. NW interlined his journal with a note to this effect: Webster Greater Journal, May 19, 1785, NN–Diaries.

8. Webster Greater Journal, May 20, 1785, NN–Diaries.

9. The advertisement, dated May 25, 1785, is reproduced in Warfel, *Noah Webster*, p. 124.

10. Mrs. Roswell Skeel, Jr., "Salesmanship of an Early American Best Seller," *The Papers of the Bibliographical Society of America*, 32 (1938): 39.

11. Webster Greater Journal, July 5, 1785, NN–Diaries.

12. Quoted in Skeel, "Salesmanship," p. 39.

13. NW to Hudson & Goodwin, August 22, 1785, NN–1.

14. Webster Greater Journal, July 19, August 4, 1785, NN–Diaries.

15. Webster Greater Journal, August 25, September 3, 12, 21, 30, and October 6, 1785, NN–Diaries.

16. Webster Greater Journal, November 4, 5, 1785, NN–Diaries.

17. Webster Greater Journal, November 17, 1785, NN–Diaries.

18. NW to Timothy Pickering, January 20, 1786, quoted in Ford, *Notes*, 1: 147–48.

19. Webster Greater Journal, January 30, 1786, NN–Diaries.

20. Webster Greater Journal, February 17, 1786, NN–Diaries.

21. See below, Chapter VI, note 57.

22. Webster Greater Journal, May 25, 1786: "Form a plan of a new Alphabet & send to Dr Franklin at the request of Dr Ramsey," NN–Diaries. Dr. "Ramsey" was Dr. David Ramsay; Warfel, *Noah Webster*, p. 138.

23. Timothy Pickering to NW, October 19, 1785, NN–2.
24. Ibid.
25. Webster Greater Journal, February 15, 1786, NN–Diaries.
26. Webster Greater Journal, February 28, 1786, NN–Diaries.
27. Webster Greater Journal, March 20–May 29, 1786, NN–Diaries.
28. NW to Mary Cox, April 14, 1786, PM.
29. Webster Greater Journal, July 2, 1786, NN–Diaries.
30. Webster Greater Journal, July 13–October 25, 1786, NN–Diaries.
31. Webster Lesser Journal, October 30, 1786, NN–Diaries.
32. NW to The Honorable the Speaker of the House of Assembly, State of Delaware, January 24, 1787, LC.
33. NW to Messrs Dunlap & Claypole, March 1, 1787, in Warfel, *Letters*, pp. 57–59. Webster here listed the copyright terms of each state.
34. Webster Greater Journal, November 23, 1786, NN–Diaries.
35. Webster Greater Journal, December 25, 1786, NN–Diaries.
36. Webster Greater Journal, December 28, 1786, NN–Diaries.
37. Webster Greater Journal, February 24, 1787, NN–Diaries.
38. Webster Greater Journal, March 15, May 28, June 14, July 18, and August 4, 1787, NN–Diaries.
39. Webster Greater Journal, April 13, 1787; Webster's salary was £200 p.a., ibid., April 10, 1787, NN–Diaries.
40. Skeel, *Bibliography*, "The 'Domestic Debt' Controversy," pp. 486–488.
41. This was NW's view of his opponent's position: "Adam" (i.e., NW), April 25, 1787 to the Printer, *Freeman's Journal* (Philadelphia), in Warfel, *Letters*, p. 59; Skeel, *Bibliography*, "The 'Seth' Controversy," pp. 488–489.
42. Skeel, *Bibliography*, "Criticism of the Third Edition of the Grammar," pp. 489–490.
43. NW to the Public, May 8, 1787, in Warfel, *Letters*, pp. 62–63.
44. Noah Webster (Senior) to NW, July 28, 1787, NN–2.
45. Warfel, *Noah Webster*, p. 160; see Skeel, *Bibliography*, p. 485.
46. Webster Greater Journal, March 1, April 2, 18, 20, May 4, June 9, 1787, NN–Diaries.
47. Skeel, *Bibliography*, pp. 10–12 (Title 7).
48. Skeel, *Bibliography*, p. 367 (Title 771). There is no extant copy.
49. [Thomas] Fitzsimmons to NW, September 15, 1787, NN–2.
50. Adrienne Koch, introd., *Notes of Debates in the Federal Convention of 1787, Reported by James Madison* (1966; rpt. New York: Norton, 1969), p. 12.
51. [Noah Webster], *An Examination into the Leading Principles of the Federal Constitution...* (Philadelphia: Prichard & Hall, 1787); Skeel, *Bibliography*, Title 718.
52. Webster Greater Journal, October 22, 23, 1787, NN–Diaries.
53. Webster Greater Journal, December 4, 1787: "make the bargain for printing the American Magazine," NN–Diaries.
54. Webster Greater Journal, October 31, 1787, NN–Diaries.
55. Webster Greater Journal, December 20, 1788, NN–Diaries.

56. Webster Greater Journal, April 7, 1788. Webster was busy with the Philological Society through the spring; NN–Diaries.
57. Webster Greater Journal, July 15, 1788: "Writing for Dr Morse Geography," NN–Diaries; Webster also offered to help Morse with the latest version of his geography in 1793: NW to Jedediah Morse, September 20, 1793, Simon Gratz Collection, HSP.
58. Noah Webster, *Dissertations on the English Language . . . to which is added, by way of Appendix, an Essay on a Reformed Mode of Spelling, with Dr. Franklin's Arguments on that subject* (Boston: for the author, Isaiah Thomas & Co., 1789); Skeel, *Bibliography*, Title 651.
59. James Greenleaf to NW, February 15, 1789, NN–2; see also James Greenleaf to NW, November 24, 1788 (ibid.).
60. James Greenleaf to NW, April 20, 1789, NN–2; see NW to James Greenleaf, August 12, 1789, Society Collection, HSP.
61. NW to James Greenleaf, September 20, 1789, Society Collection, HSP.
62. NW to Rebecca [Greenleaf], October 10, 1789, Goodrich Family Papers, Yale.
63. Webster Greater Journal, October 19, 1789, NN–Diaries.
64. Webster Greater Journal, October 26, 1789, NN–Diaries.
65. John Trumbull to Oliver Wolcott, December 9, 1789, quoted in Ford, *Notes*, 1: 269; see Goodrich, "Life and Writings," p. 16.
66. For a fuller account of the years 1789–1818, see Rollins, *The Long Journey*, pp. 55–121, and Warfel, *Noah Webster*, pp. 195–344.
67. Skeel, *Bibliography*, pp. 443–44.
68. Noah Webster, *Rudiments of English Grammar . . .* (Hartford: Elisha Babcock, 1790); Skeel, *Bibliography*, Title 445; Noah Webster, *A Collection of Essays and Fugitiv* [sic] *Writings . . .* (Boston: for the author, I. Thomas & E. T. Andrews, 1790); Skeel, *Bibliography*, Title 745.
69. Skeel, *Bibliography*, pp. 371–72 (Title 781), and Noah Webster, *The Little Reader's Assistant . . .* (Hartford: Elisha Babcock, 1790); Skeel, *Bibliography*, Title 529.
70. [Noah Webster], *The Prompter; or A Commentary on Common Sayings and Subjects* (Hartford: Hudson & Goodwin, 1791); Skeel, *Bibliography*, Title 652.
71. NW to George Washington, September 2, 1790, in Warfel, *Letters*, pp. 85–86. The secret topic was NW's theory on vegetable manure.
72. NW to James Greenleaf, July 8, 1793, Etting Collection, HSP.
73. Webster Greater Journal, December 9, 1793, NN–Diaries.
74. For an analysis of subject matter see Gary R. Coll, "Noah Webster, Journalist, 1783–1803" (Ph.D. Diss., University of Southern Illinois, 1971).
75. Dissolution of Webster–Bunce partnership, February 10, 1796, NN–9. The settlement cost NW $3,000.
76. NW to [Hudson & Goodwin], May 15, 1796, NN–1.
77. NW to Hudson & Goodwin, January 13, 1798, NN–1.
78. Babbidge, *Noah Webster: On Being American*, p. 10.

79. *Minerva and Mercantile Evening Advertiser* (New York), July 12, 1797; quoted in Rollins, *The Long Journey*, p. 83.
80. Rollins, *The Long Journey*, p. 79. Rollins dates this change from 1794. See, in general, ibid., pp. 71–88.
81. Ibid., pp. 89–94.
82. Warfel, *Noah Webster*, pp. 260, 299.
83. Noah Webster, *A Brief History of Epidemic and Pestilential Diseases . . .* 2 vols. (Hartford: Hudson & Goodwin, 1799); Skeel, *Bibliography*, Title 748.
84. NW to Benjamin Rush, September 11, 1801, in Warfel, *Letters*, pp. 235–37.
85. Noah Webster, *Elements of Useful Knowledge. Volume I* (Hartford: Hudson & Goodwin, 1802), preface, p. [7]; Skeel, *Bibliography*, Title 537.
86. Noah Webster, *Elements of Useful Knowledge. Volume II* (New Haven: for the author, 1804); Skeel, *Bibliography*, Title 544.
87. Noah Webster, *Elements of Useful Knowledge. Volume III* (New Haven: Bronson, Walter & Co., 1806); Skeel, *Bibliography*, Title 549.
88. Noah Webster, *History of Animals; being the Fourth Volume of Elements of Useful Knowledge* (New Haven: Howe & Deforest, 1812); Skeel, *Bibliography*, Title 551.
89. Elizur Goodrich to NW, September 29, 1783, NN–2.
90. Noah Webster, *A Compendious Dictionary of the English Language* (1806; rpt. New York: Crown Publishers, 1970); Skeel, *Bibliography*, Title 577. Webster acknowledges Elizur Goodrich's suggestion in his preface, p. [iii]. See ibid., p. xix, for Webster's identifying John Entick's *Spelling Dictionary* as the basis for his own. For Entick see above, Chapter II, note 62.
91. See below, Chapter VI, note 53.
92. Noah Webster, *A Dictionary of the English Language; compiled for the Use of Common Schools in the United States* (Boston: John and David West, 1807); Skeel, *Bibliography*, Title 578. Skeel (ibid., p. 229) claims that this edition was not an abridgement of the *Compendious*, but of the ongoing *American Dictionary*. Webster, however, specifically says in his preface that it was an abridgement of the former (p. iv).
93. NW to Samuel L. Mitchill, June 29, 1807, Jones.
94. NW to Thom[as] Dawes, December 20, 1808, NN–1. Reprinted in Warfel, *Letters*, pp. 309–15. Dawes' answer to this letter provoked a reply from Webster, which was eventually printed in the *Panoplist* in July, 1809: Skeel, *Bibliography*, pp. 293–94 (Title 706).
    The psychological bases for Webster's conversion are discussed in Rollins, *The Long Journey*, pp. 107–15. Rollins sees Webster's anxiety over political events—the embargo in particular—and the strains within his family, as the precipitating elements. He suggests that submission to the authority of an omnipotent God gave Webster the reassurance and emotional stability for which he longed.
95. Rollins, *The Long Journey*, p. 119. See "Reply to a Letter of David

McClure, Esq., on the Subject of the Proper Course of Study in the Girard College, Philadelphia," dated October 25, 1836, in Noah Webster, *A Collection of Papers on Political, Literary and Moral Subjects* (1843; rpt. New York: Burt Franklin, 1968), p. 291: "No truth is more evident to my mind, than that the Christian religion must be the basis of any government intended to secure the rights and privileges of a free people."

96. See Appendix VII. Totals of copies of the *American Spelling Book* recorded by Webster as licensed for the year 1810, for example, amount to 301,769. At a penny a spelling book, Webster was receiving $3,017 as his premium that year, NN–Account Books. See also note 102, for Webster's calculation that the average annual sales of the speller from 1804 to 1815 were 241,000.

97. NW to Joel Barlow, October 19, 1807: "if I can give it [the *Elements*] circulation in the middle and southern states, the profits will enable me to bear the expenses of my great work" (Warfel, *Letters*, p. 293).

98. NW to John Jay, May 19, 1813; in Warfel, *Letters*, p. 334.

99. Copy of NW to Josiah Quincy, February 12, 1811, NN–1. Similarly, NW to John M. Mason, January 3, 1811, Simon Gratz Collection, HSP.

100. Warfel, *Noah Webster*, pp. 298, 327–28.

101. Ibid., pp. 327–44. Noah Webster, "An Address, delivered at the laying of the corner stone of the building erecting for the Charity Institution in Amherst, Massachusetts, August 9, 1820," in Amherst College, *A Plea for a Miserable World* (Boston: Ezra Lincoln, 1820), pp. [7]–11; Skeel, *Bibliography*, Title 742.

102. NW's own draft of his letter to his publishers, November 20, 1815, NN–1. My arithmetic, using, like Webster, the figures in his Account Book No. I, NN–Account Books, makes the annual average total for eleven years 214,000, not 241,000 as Webster claimed. His annual average of 286,000 for the preceding two years, entered under 1814 and 1815, is close enough, given that he calculated it with missing returns from two publishers.

103. NW to George Goodwin & Sons, November 20, 1815, NN–1. The actual letter differs little from NW's draft (see note 102).

104. Contract between Noah Webster of Amherst and Hudson & Hudson of Hartford, April 19, 1816, NN–9.

105. Advance by Hudson & Co., July 1, 1817, NN–9.

106. Note by NW to contract between Noah Webster of Amherst and Hudson & Hudson of Hartford (see note 104), April 20, 1818, NN–9.

CHAPTER IV

1. Skeel, *Bibliography*, pp. 5, 141, 161.
2. Chapter II, note 69.
3. NW to Isaiah Thomas, February 23, 1784, Isaiah Thomas Papers, AAS.

4. NW to Hudson & Goodwin, May 5, 1784, NN–1.
5. Advertisement, *Connecticut Courant*, June 1, 1784.
6. The grammar is identified as "Printed and sold by Hudson and Goodwin" in its fourth edition, the reader is "Printed by Hudson and Goodwin" by its second; Skeel, *Bibliography*, pp. 144, 163 (Titles 409 and 451).
7. "Proposals to Mr. Webster by Hudson & Goodwin," July 22, 1786, Miscellaneous Manuscripts Collection, H, Yale.
8. NW to Hudson & Goodwin, July 26, PM. While the majority of Webster's letters to Hudson & Goodwin appears to have been preserved, their letters to him are no longer extant; the reconstruction of events has therefore to be inferred from his letters to them, alone.
9. NW to Hudson & Goodwin, August 9, 1786, NN–1.
10. NW to Hudson & Goodwin, August 29, 1786, PM. The Boston printer was Peter Edes; Skeel, *Bibliography*, p. 9 (Title 5). Edes had a license to print 5,000; NW to Hudson & Goodwin, September 16, 1786, NN–1.
11. NW to Hudson & Goodwin, August 29, 1786, PM.
12. NW to Hudson & Goodwin, July 26, 1786, PM.
13. Webster Lesser Journal, November 1, 1786, NN–Diaries.
14. Ibid.
15. "Proposals to Mr. Webster by Hudson & Goodwin," July 22, 1786; see note 7. These "proposals" are presumably the "proposal" of Hudson & Goodwin discussed in NW to Hudson & Goodwin, July 26, 1786, PM, and the basis for the contract signed in November. While the contract only specified Webster's freedom to sell his copyright in the southern states, this freedom extended to the middle states as well. That the contract was still being discussed in August is indicated by NW to Hudson & Goodwin, August 9, 1786, NN–1, where NW asked anxiously what would happen in the event of Hudson's or Goodwin's death: "if your kin or successors should prove less honest [than yourselves], how shall I ascertain what number of books are sold!" This must refer to the clause in the contract promising NW £5 in books per 1,000 books sold.
    The question of the royalties that Webster did or did not receive is a vexed one. It is clear that here Webster stood to gain in proportion to the number of books sold, but would receive books in lieu of cash. His arrangements with other publishers often clearly precluded a set sum per book. Peter Edes of Boston paid £5.10 per 1,000, but the payment was apparently to Hudson & Goodwin for the license, not to Webster as a royalty; NW to Hudson & Goodwin, September 16, 1786, NN–1. (Compare Webster's statement that [John] Folsom of Boston would pay £5 per 1,000; NW to Hudson & Goodwin, May 28, 1788, ibid.) That there was, at this point in the history of American publishing, no standardized system of allocating the author a certain proportion of the income from sales is suggested by NW's remark that "I have no disposition to make a bargain on the terms I once

mentioned, of receiving a certain sum for each copy" (NW to Isaiah Thomas, March 15, 1789, Isaiah Thomas Papers, AAS). Three months later, NW had changed his mind: "I have made a bargain with Mr. Thomas, for a share in the Copyright of my books, by which I shall recieve [sic] £200, perhaps £300 in the course of the next year" (NW to James Greenleaf, June 6, 1789, Etting Collection, HSP). This suggests that, for the first time, Webster would tie his income to the number of books sold, and foreshadows the arrangement he would write into his contract of 1804.

This interpretation contrasts with that of Rollins and Warfel, both of whom talk loosely of "royalties" for these years: Rollins, *The Long Journey*, pp. 40, 50; Warfel, *Noah Webster*, pp. 71–72.

16. Noah Webster and Messrs Young of Philadelphia, license dated October 24, 1787, NN–9. The edition is Skeel, *Bibliography*, Title 7. Young's contract expired in 1790. When he later wrote enquiring about a new contract, Webster informed him that he had made an agreement with Hudson & Goodwin for supplying Philadelphia with his books. Hudson & Goodwin "will do as they please, either to permit you to print, or supply you on purchase or commission" (NW to [William] Young, October 18, 1792, NN–1).

17. Skeel, *Bibliography*, p. 11.

18. Webster Greater Journal, October 31, 1787, NN–Diaries; see Chapter III, note 54.

19. This emerges from the subsequent suit brought against Campbell: sworn statement detailing the accusations against Campbell of violating Hudson & Goodwin's copyright, February 28, 1789, NN–10.

20. NW to Isaiah Thomas, June 25, 1788, Isaiah Thomas Papers, AAS.

21. NW to Hudson & Goodwin, June 22, 1788, NN–1.

22. NW to Hudson & Goodwin, May 28, 1788, NN–1. Folsom is also mentioned in NW to Hudson & Goodwin, July 24, 1786 (ibid.).

23. NW to Hudson & Goodwin, June 22, 1788, NN–1; NW to Isaiah Thomas, June 25, 1788, Isaiah Thomas Papers, AAS.

24. NW to Hudson & Goodwin, June 22, 1788, NN–1.

25. NW to [Hudson & Goodwin], August 3, 1788, PM.

26. The terms apparently involved NW in buying back from Hudson & Goodwin the rights for Massachusetts: he mentions that he purchased the right to sell in Massachusetts from Hudson & Goodwin "for a considerable price" (NW to Hudson & Goodwin, February 27, 1789, NN–1).

27. NW to Hudson & Goodwin, August 16, 1788, NN–1; Skeel, *Bibliography*, p. 14 (Title 14).

28. NW to Russel & Haswell, September 7, 1788, NN–1.

29. See notes 18–19. See also NW to Hudson & Goodwin, June 22, 1788, NN–1: "Campbell has only a *concurrent* right with other booksellers in selling, altho he has the *sole* right of printing in this state" (i.e. New York State).

30. NW to Hudson & Goodwin, February 20, 1789, NN–1: "their

honesty I have long doubted; indeed they both cheated me before they had had their grants five months." "Their" refers to Campbell and to NW's Philadelphia printer, William Young.

31. NW to [Hudson & Goodwin], February 17, 1788, NN–1.

32. Sworn statement detailing accusations against Campbell, February 28, 1789, NN–10.

33. NW to Hudson & Goodwin, February 20, 1789, NN–1. See also NW to Hudson & Goodwin, February 27, 1789, and NW to Hudson & Goodwin, n.d., filed as "probably 1791–2" (ibid.). NW's reference to the keys to his trunk in this letter, and in that of February 12, 1789, dates this letter to February 1789.

34. NW wrote in his journal, "Hudson & Goodwin recover judgement agt N Patten for selling my books" (Webster Greater Journal, January 30, 1790, NN–Diaries).

35. Nathaniel Patten, advertisement, "A Proposal to save Three hundred and thirty Pounds six shillings and eight pence" (*American Mercury* [Hartford], May 24, 1790).

36. NW, advertisement dated September 15, 1792, *Connecticut Courant*, September 17, 1792; Skeel, *Bibliography*, pp. 19–20 (Title 28).

37. Skeel, *Bibliography*, p. 20; Warfel, *Noah Webster*, p. 73.

38. NW to [Hudson & Goodwin], January 23, 1795, NN–1; NW to Hudson & Goodwin, February 20, 1797 (ibid.). William Young, the Philadelphia printer, put the number printed by Campbell at 50,000; Timothy Pickering to NW, December 8, 1791, NN–2.

39. NW to Hudson & Goodwin, February 16, 1794, NN–1.

40. NW to Hudson & Goodwin, April 10, 1796, PM.

41. NW to Hudson & Goodwin, October 21, 1796, PM.

42. NW to Hudson & Goodwin, February 20, 1797, NN–1.

43. Thomas' letter to NW of February 15, 1784 is mentioned in NW to Isaiah Thomas, February 23, 1784, Isaiah Thomas Papers, AAS. See also NW to Isaiah Thomas, March 27, 1784, NN–1.

44. NW to Isaiah Thomas, June 25, 1788, Isaiah Thomas Papers, AAS; Webster, *Dissertations on the English Language* (1789); Noah Webster, *The American Spelling Book*, Thomas and Andrews's first edition (Boston: Isaiah Thomas & Ebenezer T. Andrews, 1789); in Skeel, *Bibliography*, p. 15 (Title 16).

45. Nathaniel Appleton, who was married to Rebecca Greenleaf's sister, told Webster that he had heard that Thomas and Andrews' edition of Webster's speller was "the best extant, but that it is not correct" (Nathaniel Appleton to NW, January 17, 1790, NN–2).

46. NW to Isaiah Thomas, June 25, 1788, Isaiah Thomas Papers, AAS.

47. Tebbel, *A History of Book Publishing in the United States*, 1: 68.

48. William Perry, *The Only Sure Guide to the English Tongue*, 8th ed., Worcester 1st ed. (Worcester: Isaiah Thomas, 1785); [Isaiah Thomas], *New American Spelling Book* (Worcester: Isaiah Thomas, 1785).

49. Timothy Pickering to NW, May 2, 1786, NN–2; William Perry, *The Royal Standard English Dictionary*, First American Edition (Worcester: Isaiah Thomas, 1788).

50. Annie R. Marble, *From 'Prentice to Patron: the Life Story of Isaiah Thomas* (New York: Appleton-Century, 1953), p. 167.
51. Thomas & Andrews' twelfth edition includes in its listing of booksellers, "Thomas, Andrews & Butler, in Baltimore; ... Andrews & Penniman in Albany" (Skeel, *Bibliography*, p. 25 [Title 45]).
52. See Appendix II.
53. Skeel, *Bibliography*, pp. 13–14 (Titles 12 and 13).
54. Noah Webster, *The American Spelling Book*, the twelfth edition (Providence: John Carter, 1789); in Skeel, *Bibliography*, pp. 16–17 (Title 20). There is no evidence as to the existence of any earlier editions by this publisher.
55. NW to Mathew Carey, August 4, 1791, NW to Messrs Carey, Stewart & Co., August 14, 1791, Lee & Febiger, HSP.
56. NW, "A book called a *Practical Spelling Book* has lately been published by the Rev T H Gallaudet & the Rev H Hooker" (November 25, 1840, NN–10).
57. Timothy Pickering to NW, December 8, 1791, NN–2.
58. Skeel, *Bibliography*, pp. 21, 24 (Titles 35, 44, 34).
59. Ibid., p. 21.
60. For the terms of the contract, see legal opinion from Charles Chauncey to NW, July 31, 1805, NN–9; Skeel, *Bibliography*, p. 31 (Titles 69–70).
61. NW to Bonsal & Niles, October 2, 1804, NN–1.
62. Legal opinion from Charles Chauncey, July 31, 1805, NN–9. Chauncey charged Bonsal & Niles with printing "an extraordinary number of the work" (ibid.).
63. No copy of the speller or grammar for these years is extant, but there are extant copies of the *American Selection* of 1794 and 1795 (Skeel, *Bibliography*, pp. 173–74 [Titles 469 and 471]). NW mentions that he expects to have an impression of the spelling book out by spring 1794; NW to [Hudson & Goodwin], December 30, 1793, NN–1. Bunce advertised a "New and Improved Edition [of the spelling book], printed under the inspection of the author," in the *American Mercury*, February 25, 1794: Skeel, *Bibliography*, p. 23 (Title 40).
64. Webster bought 10,000 spelling books from Hudson & Goodwin on October 10, 1796 for 6¢ a copy. He retailed 2,000 copies to William Young, and 1,000 to, respectively, Robert Campbell, Joseph Crukshank and John Ormrod, all of Philadelphia, at 8¢ a copy, on October 24, 1796: Webster, Account Book No. I, 1788-1838, pp. 55, 58–61, NN–Account Books. See also NW to Hudson & Goodwin, March 30, 1796, NN–1.
65. NW to James Greenleaf, April 17, 1791, Etting Collection, HSP.
66. See note 15.
67. Notice of a public auction of a license to print 150,000 copies of Part I of the Institute, March 30, 1796, cited in Skeel, *Bibliography*, p. 26. NW to Jacob Johnson, December 6, 1804, quoted in Skeel, *Bibliography*, p. 34: "I am afraid also that Martin & Ogden of North Carolina have printed, under a license for 25,000, given 18

months ago, a much larger number." (See *ibid.* Titles 79 and 85.)

68. NW's own copy of his letter to Bonsal & Niles, November 24, 1803, NN–1.

69. Printed indenture on *The American Spelling Book*, NN–9. A note in NW's hand on the back of the indenture reads "used in 1804." There is a discrepancy between this notation and the implication of Webster's letter to the Websters of Albany, February 18, 1804, NN–1, where he mentions that he has found a difference in the price per dozen between their contract and that of [Jacob] Johnson of Philadelphia. He calls this an oversight. As such an oversight could hardly have arisen from the printed contract, which spells out the price per dozen, perhaps it was in part this slip that inspired him to use a printed contract. In this same letter, he also mentions that Johnson "is restricted in his sales to the *West side of the Hudson.*" The new contract, in contrast, stipulates no restrictions on where the books may be sold. Thomas & Andrews saw the new contract, as Thomas specifically mentions it: Thomas & Andrews to NW, February 13, 1804, NN–3.

70. That printers did indeed follow this method to calculate the number of copies printed emerges from NW's account book, where Webster often specifies the number of quires used. For example, alongside Asahel Seward's returns for April 1809, NW writes, "April 1809—638 [i.e. quires]—29,000." Account Book No. I, NN–Account Books.

71. Printed indenture; notation in NW's handwriting on the back reads "used in 1804," NN–9.

72. For the reassignment of licenses, see Skeel, *Bibliography*, p. 36. For the choice between West and Thomas & Andrews see Thomas & Andrews to NW, November 22, 1803; January 15, 30, February 13, 1804; and Thomas Dawes to NW, January 5, February 15, 1804, all in NN–3 (Dawes was Webster's brother-in-law); see also Thomas & Andrews to NW, February 22, 1804, PM. After the reassignment, Webster asked Thomas & Andrews for a cent per speller for stock still in hand; Eben[ezer] Andrews to Isaiah Thomas, October 5, 9, 1804, Isaiah Thomas Papers, AAS.

73. The figures for Utica, Bennington and Brattleboro, Boston, Philadelphia and Hartford derive from NW, Account Book No. I, 1788-1838, pp. 63–68, NN–Account Books. A Lexington figure of 5,000 is to be found in Henry Clay to NW, November 18, 1806, NN–3; but Webster's account book shows an entry in 1809 for Maccoun, Tilford & Co. (labeled "Assignees of Joseph Charless") of Lexington, Kentucky for 7,300 spellers. (A note by Webster reads, "no returns & the house failed." He did, however, record three small premiums received between 1809 and 1813.) The figures for the south and for Ohio and New Orleans come from NW, draft of letter to booksellers, November 20, 1815, NN–1; NW to George Goodwin & Sons, November 20, 1815 (*ibid.*). He there estimates the Lexington figure to be 7,000.

In his Account Book No. I, Webster entered annual totals

from 1804 to 1818 for each publisher, and added up the overall totals by publisher (but not by year). The former have been reproduced in Skeel, *Bibliography*, pp. 36–57 (Titles 89–172); the latter as well as the former have been tabulated in Monaghan, "Noah Webster's Speller," Appendix V. For the totals licensed by all publishers for each year, calculated by me from Webster's figures, see above, Appendix VII.

74. NW to Hudson & Goodwin, May 5, 1784, NN–1.
75. NW to Hudson & Goodwin, July 24, 1786, NN–1.
76. NW to Hudson & Goodwin, January 18, 1789, NN–1; see also NW to Hudson & Goodwin, February 16, 1794 (ibid.).
77. NW to Hudson & Goodwin, n.d. (internally dated to February 1789), NN–1; see note 33. See also Isaiah Thomas to William Young, September 1, 1789: "I have been able to do *Nothing* with the several Printers concerned in Webster's Spelling Book respecting a uniform price, but hope they will speedily find it in their interest to comply" (Isaiah Thomas, Sr., Misc. Papers, NN).
78. NW to Hudson & Goodwin, November 5, 1810, NN–1.
79. NW to Hudson & Goodwin, August 29, 1786, PM.
80. NW to Hudson & Goodwin, August 16, 1788, NN–1. The pictures ("cuts") were the illustrations of the fables which appear for the first time in the 1787 spelling book.
81. NW's own copy of his letter to Russel & Haswell, September 7, 1788, NN–1.
82. Skeel, *Bibliography*, pp. 15, 24 (Titles 17, 45).
83. Skeel, *Bibliography*, p. 53 (Title 154). Braford & Read of Boston was the publisher; see above, note 73.
84. NW to Hudson & Goodwin, August 9, 1786, NN–1.
85. NW to Hudson & Goodwin, April 3, 1786, NN–1; see also NW to Hudson & Goodwin, April 25, 1786 (ibid.).
86. NW to Hudson & Goodwin, March 7, 1787, NN–1.
87. NW to Hudson & Goodwin, July 24, 1786, NN–1; see also NW to W[illia]m Young, February 20, 1788 (ibid.).
88. NW's own copy of his letter to Bonsal & Niles, November 24, 1803, NN–1.
89. NW to Hudson & Goodwin, April 3, 1786, NN–1.
90. NW's own copy of his letter to [David] Hogan, January 10, 1804, NN–1. Hogan was a Philadelphia printer who published several editions of Webster's revised *American Selection* between 1805 and 1816; Skeel, *Bibliography*, pp. 186–90. Here, however, he was printing the revised *American Spelling Book* for the publisher Jacob Johnson. Webster instructs Hogan, in this letter, to ask Johnson to let Hogan make the same corrections in Johnson's copy.
91. Ibid.
92. Ibid.
93. NW to Ch[as.] & G. Webster, September 7, 1807, NN–1.
94. NW to [David] Hogan, January 10, 1804, NN–1.
95. NW to Webster & Skinner, March 24, 1810, PM.
96. NW to Hudson & Goodwin, September 14, 1787, NN–1.

97. NW to John Canfield, January 6, 1783, NN–1.
98. Webster, *A Grammatical Institute, Part I* [1783], p. 14.
99. *Connecticut Courant*, October 14, 1783; Skeel, *Bibliography*, p. 6.
100. Noah Webster, *A Grammatical Institute . . . Part I*, the sixth edition (Hartford: Hudson & Goodwin, 1787), pp. [iii–v].
101. Sam[uel] S. Smith to NW, September 27, 1782, NN–2. See also copy of Tapping Reeve to John Canfield, October 21, 1782 (ibid.); John Turnbull to NW, April 28, 1783 (ibid.).
102. Timothy Dwight to NW, May 6, 1784, Timothy Dwight Papers, PM.
103. Oliver Wolcott to NW, March 9, 1784, PM.
104. George Washington to NW, July 30, 1785; in Ford, *Notes*, 1: 93.
105. Benjamin West to NW, September 11, 1784, Benjamin West Papers, PM.
106. NW asked Hudson & Goodwin to send him "a Copy of the Schoolmaster's recommendation of the Spelling Book—I will insert it after an advertisement" (NW to Hudson & Goodwin, September 10, 1786, NN–1).
107. Elisha Babcock to NW, November 22, 1783, NN–2.
108. NW to Hudson & Goodwin, August 9, 1786, NN–1.
109. NW to Hudson & Goodwin, August 22, 1785, NN–1.
110. NW to Hudson & Goodwin, September 4, 1788, NYHS. For the Philological Society, see Warfel, *Noah Webster*, pp. 185–87.
111. NW to Hudson & Goodwin, April 3, 1786, NN–1.
112. Quoted in Warfel, *Noah Webster*, p. 137.
113. NW to Hudson & Goodwin, April 3, 1786, NN–1. See also NW to Hudson & Goodwin, n.d., filed as "probably 1791–2," "books are wanted. They are not sufficiently advertised" (ibid.). For the date, see note 33.
114. NW to Hudson & Goodwin, August 9, 1786, NN–1.
115. Advertisement, *The Connecticut Journal* (New Haven), November 23, 1784. For the original letter, see Joseph Willard to NW, February 2, 1784, NN–2. The italicization of some, but not all, of Dilworth's name may be explained by the original letter, which Webster faithfully reproduced: Willard underlined the phrase "*Mr. Dilworth's new Guide*" [sic], which the printers, used to italicizing titles, but not author's names, have reproduced in part. The originals of the other letters cited in the advertisement are preserved: copy of Tapping Reeve to John Canfield, October 21, 1782, NN–2; Benjamin West to NW, September 11, 1784, Benjamin West Papers, PM. Note that the newspaper advertisement dates the Reeve letter 'October 12, 1782"—presumably a typographical error. The last part of the advertisement was unquestionably written by Webster himself, and signed ex post facto by his friends.
116. Skeel, *Bibliography*, p. 8.
117. NW to [Hudson & Goodwin], December 24, 1810, NN–1.
118. Joseph Willard to NW, February 2, 1784, NN–2.
119. NW to Hudson & Goodwin, August 22, 1785, NN–1.
120. Ibid.

121. NW to "Gentlemen," June 15, 1805, Simon Gratz Collection, HSP.
122. Nath[aniel] W. Appleton to NW, February 21, 1790, NN–2.
123. Nath[aniel] W. Appleton to NW, December 6, 1789, NN–2.
124. NW to Benjamin Rush, December 4, 1789, cited in Rollins, *The Long Journey*, p. 66.
125. NW's copy, Grant to Connecticut Academy of Arts and Science, August 28, 1804, NN–9. NW's annotation states that the Academy relinquished the grant from the speller and Hudson & Goodwin paid the grant on the *Elements*.
126. Grant to Trustees of Nassau Hall, August 29, 1804, NN–9.
127. Abel Flint to NW, January 18, 1805, NN–3. NW's annotation to this letter shows that he discontinued this grant, at his own request, after one year. See also NW's own copy of Grant to Trustees of the Missionary Society of Connecticut, August 28, 1804, NN–9.
128. NW to William Young, March 12, 1790, PM. One of the three colleges mentioned was presumably Yale, to which Webster gave one percent of the sales of the *Institute*, to endow an annual prize for the best composition in Ethics, Moral Philosophy and Belles Lettres: Ezra Stiles to NW, March 16, April 9, 1790, PM.
129. Chester T. Hallenbeck, "Book-trade Publicity before 1800," *The Papers of the Bibliographical Society of America*, 32 (1938), 47–56.
130. Timothy Pickering to NW, October 19, 1785, NN–2.
131. Timothy Pickering to NW, May 2, 1786, NN–2; Skeel, *Bibliography*, pp. 135–36 (Title 397).
132. Timothy Pickering to NW, December 8, 1791, NN–2.
133. See note 73.
134. Nath[aniel] W. Appleton, December 6, 1789, NN–2.
135. Nath[aniel] W. Appleton to NW, June 6, 1790, NN–2. Appleton died in 1795: William Greenleaf to NW, April 15, 1795 (ibid.).
136. NW to [Da]niel Greenleaf, February 24, 1800, NN–1.
137. Joel Barlow to NW, August 31, 1782, in Todd, *Life and Letters of Joel Barlow*, p. 42.
138. NW to Hudson & Goodwin, August 9, 1786, NN–1.
139. Warfel, *Noah Webster*, pp. 72–73.
140. See above, Chapter II, note 29.
141. J[oseph] Buckminster to NW, November 17, 1783, NN–2.
142. Noah Webster, *The American Spelling Book... Being the First Part of a Grammatical Institute of the English Language...* 8th Connecticut ed. (Hartford: Hudson & Goodwin, [1789]), p. vii; Skeel, *Bibliography*, Title 17.
143. Appendix I.
144. NW to Hudson & Goodwin, September 28, 1786, NN–1. Webster, *A Compendious Dictionary* (1806) defines *drug* as "a medical simple, a thing of little worth."
145. Alston, *A Bibliography of the English Language*, Vol. 4, Title 734.
146. See note 48.
147. Mathew Carey, *Columbia Spelling & Reading Book*, 9th ed. (Phila-

delphia: M. Carey, 1806); in Ralph R. Shaw and Richard H. Shoemaker, *American Bibliography, a Preliminary Checklist for 1806* (New York: Scarecrow Press, 1961). This is the only extant edition found in Shaw and Shoemaker.

148. NW, "A book called a *Practical Spelling Book* has lately been published by the Rev T H Gallaudet & The Rev H Hooker," November 25, 1840, NN–10.

149. NW to [Hudson & Goodwin], May 28, 1788, NN–1.

150. NW to "Gentlemen," June 15, 1805, Simon Gratz Collection, HSP.

151. Henry Clay to NW, November 18, 1806, NN–3. The printer was Charless of Lexington, Kentucky. Charless' threat worked: NW annotated the letter that he accepted Charless' terms (ibid.); Skeel, *Bibliography*, p. 41 (Title 102). See above, note 73.

152. NW to John West, January 18, 1805, Jones.

153. NW to [Hudson & Goodwin], December 22, 1810, NN–1.

154. NW to Lemuel Shattuck, November 18, 1829, in "History of Elementary School Books," p. 475.

155. Appendixes II, III and IV.

156. Timothy Pickering to NW, October 19, 1785, NN–2.

157. NW to Timothy Pickering, October 28, [1785], in Warfel, *Letters*, p. 38. Skeel, *Bibliography*, p. 135, documents the existence of the edition, of which no copy is extant (Title 397).

158. Skeel, *Bibliography*, pp. 367–70 (Titles 771–780). After 1801, the sole printer was Ashbel Stoddard of Hudson, New York. Title 779 appeared in 1805, Title 780 in 1818. There seems no reason to believe that Webster was actively involved in these last editions.

159. Skeel, *Bibliography*, pp. 191–94 (Titles 529–535).

160. Nila Banton Smith, *American Reading Instruction* (Newark, Del.: International Reading Association, 1965), p. 45.

161. Webster, *The Little Reader's Assistant* (1790), p. [2].

162. Rollins, *The Long Journey*, p. 66.

163. Webster, *The Little Reader's Assistant*, pp. 25, 40–41, 42. The spellings are on pp. 37, 47, 52 and passim.

164. Cited in Skeel, *Bibliography*, pp. 165–67, under Titles 452 and 455. For advertisements, see ibid., p. 170, where Skeel cites the advertisement for Thomas & Andrews's first edition, in 1790 (Title 459).

165. NW to William Young, December 19, 1787, Dreer Collection, HSP.

166. Nath[aniel] W. Appleton to NW, June 6, 1790, NN–2.

167. Nath[aniel] W. Appleton to NW, June 14, 1790, NN–2. The schoolmaster concerned was Caleb Bingham, who proceeded to write a reader of his own, *The American Preceptor*; see above, Chapter II, note 84.

168. NW to Hudson & Goodwin, May 25, 1796, NN–1.

169. Noah Webster, *The American Selection*, the tenth edition with great improvements (Hartford: Hudson & Goodwin, [1796?]); in Skeel, *Bibliography*, p. 176 (Title 477).

170. Skeel, *Bibliography*, pp. 185–90 (Titles 510–27). There was, in fact, one edition by Thomas & Andrews, in 1807 (Title 515). Despite its

calling itself "a new edition," it was essentially the old text. For an example of Webster's attempts to interest other publishers in printing the improved *American Selection*, see NW to [Chas. R. and George Webster], February 18, 1804, NN–1. David Hogan was the book's publisher in Philadelphia; see above, note 90.

171. typeface: NW to Hudson & Goodwin, January 31, 1809, NN–1; recommendations and publishers: NW to Hudson & Goodwin, June 25, 1810 (ibid.).

172. NW to Websters & Skinner, November 6, 1807, NN–1.

173. Recommendation, June 22, 1810, signed Jonathon W. Kellogg, Instructor, in NW's handwriting, enclosed in NW to Hudson & Goodwin, June 25, 1810, NN–1.

174. Skeel, *Bibliography*, pp. 199–206 (Titles 537–552); NW, Account Book No. I, 1788–1838, p. 70, NN–Account Books.

175. The exceptions were *A Letter to the Honorable John Pickering . . .* (Boston: West & Richardson, 1817), reprinted in Warfel, *Letters*, pp. 341–94, and *Letters to a Young Gentleman. . .* (New Haven: Howe & Spalding, 1823). The former was a response to a publication by Pickering on vocabulary peculiar to Americans; the latter a reprint of parts of Volumes I and II of the *Elements*; Skeel, *Bibliography*, pp. 297 and 207 (Titles 712 and 553). In addition, Webster reissued, with minor changes, his school dictionary of 1807: Noah Webster, *A Dictionary of the English Language; compiled for the Use of Common Schools in the United States* (Hartford: George Goodwin & Sons, 1817); Skeel, *Bibliography*, Title 579. See above, Chapter III, note 92.

CHAPTER V

1. Sam[uel] S. Smith to NW, February 2, 1807, NN–4. Smith wrote to encourage NW in his purpose of tracing the English language to its roots.

2. Warfel, *Noah Webster*, p. 349.

3. Writing to a creditor in February, Webster stated that he was unprepared to repay his advance but hoped to have it by April. "I am barely able to subsist my family, with economy." He also said he had not even been able to buy the books he needed and was not about to return to Connecticut! (NW to William Lessingwill, February 14, 1822, NN–1.) Webster was motivated to leave Amherst because a new law would have subjected him to double taxation; NW to Harriet Webster Cobb, March 19, 1822 in Warfel, *Letters*, pp. 408–409.

4. None of the scenario reconstructed above is explicitly stated in any of the letters that relate to this incident, but it is not difficult to read between the lines: William Brown to NW, October 8, 1821, NN–4. (Brown was Horatio Southgate's brother-in-law.) Southgate wrote out a confession, which was read aloud by his pastor at the service.

5. [Julia] and [Chauncey] Goodrich to NW, July 6, 1822, NN–4.

6. Indenture between Noah Webster and David Hoadley of New

Haven, October 21, 1822, NN–9. The house cost NW $3,400 (ibid.).

7. NW to Rebecca Webster, July 10, 1824, NN–1.

8. NW to Eliza Webster, August 19, 1824, NN–1.

9. NW to Rebecca Webster, August 27, 1824, NN–1. See also [Harriet W. Cobb] to NW, July 24, 1824, NN–1 (sic); Harriet W. Cobb and Rebecca Webster to NW, August 24, [1824], NN–4.

10. Quoted in Warfel, *Noah Webster*, p. 354.

11. NW to Rebecca Webster, September 24, 1824, NN–1.

12. Ibid.

13. NW, "... Todd's Johnson ... ," July 1833, NN–7.

14. NW to Rebecca Webster, October 16, 1824, NN–1.

15. NW to Rebecca Webster, January 27, 1825, NN–1. See also NW's copy of his letter to Daniel Webster, September 30, 1826 (ibid.).

16. "Henry John Todd," *Dictionary of National Biography*, 19: 908–10.

17. Robert Baldwin to NW, April 25, 1825, NN–4. See also A. J. Valpy to NW, March 26, 1825; Messrs. Longman to NW, April 11, 1825 (ibid.).

18. NW's copy of his letter to Daniel Webster, September 30, 1826, NN–1.

19. Warfel, *Noah Webster*, p. 358.

20. Warfel, *Noah Webster*, pp. 358–60; Noah Webster, *An American Dictionary of the English Language*, 2 vols. (1828).

21. Webster, *An American Dictionary* (1828), 1: preface, n.p.

CHAPTER VI

1. Advertisement in Webster, *An American Dictionary of the English Language* (1828), 1: n.p.; Samuel Johnson, *A Dictionary of the English Language ... with numerous corrections, and with the addition of several thousand words by the Rev. H. J. Todd ...* 2nd ed. 3 vols. (London: Longman, Rees, Orme, Brown, and Green, 1827).

2. Joseph H. Friend, *The Development of American Lexicography, 1798–1864* (The Hague: Mouton, 1967), p. 36. For Friend's critique of Webster as a lexicographer see, on additions to the vocabulary, pp. 36–38; on definitions, pp. 43–46; on etymology, pp. 75–79; on pronunciation, pp. 56–75; on orthography, pp. 54–56.

3. Rollins, *The Long Journey*, pp. 131–38. Rollins is at pains to contradict the generally held notion that the *American Dictionary* is primarily the product of Webster's nationalism. I myself see no incompatibility between the two positions: granted that Webster had abandoned his early belief that Americans should develop a language distinct from the one spoken in Britain, and granted that he was primarily interested in "social control," it still seems to me that his desire for social control sprang as much from an altruistic wish to see his country at peace within itself as from a purely selfish wish to live in an ordered world.

4. Vincent P. Bynack, "Language and the Order of the World: Noah Webster and the Idea of an American Culture" (Ph.D. Diss., Yale

University, 1978), pp. 191–92, 112–19. Bynack analyzes Webster's "introduction" to the *American Dictionary*, and suggests that Webster's conversion brought order not only to his life but to his ideas on language. Bynack's thesis is that Webster believed that the language of ordinary Americans embodied the harmony of the world before the fall, and that this colloquial language gave them access to God's order.

5. Noah Webster, *A Dictionary of the English Language... for the use of Primary Schools and the Counting House* (New York: White, Gallaher & White, 1830), p. ii.
6. Both copies of an agreement between Aaron Ely of New York and NW, December 15, 1828, NN–9; see below, Chapter VII, note 14.
7. Webster, *A Dictionary of the English Language* (1830). The number of words is mentioned in an advertisement for a "Series of books for systematic instruction in the English Language" filed as if dated May, 1830, NN–5.
8. Noah Webster, *An American Dictionary of the English Language... abridged from the Quarto Edition* (New York: S. Converse, 1829); in Skeel, *Bibliography*, p. 249 (Title 608).
9. Webster, *A Dictionary of the English Language* (1830), p. ii.
10. For a more detailed exposition, see Monaghan, "Noah Webster's Speller, 1783–1843," pp. 244–53.
11. Webster, *A Grammatical Institute, Part I* [1783], p. 5.
12. John Hart, "The Opening of the Unreasonable Writing of our Inglish Toung," (1551) unpublished MS, pp. 27–28, in Bror Danielsson, "John Hart's Works on English Orthography and Pronunciation 1551, 1569, 1570. Part I, Biographical and Bibliographical Introductions, Texts and Index Verborum," *Stockholm Studies in English*, vol. 5 (Stockholm: Almqvist & Wiksell, 1955), pp. 117–18.
13. John Hart, *An Orthographie, conteyning the due order and reason, how to write or paint thimage of mannes voice, most like to the life or nature* (1569), p. 47b, in Danielsson, "John Hart's Works," p. 203.
14. Dilworth, *A New Guide to the English Tongue* (1771), p. iii.
15. Henry Bradley, Charles Hockett and the Czech linguist Joseph Vachek were among the exceptions; Richard L. Venezky, *The Structure of English Orthography* (The Hague: Mouton, 1970), pp. 27–29.
16. Leonard Bloomfield, *Language* (New York: Holt, Rinehart & Winston, 1933), pp. 22–27.
17. Ibid., pp. 21, 501. See also Leonard Bloomfield, "Linguistics and Reading," *Elementary English Review*, 19 (1942): 125–30, 183–86. Similarly, Robert A. Hall, *Sound and Spelling in English* (Philadelphia: Chilton, 1961), p. 29; Charles C. Fries, *Linguistics and Reading* (New York: Holt, Rinehart & Winston, 1962), pp. 186–87.
18. Bloomfield, *Language*, pp. 500–501.
19. Noam Chomsky, *Syntactic Structures* (The Hague: Mouton, 1957). See Noam Chomsky, *Language and Mind*, enlarged edition (New York: Harcourt Brace Jovanovich, 1968), pp. 2–5.

20. Noam Chomsky and Morris Halle, *The Sound Pattern of English* (New York: Harper & Row, 1968).
21. Chomsky and Halle go so far as to describe traditional orthography as a "near optimal system for the lexical representation of English words" (ibid., p. 49).
22. Carol Chomsky, "Reading, Writing and Phonology," *Harvard Educational Review*, 40 (1970): 294. Chomsky details many other examples. See also below, note 81.
23. Venezky, *The Structure of English Orthography*, p. 11.
24. Ibid., pp. 120–21. For example, the doubling of the final consonant in forms like *hop*: *hopping* (but not in *hope*: *hoping*), consistently indicates vowel quantity. Even the spelling of words borrowed from foreign languages is not wholly unmotivated, for it often indicates the language of origin (ibid., pp. 121–22). (*Fil*(i) derives from Latin, for instance, as in *filial*, but *phil*(o) from the Greek, as in *philosophy*. The spelling distinction points to a difference in meaning, not sound.)
25. Webster, *A Grammatical Institute, Part I* [1783], p. 5.
26. Ibid., p. 18.
27. Ibid., pp. 11–12, note.
28. See below, note 57.
29. Modern copy of NW to George Washington, March 31, 1786, NN–1; reprinted in Warfel, *Letters*, p. 46.
30. NW to Benjamin Franklin, May 24, 1786; in Ford, *Notes*, 1: 455–56; reprinted in Warfel, *Letters*, pp. 49–51.
31. NW to Timothy Pickering, May 25, 1786; in Warfel, *Letters*, pp. 51–52.
32. Benjamin Franklin to NW, June 18, 1786; in Ford, *Notes*, 1: 459.
33. NW to Benjamin Franklin, June 23, 1786; in Ford, *Notes*, 1: 459; reprinted in Warfel, *Letters*, pp. 52–53.
34. Benjamin Franklin to NW, July 9, 1786; in Ford, *Notes*, 1: 455.
35. Webster Greater Journal, December 28, 1786, NN–Diaries.
36. Webster Greater Journal, February 24, 1787, NN–Diaries.
37. Webster, *Dissertations*, p. 20.
38. Ibid., p. 21.
39. Ibid., pp. 22–23.
40. NW's annotated copy is in the New York Public Library Rare Book Room. The annotations are undated, but in the hand of Webster's old age.
41. Webster, *Dissertations*, p. 36.
42. Venezky, *The Structure of English Orthography*, p. 126.
43. Webster, *Dissertations*, pp. 394–96. Webster's suggestions, and his refutation of the objections he anticipates, are reproduced fully in Rosenberg, "The Influence and Contribution of Noah Webster," pp. 102–105.
44. Webster, *A Collection of Essays and Fugitiv* [sic] *Writings*, pp. [ix], x, xi.
45. Ibid., pp. 249–414.
46. Ibid., p. 408.
47. Ezra Stiles to NW, August 27, 1790, NN–2.

48. N[athaniel] W. Appleton to NW, April 25, 1790, NN–2.
49. Daniel George to NW, September 27, 1790, NN–2.
50. NW's reply seems not to be extant, but can be inferred from references to it in Daniel George to NW, November 23, 1790, NN–2.
51. Announcement inserted into the New Haven papers, June 4, 1800; reproduced in Warfel, *Noah Webster*, p. 289. Cf. "no human means can prevent some changes and the adaptation of language to diversities of condition and improvement. The process of a living language is like the motion of a broad river which flows with a slow, silent, *irresistible* current" (Webster, *A Letter to the Honorable John Pickering*, p. 29).
52. Webster, *Dissertations*, p. 29.
53. Quoted in Warfel, *Noah Webster*, p. 292.
54. NW's reply to yet another attack appeared in the Boston *Palladium*; his letter is dated November 10, 1801. It is reproduced in Warfel, *Noah Webster*, pp. 294–96.
55. Quoted in Warfel, *Noah Webster*, pp. 290–91.
56. Webster, *A Compendious Dictionary*.
57. Ibid., p. vi n.
58. Ibid., pp. vi–vii.
59. Webster, *Dissertations*, p. 30.
60. For a discussion of Webster's spelling reforms in his various works, see Rosenberg, "Influence and Contribution," pp. 98–121.
61. Webster, *The American Spelling Book*, 8th Connecticut edition, [1789], p. vi.
62. Webster, *A Dictionary of the English Language* (1830), pp. ii–iv.
63. NW, "A list of words spelled according to rules of uniformity in Dr Websters elementary books," n.d., PM.
64. See above, note 22.
65. NW's own copy of his letter to Rev. Samuel Lee, December 20, 1824, NN–1. The letter was reprinted in Noah Webster, *A Collection of Papers on Political, Literary and Moral Subjects* (1843; rpt. New York: Burt Franklin, 1968), pp. 289–90. A note at the end of the letter reads, "A copy of this letter was sent to Oxford, but no answer was returned" (ibid., p. 290).
66. Ibid., p. 289.
67. There are several approaches that may be taken to Webster's work on pronunciation. His 1783 spelling book has been used as a source for contemporary New England pronunciation by Joshua H. Neumann, "American Pronunciation According to Noah Webster (1783)" (Ph.D. Diss., Columbia University, 1924). Friend, *The Development of American Lexicography*, pp. 79–81, has offered a tentative analysis of Webster's phonemic system. Second, Webster's work can be used as a source for what he considered "correct" pronunciation, given that some dialects are accorded higher prestige than others in a given society. (Note that linguistically no one dialect can be considered more "correct" than any other dialect.) The approach adopted here is to focus on Webster's work on pronunciation as a guide to his views on letter-

sound correspondences, which, as I have argued all along, his spelling books were designed to teach.

68. Webster, *A Compendious Dictionary* (1806), pp. vi–x (on orthography); pp. x–xvi (on pronunciation).
69. Webster, *A Grammatical Institute, Part I* [1783], p. 6.
70. Ibid., pp. 33, 52.
71. Webster, *Dissertations*, p. 111. For a list of what Webster called "improprieties," see Rosenberg, "Influence and Contribution," pp. 180–82.
72. Webster, *Dissertations*, pp. 108, 105, 116–17. See also Rosenberg, "Influence and Contribution," p. 125–27.
73. Our source for Webster's lectures is his *Dissertations* (1789), which represents his revision of them.
74. Webster, *A Compendious Dictionary*, p. xii.
75. NW, "Investigation into the Origins and Principles of the English Language, and how this investigation throws light on our ancestors," n.d. (internally dated to late in his life), NN–7.
76. NW, "A Letter to a gentleman in Andover," internally dated to post 1841, PM.
77. Webster, *Dissertations*, p. 27.
78. Ibid., p. 95.
79. Ibid., pp. 95–97.
80. Ibid., pp. 98–101.
81. Webster, *The American Spelling Book* (1831), n.p., in Commager, introd., *Noah Webster's American Spelling Book*, p. 16. The quotation comes from Webster's preface, dated 1803.

   Webster was in good company in omitting his rules on stress. Noam Chomsky has pointed out that the phonological rules for mapping a given item in the lexicon (such as *photograph-*) into its different phonetic realizations (such as /fótəgræf/ [photograph]; /fətágrəf/ [photograph-y]; /fotəgrǽf/ [photograph-ic] are perfectly automatic, and an integral part of the child's linguistic system. It is therefore, he suggests, unnecessary to attempt to teach children the rules; Noam Chomsky, "Phonology and Reading," in Harry Levin and Joanna P. Williams, eds., *Basic Studies on Reading* (New York: Basic Books, 1970), pp. 3–18.
82. Webster, *A Compendious Dictionary*, p. [xxiv].
83. See Appendix IX.
84. John Walker, *A Pronouncing Dictionary and Expositor of the English Language* (New London: W. & J. Bolles, 1836).
85. Webster, *A Dictionary of the English Language* (1830).
86. Noah Webster, *The Elementary Spelling Book* (Cincinnati: Corey & Fairbank, 1834), Tables 121, 141, 143; Skeel, *Bibliography*, Title 294.
87. Webster, *The Elementary Spelling Book* (1834), Tables 16, 73, 121.
88. Oscar Tinglestad, "The Religious Element in American School Readers up to 1830; a Bibliographical and Statistical Study," (Diss., University of Chicago, 1925); cited in Rosenberg, "Influence and Contribution," p. 55. Tinglestad calculated that the percentage of religious content in Webster's spellers was, from

1783 to 1804, thirty-three per cent; 1804 to 1829, forty-seven percent; 1829 on, ten per cent.
89. Chauncey Goodrich to NW, n.d.; internally dated to post 1829, NN–10.
90. Ibid.
91. Contrast the spellings in an 1842 *Elementary* (Lawrenceburgh) with those in an 1831 *Elementary* (Wells River). The pagination of both is identical, as is the content, except for the following words:

	1831	*1842*
p. 43	maiz	maiz
p. 58	sleez y	sleaz y
p. 59	me läs ses	me läs ses
p. 65	rib in	sav in

92. Corey & Fairbank to NW, July 23, 1833, NN–5. Similarly, Gideon J. Newton to NW, January 21, 1834 (ibid.).
93. Skeel, *Bibliography*, p. 90 (Title 273).

CHAPTER VII

1. Noah Webster, letter, *The American Journal of Education*, 1 (1826): 315.
2. [William Russell, ed.], *The American Journal of Education*, 1 (1826): 2.
3. Ibid., p. 384.
4. Thomas J. Lee, *A Spelling Book, containing the Rudiments of the English Language* (Boston: [Monroe & Frances], 1825); James H. Sears, *A Standard Spelling-Book, or the Scholar's Guide to an accurate Pronunciation of the English Language*, rev. ed. (New Haven: [Durrie & Peck], 1825); William Bolles, *A Spelling Book Containing Exercises in Orthography, Pronunciation, and Reading* (New London: Printed by Samuel Green for the author, 1825); Elihu F. Marshall, [*Marshall's*] *Spelling Book of the English Language*, 1st rev. ed. (Concord, N.H.: Jacob B. Moore, 1826); Lyman Cobb, *A Just Standard for Pronouncing the English Language*, rev. ed. (Ithaca: Mack & Andrus, 1825); Noyes P. Hawes, *The United States Spelling Book; or English Orthoepist* (Portland: Adams & Paine, 1824); Hall J. Kelley, *Kelley's First Spelling Book*, sixth edition (Boston: Lincoln and Edmands, 1826); B[enjamin] D. Emerson, *The National Spelling Book and Pronouncing Tutor* (Boston: Richardson and Lord, 1828).
   Note that not all these editions are now extant. Their existence is authenticated by their being cited in the *American Journal of Education* (see below). Missing bibliographical information has been supplied from later editions found in Richard H. Shoemaker, *A Checklist of American Imprints for 1825, 1826, 1827* and *1828* (Metuchen, N.J.: The Scarecrow Press, 1969–1971).
   The *American Journal of Education* reviewed these works as follows: Lee's speller was reviewed in 1826, Vol. 1, p. 125; Sears' in ibid., p. 190; Bolles' in ibid., p. 254; Marshall's in ibid., p. 511; Cobb's in ibid., p. 639; Hawes' in 1827, Vol. 2, p. 63; Kelley's in ibid., p. 639; Emerson's in 1828, Vol. 3, p. 256.

5. Martin Ruter, *The New American Spelling Book and Juvenile Preceptor...* (Cincinnati: Morgan & Lodge, 1825); in Richard H. Shoemaker, *A Checklist of American Imprints for 1825* (Metuchen, N.J.: Scarecrow Press, 1969).
6. The spelling books by James H. Sears, Elihu F. Marshall, Lyman Cobb, Noyes P. Hawes, Hall J. Kelley and B. D. Emerson all mentioned Walker's dictionary or Walker's orthoepy in their titles. Bolles used Walker's notations.
7. Rev. of *A Standard Spelling-book, or the Scholar's Guide to an Accurate Pronunciation of the English Language*, by James H. Sears, *The American Journal of Education*, 1 (1826): 190.
8. "John Walker," *Dictionary of National Biography*, 20: 531–32; John Walker, *A Critical Pronouncing Dictionary of the English Language* (Philadelphia: M. Carey, 1803); in Ralph R. Shaw and Richard H. Shoemaker, *American Bibliography, a Preliminary Checklist for 1803* (New York: Scarecrow Press, 1959).
9. NW responded to the Superintendent of New York State in NW's own copy, NW to Hudson & Co., September 22, 1820, NN–1.
10. Ibid.
11. NW to W. C. Fowler, quoted in Warfel, *Noah Webster*, p. 386.
12. NW, March 1826, quoted in Warfel, *Noah Webster*, pp. 385–86; Skeel, *Bibliography*, p. 461, no. 198.
13. Warfel, *Noah Webster*, p. 390.
14. Both copies of an agreement between Aaron Ely of New York and Noah Webster, December 15, 1828, NN–9.
15. NW to Lemuel Shattuck, November 18, 1829, in "History of Elementary School Books," *New-England Magazine*, 2 (1832): 476: "Many Spelling-Books have appeared, since the publication of mine; but no great impression was made on the sales of mine, till Walker's Dictionary became popular in this country." For "Elocution Walker," see Edward Everett to NW, June 19, 1827, NN–5.
16. NW's letter of July 7, 1827, is mentioned in Henry Hudson to NW, August 7, 1827, NN–5.
17. NW kept a copy of his letter to Henry Hudson, dated September 14, 1831, together with a summary of the whole correspondence. He also kept a record of "complaints of copy-owners of Mr. Hudson's management," a list of the copyholders of *The American Spelling Book*, and a summary of the total copies printed by each firm over the period; all are in NN–10.

The latter, Webster's summary (undated, but presumably post September 1831), is reproduced below. (Place of publication has been supplied.)

Webster & Skinner (Albany) 60,000 a year 840,000
Holbrook & Fessenden (Brattleboro) 950,000
Richardson & Lord (Boston) 350,000
Cushing & Sons (Baltimore) 40,000 a year 280,000
Kimber & Sharpless (Philadelphia) 70,000 400,000 a year

Worsley (Lexington, Ky.) 50,000 a year   160,000
E[phraim] Morgan (Cincinnati) 40,000
Niles (Middletown, Conn.) 60,000 a year
Terhune & Letson (New Brunswick, N.J.)
50,000 a year, say 187,000

18. H[enry] Hudson to NW, August 7, 1827, NN–5.
19. H[enry] Hudson to NW, August 28, 1828, NN–5. (Hudson wrote in answer to NW's letter of August 9.)
20. Ibid.
21. H[enry] Hudson to NW, October 24, 1828, NN–5.
22. H[enry] Hudson to NW, February 24, 1830, NN–5.
23. H[enry] Hudson to NW, October 29, 1828, NN–5.
24. NW's own copy of his letter to H[enry] Hudson, March 19, 1829, NN–1.
25. H[enry] Hudson to NW, February 20, 1830, NN–5.
26. NW to H[enry] Hudson, February 22, 1830, NN–1.
27. H[enry] Hudson to NW, February 24, 1830, NN–5.
28. See Appendixes V and VII.
29. H[enry] Hudson to NW, September 11, 1828, NN–5.
30. H[enry] Hudson to NW, February 24, 1830, NN–5. The figures Hudson gave in this letter confirmed his claim that the purchaser of a license would purchase as small a license as possible and then overprint. West, Richardson & Lord of Boston, for example, had a license for 50,000 spellers p.a. According to Hudson, they printed no fewer than 63,000 annually (except for one year of 57,000), and once went as high as 105,000 spellers. Holbrook & Fessenden of Brattleboro, whose license was also for 50,000 p.a., actually averaged over 89,000 copies annually from 1818 to 1825, for a seven-year total of 623,522. Hudson's figures also demonstrated the damage that the new speller was inflicting on him: the same firm printed 61,000 copies in 1826, but only 49,600 in 1829.
31. NW's own copy of his letter to Henry Hudson, September 14, 1831, NN–10.
32. N[oah] Webster, *Series of Books for Systematic Instruction in the English Language* [New Haven: n.p., 1830?], p. 6. As Cobb's reply to this is dated 1831, and as the dictionary for schools (advertised in this brochure) was published in 1830, the date must be 1830 or early 1831. Skeel argues for a date in late March or early April, 1830; Skeel, *Bibliography*, p. 356 (Title 755).
33. H[enry] Hudson to NW, September 22, 1831, NN–5.
34. The speller's progress is revealed in NW to W[illiam] C. Fowler, April 24, May 7 (when NW is "preparing the way"), June 30, 1829; Skeel, *Bibliography*, pp. 85–86. For the controversy, see Skeel's numbered items in *ibid.*, pp. 501–502, and the corresponding articles in the 1829 *New York Evening Post*: "Webster's Dictionary," May 28 (Skeel no. 1); [Lyman Cobb], "Webster Dictionary and Spelling Book," June 27 (Skeel no. 2); John Borland, A. Mills and A. M. Merchant (the committee members), letter, July 1 (Skeel no. 3); "Candour," "Webster's Spelling Book compiled by Aaron

Ely," August 22 (Skeel no. 7); Aaron Ely, letter, August 26, 1829 (Skeel no. 8). Skeel believes that "Candour," because he states that he is not the author of any textbooks, is not Lyman Cobb. Internal evidence, however—the *-our* spelling and Candour's obsession with the differences in spelling between the Webster dictionaries of 1806 and 1817—strongly suggest Cobb's authorship. On Ely's death see Susan Ely to NW, October 27, 1831, NN–5.

35. Noah Webster, *The Elementary Spelling Book; being an Improvement on the American Spelling Book* (New York: J. P. Haven & R. Lockwood, 1829); in Skeel, *Bibliography*, p. 86 (Title 261); Noah Webster, *A Dictionary of the English Language* (1830); Skeel, *Bibliography*, Title 592.

36. S[herman] Converse to NW, May 20, 1828, Ellsworth Papers, CHS.

37. Contract betwen NW and Elihu White, William Gallaher & Norman White, booksellers, in New York, June 7, 1831, NN–9.

38. Contract between NW and White, Gallaher & White, June 7, 1831, NN–9. (This is a different contract from the one cited in the preceding note.)

39. Printed indenture, NN–9; see above, Chapter IV, notes 69–71.

40. NW's MS "draft of the contract which is to be printed up, of the Elementary Spelling Book," April 20, 1830, NN–9. There is also a copy of the printed contract used by the successor firm N. & J. White: NW had to get a license from them himself to print 90,000 copies. Contract between NW and N. & J. White, February 23, 1832, NN–9.

41. Contract between NW and N. & J. White, February 23, 1832, NN–9.

42. The foundry of Adoniram Chandler is not written into the printed contract used by N. & J. White, but is mentioned in NW's draft copy of his contract, April 20, 1830, NN–9.

43. For example, *The American Spelling Book*, the revised impression, was stereotyped by E. & J. White for a Canandaigua publisher in 1820; Skeel, *Bibliography*, p. 61 (Title 184). A Cincinnati edition was stereotyped by B. & I. Collins in 1821; Skeel, *Bibliography*, p. 62 (Title 190).

44. NW to William G. Webster (hereafter cited as WW), September 5, 1831, NN–1.

45. NW's own copy of letter to Daniel Webster, September 30, 1826, NN–1.

46. NW's copy of Daniel Webster to NW, October 14, 1826, added by NW to the letter cited in the preceding note, NN–1.

47. NW to Harriet Fowler, December 1830, quoted in Warfel, *Noah Webster*, pp. 391–92.

48. Warfel, *Noah Webster*, p. 392.

49. NW to Rebecca Webster, January 4, 1831, NN–1.

50. Ibid.

51. Quoted in Warfel, *Noah Webster*, p. 393.

52. NW to Rebecca Webster, January 7, 1831, NN–1.

53. NW to Rebecca Webster, February 7, 1832, NN–1. Note that NW has dated his letter incorrectly: the year should read 1831.

Internal evidence (Webster was fussing about the winter's wood supply in this and his earlier letters) and Webster's letter from New Haven in February, 1832 (typewritten copy NW to Eliza [Jones], February 15, 1832, NN–1) make this correction necessary. Due to an error in drafting the copyright law, authors were not given the right to renew the copyright themselves after twenty-eight years; see below, note 101.

54. NW to Rebecca Webster, January 26, 1831, NN–1.
55. NW to Rebecca Webster, February 16, 1831, Facsimile, CHS.
56. Ibid.
57. Noah Webster, *To the Friends of Literature* (New Haven: n.p., October 1836); Skeel, *Bibliography*, Title 762.
58. Ibid.
59. Advertisements for the *Elementary Spelling Book* first appeared in a New York paper in July, 1829. In the New Haven *Daily Advertiser*, testimonials were added to the advertisement by January, 1830; Skeel, *Bibliography*, p. 86.
60. NW's own copy to Henry Hudson, September 14, 1831, NN–10.
61. Contract between NW and Walter H. Bidwell, April 20, 1830, NN–9. The terms of the contract for licenses are the same as those printed by N. & J. White (see note 40).
62. The journal is written in the first person, and the name of its author is not given. The date at which the journal begins (April 22, 1830, in New Haven) and the date of the Webster-Bidwell agreement (April 20, 1830) make the ascription certain. In addition, internal evidence supports the ascription. For example, both the contract and the journal refer to the Rev. Ornan Eastman, who was authorized to make contracts in Tennessee, Mississippi and Alabama, according to the contract; the journal mentions that the writer gave Eastman power of attorney. See below, note 64.
63. Walter Sutton, *The Western Book Trade: Cincinnati as a Nineteenth Century Publishing and Trade-Book Center* (Columbus, Ohio: Ohio Historical Society, 1961).
64. Anonymous journal, titled "Signed Endorsements, Journal of a tour," first entry April 22, 1830, NN–Account/Endorsements/ Journal. Bidwell calls the College of Teachers the "Society of Teachers."
65. NW to WW, September 5, 1831, NN–1.
66. WW to NW, May 28, 1831, NN–5.
67. Typewritten copy, NW to Eliza [Jones], February 15, 1832, NN–1.
68. W[illiam] C. Fowler to NW, December 24, 1829, NN–5. See also W[illiam] C. Fowler to NW, June 9, 1830 (ibid.).
69. Because the Goodriches and the Websters both lived in New Haven, there was naturally little correspondence between them. Chauncey Goodrich emerged as the victor, in the struggle between the sons-in-law after Webster's death, and took over the editorship, with William Webster, of the *American Dictionary*, and of its later revisions.
70. NW to Horatio Southgate, May 17, 1830, NYHS.

71. Horatio Southgate to NW, June 2, 1830, NN–5.
72. Moses G. Atwood to NW, June 12, 1833, NN–5.
73. Gideon J. Newton to NW, January 21, 1834, NN–5.
74. NW to H[enry] Hudson, February 22, 1830, NN–1.
75. For another account of the "Spelling Book War," see the chapter with that title in Warfel, *Noah Webster*, pp. 378–400.
76. Quoted in Warfel, *Noah Webster*, pp. 386–87. (See note 12.) Cobb mentions the date, March, 1826, and place, New Haven, in his pamphlet, pp. 30–31. (See below, note 78.)
77. Elihu F. Marshall, *Marshall's Spelling Book* (1826). This is the earliest extant edition, but being itself a revised edition, implies a yet earlier one. (See note 4.)
78. Examinator, *A Critical Review of Noah Webster's Spelling Book first published in a series of numbers in the Albany Argus in 1827 and 1828* (n.p., 1828), p. 4.
79. Ibid., p. 3.
80. Ibid., p. 4.
81. Ibid., p. 5.
82. Ibid., pp. 8–31. (NW's common school dictionary first appeared in 1807 and was republished in 1817; see above, Chapter III, note 92 and Chapter IV, note 175.)
83. Ibid., pp. 31–32.
84. Ibid., pp. 33–34. Cobb reproduced Webster's reply, which was dated December 1827.
85. Ibid., pp. 34–45.
86. Warfel, *Noah Webster*, pp. 389–90. For mention of a six-month trip from Washington to Portland in the summer of 1831, see NW's own copy of his letter to Henry Hudson, September 14, 1831, NN–10.
87. Webster, *Series of Books for Systematic Instruction*. See note 32 above.
88. Lyman Cobb, *A Critical Review of the Orthography of Dr. Webster's Series of Books for Systematick Instruction in the English Language...* (New York: Collins & Hannay, 1831), p. 25.
89. Noah Webster, *To the Friends of American Literature* (n.p., November 1831), p. 1. See also Noah Webster, *To the Public* (n.p., November 15, 1831), in a similar vein. A note by NW on the back of the latter reads "Few of these circulars were sent." For his MS proof corrections of this see the copy in NN–9. See also Skeel, *Bibliography*, pp. 357–59.
90. Skeel, *Bibliography*, pp. 568–70; H[enry] Hudson to NW, August 18, 27, 1831, NN–5.
91. N[oah] Webster, *Biography, for the Use of Schools* (New Haven: Hezekiah Howe, 1830); Skeel, *Bibliography*, Title 554.
92. Noah Webster, *The Elementary Primer, or First Lessons for Children: being an Introduction to the Elementary Spelling Book* (New York: M'Elrath and Bangs, 1831), p. 13; Skeel, *Bibliography*, Title 399.
93. Noah Webster, *An Improved Grammar of the English Language* (New Haven: Hezekiah Howe, 1831); Skeel, *Bibliography*, Title 435.

94. Noah Webster, *History of the United States. . .* (New Haven: Durrie & Peck, 1832); Skeel, *Bibliography*, Title 555.
95. NW's own copy of his letter to Durrie & Peck, March 12, 1832, NN–1. See also contract between Noah Webster and Durrie & Peck, for exclusive right to print the *History of the United States*, October 1, 1831, NN–9. William Webster is cited as a partner in the firm.
96. NW to Daniel Webster, March 30, 1837, in Warfel, *Letters*, pp. 459–60.
97. NW to Messrs Morse, February 24, 1834, NN–1.
98. Berries & Ward to NW, January 16, 1833, NN–5. For the same criticism—that the price of the dictionary was too high—see also Moses G. Atwood to NW, June 12, 1833 (ibid.).
99. The contract between NW and N. & J. White seems to be missing from NW's papers. The caption "sold also by N. & J. White" appears, however, on 1832 texts (e.g. the Concord edition published by Moses G. Atwood in 1832, Skeel, *Bibliography*, p. 94 [Title 284]) of the *Elementary Spelling Book*. In addition, the firm of N. & J. White had a printed contract before February 1832. Webster himself bought a license from them for 90,000 copies: Contract between NW and N. & J. White, February 23, 1832, NN–9.

    See also the Revocation of instrument of June 7, 1831 (which had made White, Gallaher & White NW's sole agents), February 4, 1833, NN–Photostats of agreements and contracts. Webster took legal advice on whether the dissolution of the partnership justified him in revoking White, Gallaher & White's power of attorney, and their agency. He was advised that it did. See Seth P. Staples to NW, February 7, 16, 20, 23, 1833, NN–5.
100. NW to Messrs White, March 17, 1832, NYHS.
101. Moses Atwood to NW, August 20, 1833, said he was glad that Webster was prepared to have the old spelling book cease (NN–5). In fact, Webster did not hold the copyright to the old speller, due to an error in the drafting of the copyright law of 1831: NW, in an annotation to H.R. 140, February 1, 1828, "A Bill to amend the act for the encouragement of learning," stated that in redrafting the 16th section of this bill in order to allow the privilege of renewal to the widow and heirs of an author (an improvement suggested by Webster himself), his son-in-law William Ellsworth "omitted the words *to him* before the words, *the widow*—by which I lost the right of renewal of the American Spelling Book" (NN–8).
102. Corey & Fairbank to NW, May 27, 1833, NN–5.
103. Corey & Fairbank to NW, July 23, 1833, NN–5.
104. Corey & Fairbank to NW, November 5, 1834, NN–5.
105. *Gazette*, October 6, 1838; cited in Sutton, *The Western Book Trade*, p. 181.
106. Sutton, *The Western Book Trade*, p. 46.

107. Indemnity, Thomas Welton of Waterbury, "I . . . agree not to trouble or molest Wm G Webster of the firm of Haydens & Co for any debt due me from sd firm," November 13, 1832; similarly, an indemnity from Austin Steele, re "the late firm of Haydens," May 14, 1832; from the Merchants Bank, New York; the firm of Nicholson & Manuel, February 1, 1832; and a "Statement of Monies rec & disbursed on a/c of T. H. Bond and W. G. Webster," by Mrs. Bond and N. Webster, for $1,180.00, May 15, 1832; all in NN–9. William's connection with the firm of Haydens & Co. of Waterbury seems to have begun in 1826; a note from his father certifies that he owns $3,000 in Haydens' stocks; NW, "This certifies that William G Webster . . . ," July 31, 1826, NN–9.

CHAPTER VIII

1. WW to NW, May 4, 1835, NN–5. The Pittsburgh publishers were Johnston & Stockton.
2. Or so William thought. In fact, Corey & Fairbank announced the date of the partnership as July 1: WW to NW, July 7, 1835, NN–5. For a fuller account of William's publishing venture, see Sutton, *The Western Book Trade*, pp. 166–78.
3. WW to NW, August 5, 1835, NN–5.
4. WW to NW, February 17, 1817, NN–4.
5. WW to NW, October 22, 1820, NN–4.
6. NW to Lucius Boltwood, March 27, 1824, NN–1.
7. For William's description of his wedding, see his letter in Ford, *Notes*, 2: 514–16; for his business involvement, see above, Chapter VII, note 107.
8. WW to NW, July 7, 15, 1835, NN–5; NW to WW, September 9, 1835, PM.
9. WW to NW, July 15, October 10, 1835, NN–5.
10. NW to Corey, Fairbank & Webster, August 29, 1835, NN–1.
11. WW to NW, October 16, 1835, NN–5.
12. WW to NW, November 5, 1835, NN–5.
13. WW to NW, February 15, 1836, NN–5.
14. WW to NW, February 15, March 5, 1836, NN–5.
15. WW to NW, March 14, 1836, NN–5.
16. NW to WW, April 6, 1836, PM.
17. WW to NW, April 24, 1836, NN–5.
18. Account labeled "stock on hand March 21, 1837," NN–9.
19. WW to Rebecca Webster, June 14, 1836, NN–5.
20. NW to WW, July 7, 1836, NN–1.
21. W[illiam] C. Fowler to NW, July 14, 1836, NN–5. See also NW to WW, July 26, 1836, NN–1; W[illiam] C. Fowler to NW, July 28, 1836, NN–5.
22. NW to WW, July 7, 1836, NN–1.
23. WW to NW, July 16, 1836, NN–5.
24. WW to NW, July 28, 1836, NN–5.
25. WW to NW, August 5, September 7, 1836, NN–5.

26. WW to NW, August 5, 1836, NN–5.
27. WW to NW, August 12, 1836, NN–5.
28. WW to NW, August 12, September 7 (bis), 22, 1836, NN–5; NW to WW, September 8, 13, 1836, PM.
29. WW to NW, October 10, 11, 1836, NN–5. Webster sanctioned the arrangement in letters dated October 18 and 19 (mentioned in WW to NW, October 27, 1836 [ibid.]).
30. WW to NW, November 30, 1836, NN–5.
31. WW to NW, July 15, 1836, NN–5. For the strawberry mark see WW to NW, October 27, November 7, 15, 24, December 13, 1836, (ibid.), January 30, 1837, NN–6; NW to WW, November 4, 1836, NN–1.
32. "I find that the impression is very general that you are not the author of the Elementary Sp. Bk; your circular contradicting the report did not get out here" (WW to NW, November 18, 1835, NN–5). Skeel, *Bibliography*, p. 101, calls this circular, of which she has been unable to locate a copy, Title 306. I believe William to be referring to an extant circular, Noah Webster, *To the Public* (n.p., November 15, 1831), which is Skeel, *Bibliography*, Title 758. In this attack against Lyman Cobb, Webster states that his "School Dictionary and Elementary Spelling Book, are compilations entirely my own. I employed a person to write for me; but every part of these works was corrected, arranged, and the words marked for pronunciation, by my own hand."
33. WW to NW, December 3, 1835, NN–5.
34. WW to NW, May 4, 1835, NN–5; see above, note 1.
35. WW to NW, July 22, 29, 1835, NN–5; Skeel, *Bibliography*, p. 359 (Title 761).
36. WW to NW, December 20, 1835, NN–5.
37. WW to NW, July 29, NN–5.
38. WW to NW, July 22, 1835, NN–5. See Chapter VII, note 93. Corey & Webster put out an edition of this grammar in 1836; Skeel, *Bibliography*, p. 155 (Title 438).
39. Scully, "A Biography of William Holmes McGuffey," pp. 91, 103; Charles Cist, *Cincinnati in 1841: its Early Annals and Future Prospects* (Cincinnati: for the author, 1841), p. 121.
40. WW to NW, October 10, 1835, NN–5.
41. WW to NW, November 7, 1835, NN–5.
42. NW to WW, November 9, 1835, NN–1; similarly, NW to WW, November 17, 1835, Jones. For an example of a title that had the best of all worlds, see Nathan Guilford's *The Western Spelling Book; being an improvement of The American Spelling Book, by Noah Webster,* mentioned in WW to NW, November 18, 1835, NN–5; Skeel, *Bibliography*, pp. 568–69.
43. WW to NW, November 24, 1835, NN–5.
44. NW to WW, July 14, 1835, NN–1; WW to NW, July 22, 1835, NN–5.
45. NW to WW, August 29, 1835, NN–1; WW to NW, September 29, 1835, NN–5.

46. NW to WW, n.d. (internally dated to post December 18, 1835), PM; WW to NW, January 7, 1836, NN–5; printed testimonial, dated Yale College, December 18, 1835 and signed by President Jeremiah Day and several faculty members, including Chauncey Goodrich, Simon Gratz Collection, HSP.
47. NW to WW, October 17, 1835, NN–1. See also NW to WW, October 8, 1835, PM.
48. NW to WW, November 28, 1835, NN–1.
49. WW to NW, December 3, 1835, NN–5.
50. Ibid.
51. WW to NW, July 22, 1835, NN–5.
52. WW to NW, November 30, 1836, NN–5.
53. WW to NW, January 18, 1836, NN–5.
54. WW to NW, February 6, 1836, NN–5.
55. WW to NW, October 10, 1836, NN–5.
56. WW to NW, December 13, 1836, NN–5.
57. WW to NW, January 30, 1837, NN–6.
58. NW to WW, January 5, 1837, NN–1. Noah Webster, *To Messrs. A. Picket and J. W. Picket* (New Haven: n.p., November, 1836); Skeel, *Bibliography*, Title 307.
59. WW to NW, January 30, 1837, NN–6.
60. WW to NW, February 1, 1837, NN–6.
61. WW to NW, February 22, 1837, NN–6.
62. Emily W. Ellsworth to NW, October 31, 1836, NN–5.
63. W[illiam] C. and Harriet Fowler to NW, February 13, 1837, NN–6.
64. WW to NW, February 22, 1837, NN–6.
65. NW to WW, March 1, 1837, NN–1.
66. NW to WW, January 7, 1837, NN–1.
67. WW to NW, February 1, 1837, NN–6.
68. WW to NW, March 21, April 14, 1837, NN–6.
69. WW to NW, April 26, 1837, NN–6; NW to Rosalie Webster, May 6, 1837, NN–1.
70. WW to NW, May 22, 1837, NN–6.
71. WW to NW, July 31, 1837, NN–6.
72. NW to WW, April 8, 1837, NN–1.
73. NW to WW, October 14, 1837, Yale.
74. WW to NW, November 9, 1837, NN–6.
75. WW to NW, June 8, 1838, NN–6.
76. WW to NW, January 5, 1839, NN–6.
77. NW to WW, April 8, 1839, NN–1; WW to NW, April 8, 1839, NN–6.
78. WW to NW, May 8, 1838, NN–6.
79. WW to NW, July 8, 1837, NN–6; NW to Emily Ellsworth, June 27, 1837, Ellsworth Papers, CHS.
80. Rosalie Webster to NW, May 5, 1838, NN–6; NW to Emily Ellsworth, May 7, 1838, Ellsworth Papers, CHS.
81. WW to NW, June 8, July 23, 1838, NN–6.
82. WW to NW, December 29, 1838, NN–6.

83. WW to NW, June 16, 1839, NN–6.
84. WW to NW, April 19, 1839, NN–6.
85. NW to WW, June 27, 1835, Yale.
86. NW to WW, May 1, 1839, PM.

CHAPTER IX

1. NW to WW, May 1, 1839, PM.
2. WW to NW, June 23, 1839, NN–6.
3. NW to WW, July 5, 1839, NN–1.
4. See Chapter VII, note 99. NW kept the letters N. & J. White sent him; their letters are dated from January 15, 1835 to December 14, 1837, CHS.
5. NW to WW, July 5, 1839, NN–1.
6. WW to NW, June 16, 1839, NN–6.
7. Harriet Fowler to NW, July 18, [1839], NN–6.
8. WW to Emily Ellsworth, September 23, 1839, Ellsworth Papers, CHS.
9. N. & J. White passed on a report that 100,000 copies of *The American Spelling Book* had been printed in Concord since January 1, 1834; N. & J. White to NW, January 30, 1835, CHS. See also Skeel, *Bibliography*, pp. 79–80.
10. N. & J. White to NW, August 26, 1835, CHS; Skeel, *Bibliography*, pp. 100–101 (Title 305).
11. N. & J. White to NW, October 12, 1835, CHS. See above, Chapter VIII, note 36.
12. N. & J. White to NW, February 12, 18, July 9, 1835; January 7, 1836, CHS.
13. NW's own copy of his letter to N. White, September 16, 1839, PM; see also a printed circular announcing that N. & J. White had relinquished the agency of the *Elementary Spelling Book*, and that applications for licenses were to be made to N. Webster, November, 1839, NN–10; Skeel, *Bibliography*, Title 334.
14. Contract constituting Ephraim Morgan of Cincinnati as NW's attorney & sole agent west of the Allegany [sic] mountains, May 19, 1840, Ellsworth Papers, CHS.
15. Noah Webster, *The Teacher; A Supplement to the Elementary Spelling Book* (New Haven: S. Babcock, 1836); Noah Webster, *The Little Franklin: Teaching Children to Read* (New Haven: S. Babcock, 1836). The copyrights to each are dated March 24, 1836 and December 6, 1836, respectively, Ellsworth Papers, CHS. There is a review of *The Teacher* in a clipping from the *Hartford Courant*, n.d., NN–10.
16. Webster, *The Teacher*, pp. 7, 34, 57, 81, 151.
17. Webster, *The Little Franklin*, pp. ii, 7, 11, 15, 24, 60.
18. Noah Webster, *A Manual of Useful Studies...* (New Haven: S. Babcock, 1839), Chapters, I, VII, XII.
19. See Skeel, *Bibliography*, Titles 569–73 (*The Teacher*); Title 536 (*The Little Franklin*); Titles 574–76 (*A Manual of Useful Studies*); Titles 785 and 787 (*The New Testament*); Titles 435–42 (*An Improved*

Grammar). The exceptions were a Philadelphia edition of the *Manual* in 1846 and William Webster's editions of the *Improved Grammar* in Cincinnati (1836) and New York (1843); Skeel, *Bibliography*, Titles 576, 438 and 442 respectively.

20. Warfel, *Noah Webster*, pp. 365, 417.

21. WW to Emily Ellsworth, September 23, 1839, Ellsworth Papers, CHS.

22. Noah Webster, *An American Dictionary of the English Language; first edition in octavo . . .* 2 vols. (New Haven: published by the author, 1841); Skeel, *Bibliography*, pp. 237–38 (Title 586).

23. License to Cushing & Brothers, Baltimore, August 7, 1841, Ellsworth Papers, CHS. See also a circular, stating that NW and his publishers had been injured by sales of copies at auctions and trade sales, and that in future licenses would be granted only on condition that no copies would be sent to either, NN–10. For a discussion of the threat that trade sales posed to profits, see Sutton, *The Western Book Trade*, pp. 262–76.

24. On binding: NW to J. G. Rogers, January 4, 1841, Jones; on typeface and stereotyping: NW to [Samuel] Parker, May 11, 1843, PM; on corrections: NW to J. G. Rogers, January 4, 1841, Jones. The new edition of the Bible appeared in 1841; Skeel, *Bibliography*, p. 381 (Title 786).

25. See, for example, NW's query on the sales of the *Manual of Useful Studies*, NW to Messrs Wiley & Putnam, November 12, 1839, PM.

26. NW to WW, January 22, [1836], PM.

27. For example, NW to Emily Ellsworth, June 8, 1840, "I will thank Oliver to deliver the inclosed letter to the printer—it contains an advertisement & money to pay for printing it" (Ellsworth Papers, CHS). For a Webster letter to the editor on the *Elementary*, to be submitted by Fowler in his handwriting, see NW to W[illiam] C. Fowler, February 27, 1841; in Warfel, *Letters*, pp. 518–20.

28. W[illiam] C. Fowler to NW, September 28, October 17, 26, 1837: Fowler was writing a review of NW's *History of the United States* for the *American Annals of Education*, NN–6.

29. W[illiam] C. Fowler to NW, October 26, 1837, NN–6. Webster toyed with the idea of making Fowler an agent in a semi-official capacity: NW to Prof. Fowler, October 30, 1837; in Warfel, *Letters*, pp. 506–509.

30. W[illiam] C. Fowler to NW, April 1, 1843: "I have learned recently that Mr Perkins produced a change from Websters to Gallaudets Spelling Book" (NN–6).

31. NW to W[illiam] W. Ellsworth, November 26, 1839, PM.

32. Rev. Henry Jones to NW, September 11, 1839, NN–6.

33. Jerusha L. Parker to NW, December 2, 1840, NN–6. See also Jerusha L. Parker to NW, March 25, 1842 (ibid.).

34. NW to Samuel Parker, May 3, 1839, NN–1.

35. J. W. Webster to NW, April 10, 1841, NN–6.

36. J. W. Webster to NW, April 30, 1841, NN–6.

37. J. W. Webster to NW, May 24, 1841, NN–6.

38. "Account of Towns visited, & Books sold & presented for Dr. N. Webster, by Wm Goodwin of New Haven, from Thursday October 21st, to Wednesday November 17, 1841," NN–Accounts/ Endorsements/Journal.
39. Accounts, Constantine McMahon, October 6 to October 16, 1841, NN–9.
40. Accounts, Constantine McMahon, September 23, 1841, NN–9. There are four separate accounts kept by McMahon: for September 21 to 25, 1841 (when he toured Fairfield County); October 6 to 16, 1841 (when he concentrated on Litchfield County); October 18 to November 6, 1841 (when he toured mainly New Haven County); and December 27, 1841 to March 24, 1842 (when he traveled from New Jersey to Maryland). (All are in NN–9.) There is also a "List of expenses" for C McMahon... March 24, 1842, NN–Accounts/Endorsements/Journal. Although the dates in the latter are listed as March 24, 1842, and again as December 27, 1842 to March 24, *1843*, this must surely refer to the same trip, that is, the tour from December 27, *1841* to March 24, *1842*. It seems unlikely that Webster would send an agent twice to cover the same ground and too much of a coincidence that the dates for both supposed trips are identical. Letters to Webster from Constantine McMahon, January 9, 1842, from Rahway, New Jersey; January 30, 1842, from Newark, Delaware; February 8, 1842, from Baltimore, Maryland; and February 27, 1842 from Frederick City, Maryland, confirm the earlier dating, and indicate McMahon's progress, NN–6.
41. Con[stanti]ne McMahon to NW, January 9, 1842, NN–6.
42. Constantine McMahon to NW, January 30, 1842, NN–6.
43. Constantine McMahon to NW, February 8, 1842, NN–6.
44. Accounts, Constantine McMahon, December 27, 1841 to March 24, 1842, NN–9.
45. Jerusha L. Parker to NW, March 25, 1842, NN–6.
46. "Instructions," NW to Mr. Dayton, April 7, 1842, NN–1.
47. WW to NW, July 7, 1842: "Mr. Dayton spent two days in N York without success—& he has now gone into the country for a trial" (NN–6).
48. Noah Webster, *Observations on Language and on the Errors of Class-Books; addressed to the members of the New York Lyceum...* (New Haven: S. Babcock, 1839); Skeel, *Bibliography*, Title 716.
49. These undated MS attacks are all in the Noah Webster Collection, PM.
50. NW, "...a brief sketch of the errors contained in certain elementary books," n.d. (post-October 1840; the sketch is written on the back of an advertisement for Webster's new edition of the American dictionary, dated October 1840), NN–7.
51. NW, "History of Spelling Books," n.d., NN–10. In this, Webster names the compilations of Marshall, Cobb, Sears, Crandall, Bolles, Picket, Emerson and Bentley. These authors are also named in Webster's undated "The Age of Spelling Books," (ibid.). See also

the MS beginning "A book called a *Practical Spelling Book* has been lately published by the Rev T H Gallaudet & the Rev H Hooker," November 25, 1840 (ibid.). In this Webster names the works of E. H. Marshall, Lyman Cobb, Sears, Crandall, Picket, Bentley, Bolles, Ruter and Burhan as reproducing Walker's orthography and/or pronunciation; and the "more recently... appeared" spellers of Worcester, Leonard, Charles W. Sanders, Salem Town, a new one by Bentley, and the "little book" of McGuffey. He also mentions Emerson's speller, and John Comly's book, used in the middle states. Versions of some of these MS attacks appeared in various newspapers between 1838 and 1843; see Skeel, *Bibliography*, pp. 474–80, nos. 306–308, 324–25, 344, 363–64.

52. Alonzo B. Chapin, *An English Spelling Book*... (New Haven: Durrie & Peck, 1841).

53. Printed pamphlet, signed "Americanus," January 1842, NN–10. NW has written "WGW" on top of the page. For the controversy see Skeel, *Bibliography*, pp. 516–17. The relevant copies of the New Haven *Daily Herald*, which printed the exchange from November 29, 1841 to January 29, 1842, are in NN–10. William's disavowal that his father sanctioned the altercation is to be found in the *Practical Christian and Church Chronicle*, February 4, 1842; this too is in NN–10.

   For another example of an attack by Webster on an individual spelling book, see an MS letter prepared for a newspaper, which attacks Lee's spelling book, n.d., NN–7.

54. NW's own copy of his letter to Knowlton & Rice, January 15, 1840, PM.

55. Skeel has reproduced the figures recorded in Webster's Account Book (NN–Accounts) and in his papers in the Connecticut Historical Society, both for individual publishers and for totals by the year: Skeel, *Bibliography*, pp. 92, 98, 107–108, 111–12. For 1839 she has consolidated, and where necessary, corrected the figures from three of NW's lists (pp. 107–108); for the period January 1, 1840 to October 20, 1842, she has consolidated two lists (pp. 111–12). See Appendixes VI and VII. The slight discrepancies between Skeel's figures and my own for the years, 1832, 1835 and 1839 arise from our different interpretations of Webster's handwriting. The discrepancy between Webster's total of 998,000 for the years 1840 to 1842 and those recorded in Appendix VII reflects the fact that the figures in Appendix VII include copies of spellers mentioned in Webster's correspondence, but not included in his account book (presumably the source for his own grand total).

56. Contract, in WW's handwriting, between NW and Ephraim Morgan, May 19, 1840, Ellsworth Papers, CHS. A note on the back, in NW's hand, reads, "Ephraim Morgan's contract. Revoked Jany 6 1843."

57. Skeel, *Bibliography*, pp. 107–111.

58. Skeel, *Bibliography*, p. 109 (Title 327).

59. Skeel, *Bibliography*, pp. 121, 126 (Titles 367, 385).
60. NW, "A book called a *Practical Spelling Book* has been lately published by the Rev T H Gallaudet & the Rev H Hooker," November 25, 1840, NN–10.
61. Newspaper clipping, *New York Tribune*, n.d., NN–9.
62. Newspaper clipping, *New York Tribune*, n.d.: NW's reply is dated March 22, 1843, NN–9. See Skeel, *Bibliography*, p. 482, no. 381.
63. Newspaper clipping, *New York Tribune*, n.d.: "Old Dilworth's" reply is dated March 24, 1843, NN–9.
64. Noah Webster, *A Collection of Papers on Political, Literary and Moral Subjects* (New York: Webster & Clark, 1843). NW's discussion of reading is titled "Modes of Teaching the English Language," pp. 307–10.
65. NW to [Samuel] Parker, May 11, 1843, PM.
66. NW to George F. Cooledge, December 6, 1842, PM. See also Skeel, *Bibliography*, p. 122 (Title 369). Webster had a contract drawn up, ready for Ephraim Morgan to sign, in which Morgan was to surrender the right of printing and publishing, and of granting licenses for the *Elementary Spelling Book* within the United States to "Ide & Webster": NW's own copy, Instrument of Revocation, January 6, 1843, Ellsworth Collection, CHS.
67. NW to George F. Cooledge, December 6, 1842, PM.
68. NW to C. Harris, January 12, 1842, PM. Webster's own accounts show that Cooledge did *not* print more books than any other firm; see figures reproduced in Monaghan, "Noah Webster's Speller," pp. 279–80.
69. WW to NW, May 5, 1843, NN–6.
70. W[illiam] W. Ellsworth to NW, October 14, 1842, NN–6.
71. WW to NW, May 5, 1843, NN–6.
72. NW to Webster & Clark, May 8, 1843, PM.
73. NW to Webster & Clark, May 5, 1843, PM.
74. WW to NW, May 8, May 9, 1843, NN–6; NW to WW, May 9, 1843, NN–1.
75. NW to WW, May 18, 1843, NN–1.
76. NW to WW, May 22, 1843, NN–1.
77. Goodrich, "Memoir of the Author," p. xxii.
78. Ibid.
79. NW to WW, May 9, 1843, NN–1.
80. Ephraim Morgan to NW, May 18, 1843, NN–6.
81. Eliza Jones, quoted in Ford, *Notes*, 2: 365, 369.

X. EPILOGUE

1. Skeel, *Bibliography*, p. 126.
2. H. L. Mencken, *The American Language* (New York: Alfred Knopf, 1936), p. 385. See Babbidge, *On Being American*, pp. 177–78, for sources on the fate of the speller after Webster's death.
3. Skeel, *Bibliography*, p. 129.
4. Newspaper clipping, "Who Reads an American Book?" no name,

n.d. (dated internally to 1859 or thereafter), NN–10.

5. Newspaper clipping, no name, n.d. (dated internally to June 1866 or thereafter), NN–10; for the Georgia editions see Skeel, *Bibliography*, pp. 132–33 (Titles 391–92, 394).

6. Newspaper clipping, "Book Making," *Eagle* (Brooklyn), n.d., NN–10. President Grant is mentioned, which suggests a date between 1868 and 1876. As the press, according to the clipping, had been in operation for about twelve years, and as the Appleton firm began printing in 1857, the date must be 1869 or later.

7. "A Million Copies a Year," *Youth's Companion*, May 27, 1880, p. 182.

8. Joel Benton, "The Webster Spelling-Book: Its Centennial Anniversary," *Magazine of American History* 10 (1883): 306.

9. Mark Sullivan, *Our Times: The United States, 1900–1925*. Vol. 2. *America Finding Herself* (New York: Charles Scribner's Sons, 1927), p. 125. Balmuth cites Clifton Johnson, *Old-Time Schools and Schoolbooks* (1904; rpt. New York: Dover, 1963), p. 184, as a witness to the use of the blue-back speller in the classroom as late as 1904; Miriam Balmuth, *The Roots of Phonics: A Historical Introduction* (New York: McGraw-Hill, 1982), p. 154.

10. Webster's *Elementary* was the arbiter, for example, in the spelling school described in Edward Eggleston, *The Hoosier Schoolmaster* (1871; rpt. New York: Hart, 1976), pp. 38–54.

11. See above, note 7. See also note 5 for another reference to the fifty percent increase in sales in 1866.

CONCLUSION

1. Chapter I, note 44; Chapter III, note 24.
2. Chapter II, notes 46–47, 61.
3. Chapter IV, note 48.
4. Chapter IV, passim.
5. Chapter I, notes 38, 41.
6. Chapter II, notes 31–32. See also Chapter IV, note 110.
7. Chapter II, notes 33, 36, 39–40.
8. Chapter IV, notes 44, 46, 50.
9. Chapter IV, notes 55–56, 148.
10. Appendix I.
11. Chapter VII, note 80.
12. Chapter I, note 63.
13. Ibid.; Chapter II, note 68.
14. Chapter II, note 69.
15. Chapter IV, notes 99, 116.
16. Chapter II, notes 83–85.
17. Chapter II, notes 85–86.
18. Chapter IV, note 163; Chapter VI, notes 47–48, 53.
19. Chapter IV, notes 162–163.
20. Chapter IV, note 158.
21. Ruth Elson, *Guardians of Tradition: American Schoolbooks of the*

Nineteenth Century (Lincoln, Neb.: University of Nebraska Press, 1964).

22. "Plagiarism," Chapter II, note 59; "sanctimony," Chapter II, note 67; "pedantic," Chapter IV, note 37; "dull," Chapter I, note 30; and "arrogant," Chapter II, notes 68, 70. See also Chapter III, notes 43–45. For "diffidence" see Chapter IV, note 112.

23. Chapter III, note 71. Books published anonymously, Chapter III, notes 51, 70.

24. Chapter VII, notes 4–5.

25. Appendix V shows a hypothetical rate of increase in numbers of copies of *The American Spelling Book* licensed, contrasted with actual copies licensed, 1804 to 1828.

26. Chapter VII, notes 31, 71–74.

27. Chapter VI, note 88. Tinglestad, "The Religious Element in American School Readers up to 1830," tabulated, for American spellers and readers overall, a period of religious dominance up to 1775; a sharp decline in religious content from 1775 to 1792; a first reaction from the decline, 1795 to 1812; and then a second and stronger reaction beginning about 1815, but declining consistently after 1820, sharply after 1827; cited in Rosenberg, "Influence and Contribution," p. 55.

28. Chapter VI, note 92.

29. Chapter VI, notes 83–85; Chapter VII, notes 6–7; see also text to ibid., note 80 for spelling of "superiour"; to note 85 for "publick"; and note 88 for "errours," all in essays by Lyman Cobb.

30. Chapter VI, notes 83, 90–91, 93.

31. Chapter VIII, notes 57–58.

32. Chapter VI, note 87; Chapter X, note 8; Eggleston, *The Hoosier Schoolmaster*, p. 50.

33. Chapter VII, note 42.

34. Chapter VIII, note 33.

35. Chapter VII, notes 105–106; Chapter VIII, notes 41–43, 55.

36. Chapter VII, passim.

37. Chapter VIII, notes 38, 44; Chapter IX, notes 24, 26, 29, 33–47.

38. Chapter VIII, note 75. See also ibid., note 73; Chapter IX, notes 55–59.

39. Chapter VII, note 47.

40. Chapter IX, note 40.

41. Chapter VIII, note 33.

42. Chapter VII, note 14.

43. Chapter VII, note 34; Chapter VIII, note 32.

44. Chapter VI, passim.

45. Chapter IX, notes 48–51.

46. E. Jennifer Monaghan, "Reading Instruction in the Early American Republic: The Spelling Book and Its Critics, 1780–1840," paper presented at the Library of Congress Center for the Book, Washington, D.C., July 1980.

47. Chapter VIII, notes 85–86.

48. Chapter I, note 19; Chapter IX, notes 6–8.

49. Chapter VII, notes 16–33.
50. Chapter VIII, note 4.
51. Chapter VII, note 36.
52. Chapter VI, note 91.
53. Chapter III, notes 54, 84, 104–106; Chapter IX, notes 20–22.
54. Rollins, *The Long Journey*, pp. 140–42.
55. Goodrich, "Memoir of the Author"; Goodrich, "Life and Writings of Noah Webster."
56. Chapter IX, notes 69–81.
57. Chapter VIII, note 42.
58. Chapter VIII, note 57.
59. Chapter X, note 11.
60. Bugbee's assessment of Webster's contribution to the state laws of the 1780s is that "the share of accomplishment which he claimed for himself shrinks in the light of the evidence"; Bugbee, *Genesis of American Patent and Copyright Law*, p. 123.
61. Chapter IV, note 70.
62. Teachers: Chapter III, note 13 and passim; children: Chapter IX, note 43.
63. Chapter VIII, notes 49–52.
64. Chapter IX, notes 52–53.
65. Chapter VIII, notes 40–41, 43, 57.
66. E.g. Truman & Smith's *School Advocate*: Chapter VIII, note 57.
67. Chapter VII, notes 34, 55–58.
68. Chapter IX, note 33.

APPENDIXES

1. Chapter II, note 71.
2. Webster's first edition, for example, was of 5,000 copies; Chapter I, note 63. See also Chapter IV, note 22.
3. Chapter IV, note 38.
4. Chapter IV, note 35.
5. Chapter IV, note 64.
6. Chapter IV, note 67.
7. Chapter IV, notes 60–62.
8. NW, Account Book No. I, 1788–1838 (figures for Holbrook, Fessenden & Porter), NN–Account Books.
9. These details are given in the letter in Chapter III, note 102; see Chapter IV, note 73.
10. Chapter VII, note 17.
11. Chapter VII, note 30.
12. Introduction, note 6.
13. See above, note 9.
14. NW, Account Book No. I, NN–Account Books; Journal, "Statement of licenses," CHS; "Licenses for Spellers," November 4, 1839, CHS; list of figures for spelling book in 1839, NN–10.
15. Skeel, *Bibliography*, pp. 111–12.
16. Chapter VII, note 101.

17. Goodrich, "Memoir of the Author," p. xvi.
18. Epilogue, note 2.
19. Epilogue, note 4.
20. Epilogue, note 6.
21. Epilogue, notes 5 and 11.
22. Grant Overton, *Portrait of a Publisher and The First Hundred Years of the House of Appleton, 1825–1925* (New York: D. Appleton, 1925), p. 44. Overton mistakenly assigns the Appleton adoption of the speller to the year 1855, instead of 1857.
23. Introduction, note 1.

Bibliography

Advertisement for *A Grammatical Institute, Part I*. *Connecticut Courant* (Hartford), October 14, 1783.

Advertisement for *A Grammatical Institute, Part I*. *The Connecticut Journal* (New Haven), November 23, 1784.

Alston, R. C. *A Bibliography of the English Language from the Invention of Printing to the Year 1800*. Vol. 4, *Spelling Books*. Bradford: for the author, 1967.

Ash, John. *Grammatical Institutes, or, An Easy Introduction to Dr. Lowth's English Grammar*. Worcester: Battelle & Green, 1785.

Babbidge, Homer D., Jr., ed. *Noah Webster: On Being American. Selected Writings, 1783–1828*. New York: Praeger, 1967.

Balmuth, Miriam. *The Roots of Phonics: A Historical Introduction*. New York: McGraw-Hill, 1982.

Benezet, Anthony. *A First book for Children*. Philadelphia: [Joseph] Crukshank, 1779.

———— *The Pennsylvania Spelling Book*, 2nd ed. Philadelphia: Joseph Crukshank, 1779.

Benton, Joel. "The Webster Spelling-Book: Its Centennial Anniversary." *Magazine of American History*, 10 (1883): 299–306.

———— "An unwritten chapter in Noah Webster's life. Love and the spelling-book." *Magazine of American History*, 10 (1883): 52–56.

Bingham, Caleb. *The American Preceptor, being a new Selection of Lessons for Reading and Speaking*. 4th ed. Boston: Manning & Loring, for the author, 1797.

Bloomfield, Leonard. *Language*. New York: Holt, Rinehart & Winston, 1933.

———— "Linguistics and Reading." *Elementary English Review*, 19 (1942), 125–130, 183–186.

Bristol, Roger P. *Supplement to Charles Evans' American Bibliography*. Charlottesville: Bibliographical Society of America, 1970.

Bugbee, Bruce W. *Genesis of American Patent and Copyright Law.*
Washington: Public Affairs Press, 1967.

[Burgh, James]. *The Art of Speaking* . . . 4th ed. Philadelphia:
Aitken, 1775.

Bynack, Vincent P. "Language and the Order of the World:
Noah Webster and the Idea of an American Culture." Ph.D.
Diss., Yale University, 1978.

"Candour." "Webster's Spelling Book compiled by Aaron Ely."
New York Evening Post, August 22, 1829.

Carpenter, Charles. *History of American Schoolbooks.* Philadelphia:
University of Pennsylvania Press, 1963.

Chew, Samuel C., edited with an historical introduction. *Fruit
Among the Leaves: An Anniversary Anthology.* New York:
Appleton–Century–Crofts, 1950.

Chomsky, Carol. "Reading, Writing and Phonology." *Harvard
Educational Review,* 40 (1970): 287–309.

Chomsky, Noam. *Syntactic Structures.* The Hague: Mouton, 1957.

——— *Language and Mind,* enlarged edition. New York: Harcourt
Brace Jovanovich, 1968.

——— "Phonology and Reading." in Harry Levin and Joanna P.
Williams, eds., *Basic Studies on Reading.* New York: Basic
Books, 1970, pp. 3–18.

——— and Morris Halle. *The Sound Pattern of English.* New York:
Harper & Row, 1968.

Cist, Charles. *Cincinnati in 1841: its Early Annals and Future
Prospects.* Cincinnati: for the author, 1841.

Cobb, Lyman. *A Critical Review of the Orthography of Dr. Webster's
Series of Books for Systematick Instruction in the English Language* . . . .
New York: Collins & Hannay, 1831.

——— *A Just Standard for Pronouncing the English Language* . . . rev. ed.
Ithaca, N.Y.: Mack & Andrus, 1825.

Coll, Gary R. "Noah Webster, Journalist, 1783–1803." Ph.D.
Diss., University of Southern Illinois, 1971.

Colton, A. M. "Our Old Webster's Spelling Book." *Magazine of
American History*, 24 (1890): 465–66.

Commager, Henry S., introd. *Noah Webster's American Spelling
Book.* New York: Teachers College, Columbia University,
1962.

Cremin, Lawrence A. *American Education: The Colonial Experience,
1607–1783.* New York: Harper & Row, 1970.

——— *American Education: The National Experience, 1783–1876.*
New York: Harper & Row, 1980.

Danielsson, Bror. "John Hart's Works on English Orthography and Pronunciation, 1551, 1569, 1570. Part I, Biographical and Bibliographical Introductions, Texts and Index Verborum." *Stockholm Studies in English*, vol. 5. Stockholm: Almqvist & Wiksell, 1955.

"Dilworth, Thomas," Letter. *The Connecticut Journal* (New Haven), July 14, 1784.

Dilworth, Thomas. *A New Guide to the English Tongue....* Boston: William McAlpine, 1771.

"Dilworth's Ghost." Letter. *Connecticut Journal* (New Haven), June 30, 1784.

D[ilworth's] G[host]." Letter. *Connecticut Journal* (New Haven), January 12, 1785.

D[ilworth's] G[host]. Letter. *Weekly Monitor and American Advertiser* (Litchfield, Conn.), January 25, 1785.

Dixon, H. *The Youth's Instructor in the English Tongue; or, The Art of Spelling Improved.... collected from Dixon, Bailey, Watts, Owen, and Strong.* Boston: n.p., 1767.

Eggleston, Edward. *The Hoosier Schoolmaster.* 1871; rpt. New York: Hart, 1976.

Elson, Ruth. *Guardians of Tradition: American Schoolbooks of the Nineteenth Century.* Lincoln, Neb.: University of Nebraska Press, 1964.

Ely, Aaron. Letter. *New York Evening Post*, August 26, 1829.

Entick, John. *[Entick's] Spelling Dictionary, Teaching to Write and Pronounce the English Tongue with Ease and Propriety ...* a new edition by William Crakelt. London; Wilmington: Peter Brynberg, 1800.

"Entity." Letter. *Weekly Monitor* (Litchfield, Conn.), December 21, 1784.

Evans, Charles. *American Bibliography*, 14 vols. Chicago: privately printed, 1903–1959.

Examinator [Lyman Cobb]. *A Critical Review of Noah Webster's Spelling Book first published in a series of numbers in the Albany Argus in 1827 and 1828.* N.p., 1828.

Fenning, D[aniel]. *The Universal Spelling Book: or, a New and Easy Guide to the English Language.* New York: Loudon, 1787.

Ford, Emily Ellsworth Fowler. *Notes on the Life of Noah Webster.* 2 vols. New York: privately printed, 1912.

Ford, Paul L. *The New-England Primer: A History of Its Origin and Development with a Reprint of the Unique Copy of the Earliest Known Edition.* New York: Dodd, Mead, 1897.

Friend, Joseph H. *The Development of American Lexicography, 1798-1864.* The Hague: Mouton, 1967.

Fries, Charles C. *Linguistics and Reading.* New York: Holt, Rinehart & Winston, 1962.

Goodrich, Chauncey A. "Life and Writings of Noah Webster, LL.D." *American Literary Magazine,* 2 (1848): [5]–32.

———— "Memoir of the Author." In Noah Webster, *An American Dictionary of the English Language...* revised and enlarged. Springfield, Mass.: George & Charles Merriam, 1848.

Hall, Robert A. *Sound and Spelling in English.* Philadelphia: Chilton, 1961.

Hallenbeck, Chester T. "Book-trade Publicity before 1800." *The Papers of the Bibliographical Society of America,* 32 (1938):47–56.

Hansen, Allen O. *Liberalism and American Education.* 1926; rpt. New York: Octagon Books, 1965.

Hart, John. *An Orthographie, conteyning the due order and reason, how to write or paint thimage of mannes voice, most like to the life or nature* (1569) in Bror Danielsson, "John Hart's Works on English Orthography and Pronunciation, 1551, 1569, 1570. Part I, Biographical and Bibliographical Introductions, Texts and Index Verborum." *Stockholm Studies in English,* vol. 5. Stockholm: Almqvist & Wiksell, 1955.

Hart, William P. *"The English Schoole-Maister* by Edmund Coote: an Edition of the Text with Critical Notes and Introductions." Ph.D. Diss., University of Michigan, 1963.

Heartman, Charles F. *American Primers, Indian Primers, Royal Primers, and Thirty-Seven Other Types of Non-New England Primers Issued Prior to 1830.* Highland Park, N.J.: H. B. Weiss, 1935.

———— *The New-England Primer Issued Prior to 1830.* New York: R. R. Bowker, 1934.

"History of Elementary School Books." *New England Magazine,* 2 (1832): 473–78.

Hodges, Richard E. "In Adam's Fall: A Brief History of Spelling Instruction in the United States." In *Reading & Writing Instruction in the United States: Historical Trends.* Ed. H. Alan Robinson. Newark, Del.: International Reading Association, 1977.

Johnson, Clifton. *Old-Time Schools and School-books.* 1904; rpt. New York: Dover, 1963.

Johnson, Samuel. *A Dictionary of the English Language... Abstracted from the Folio Edition. To which is prefixed, a Grammar of the*

English Language. 7th ed. 2 vols. London: W. Strahan, 1783.

————— *A Dictionary of the English Language . . . with numerous corrections, and with the addition of several thousand words by the Rev. H. J. Todd . . .* 2nd ed. 3 vols. London: Longman, Rees, Orme, Brown, and Green, 1827.

[Johnson, Samuel]. *The First Easy Rudiments of Grammar, Applied to the English Tongue.* New York: Holt, 1765.

Koch, Adrienne, introd. *Notes of Debates in the Federal Convention of 1787, Reported by James Madison.* 1966; rpt. New York: Norton, 1969.

Lamport, Harold. "A History of the Teaching of Begininng Reading." Diss., University of Chicago, 1935.

Ledyard, John. *A Journal of Captain Cooke's Last Voyage to the Pacific Ocean . . .* Hartford: Nathaniel Patten, 1783.

Lindberg, Stanley W. *The Annotated McGuffey: Selections from the McGuffey Eclectic Readers, 1836–1920.* New York: Van Nostrand Reinhold, 1976.

"Literary Plagiarisms." *American Annals of Education,* 8 (1838): 563–64.

Livengood, W. W. *Our Textbooks, Yesterday and Today.* New York: Textbook Clinic, American Institute of Graphic Arts, 1953.

Lowth, Robert. *A Short Introduction to English Grammar, with Critical Notes.* Philadelphia: R. Aitken, 1775.

Marble, Annie R. *From 'Prentice to Patron: the Life Story of Isaiah Thomas.* New York: Appleton-Century, 1953.

Mathews, Mitford M. *Teaching to Read, Historically Considered.* Chicago: University of Chicago Press, 1966.

M[c]Guffey, W[illiam] H[olmes]. *The Eclectic First Reader, for Young Children, Consisting of Progressive Lessons in Reading and Spelling, mostly in Easy Words of One and Two Syllables.* Cincinnati: Truman & Smith, 1836.

Mencken, H. L. *The American Language.* New York: Alfred Knopf, 1936.

"A Million Copies a Year." *Youth's Companion,* May 27, 1880, p. 182.

Monaghan, E. Jennifer. "Noah Webster's Speller, 1783–1843: Causes of Its Success as Reading Text." Ed.D. Diss., Yeshiva University, 1980.

————— "Reading Instruction in the Early American Republic: The Spelling Book and Its Critics, 1780–1840." Paper presented at the Library of Congress Center for the Book, Washington, D.C., July 1980.

Morgan, John S. *Noah Webster.* New York: Mason Charter, 1975.

Mott, Frank L. *Golden Multitudes: the Story of Best Sellers in the United States.* New York: MacMillan, 1947.

Murray, Lindley. *English Grammar, adapted to the different classes of Learners.* 3rd ed. New York: Isaac Collins, 1800.

———— *The English Reader, or, Pieces in Prose and Poetry, selected from the Best Writers.* New York: Isaac Collins, 1800.

Neumann, Joshua H. "American Pronunciation according to Noah Webster (1783)." Ph.D. Diss., Columbia University, 1924.

Nietz, John. *Old Textbooks.* Pittsburgh: University of Pittsburgh Press, 1961.

Overton, Grant. *Portrait of a Publisher and the First Hundred Years of the House of Appleton, 1825–1925.* New York: D. Appleton, 1925.

Palmer, Thomas H. "The Teacher's Manual," (Prize Essay). *Common School Journal,* 2 (1840): 297–302.

Pastorius, F[ranz] D[aniel]. *A New Primmer or Methodical Directions to attain the True, Spelling, Reading & Writing of English* . . . . New York: William Bradford, 1698.

Pepper, Robert D. *Four Tudor Books on Education: Sir Thomas Elyot,* Tr., The Education or Bringing Vp of Children (1533), *Francis Clement,* The Petie Schole with an English Orthographie (1587), *Dudley Fenner,* The Artes of Logike and Rethorike (1584), *William Kempe,* The Education of Children in Learning (1588), *Facsimile Reproductions.* Gainesville: Scholars Facsimiles & Reprints, 1966.

Perry, William. *The Only Sure Guide to the English Tongue* . . . 8th ed., Worcster. 1st ed. Worcester: Isaiah Thomas, 1785.

———— *The Royal Standard English Dictionary* . . . *the Second American Worcester edition, carefully revised and corrected.* Worcester: Isaiah Thomas, 1793.

Pickering, Octavius. *The Life of Timothy Pickering.* Vol. 1. Boston: Little, Brown, 1867.

Picket, A[lbert]. *Picket's Juvenile Spelling-Book* . . . . New York: S. Lewis, 1823.

Plimpton, George A. "The Hornbook and Its Use in America." *The Proceedings of the American Antiquarian Society,* new ser., 26 (1916): 264.

Provenzo, Eugene F. "Education and the Aesopic Tradition." Ph.D. Diss., Washington University, 1976.

Reeder, Rudolph R. *The Historical Development of School Readers and of Method in Teaching Reading.* New York: Macmillan, 1900.

Rev. of *A Just Standard for pronouncing the English Language . . .* rev. ed., by Lyman Cobb. *American Journal of Education,* 1 (1826): 639.

Rev. of *Kelly's First Spelling Book, or Child's Instructor . . .* 6th ed., by Hall J. Kelley. *American Journal of Education,* 2 (1827): 639.

Rev. of *The National Spelling Book and Pronouncing Tutor . . .* by B. D. Emerson. *American Journal of Education,* 3 (1829): 256.

Rev. of *A Spelling Book Containing Exercises in orthography, Pronunciation, and Reading,* by William Bolles. *American Journal of Education,* 1 (1826): 254.

Rev. of *A Spelling-Book, containing the Rudiments of the English Language, with Appropriate Reading Lessons,* by Thomas J. Lee. *American Journal of Education,* 1 (1826): 125.

Rev. of *A Spelling Book of the English Language; or, the American Tutor's Assistant . . .* rev. ed., by Elihu F. Marshall. *American Journal of Education,* 1 (1826): 511.

Rev. of *A Standard Spelling-Book, or the Scholar's Guide to an Accurate Pronunciation of the English Language, . . .* rev. ed., by James H. Sears. *American Journal of Education,* 1 (1826): 190.

Rev. of *The United States Spelling Book; or English Orthoepist . . .* by Noyes P. Hawes. *American Journal of Education,* 2 (1827): 63.

Roden, Robert F. *The Cambridge Press, 1638–1692: A History of the First Printing Press Established in English America, together with a Bibliographical List of the Issues of the Press.* New York: Dodd, Mead, 1905.

Rollins, Richard M. *The Long Journey of Noah Webster.* Philadelphia: University of Pennsylvania Press, 1980.

Rosenberg, William A. "The Influence and Contribution of Noah Webster upon Language Arts Teaching in the Nineteenth Century." Ph.D. Diss., University of Connecticut, 1967.

Rush, Benjamin. "Thoughts upon the Mode of Education proper in a Republic." In *Essays on Education in the Early Republic.* Ed. Frederick Rudolph. Cambridge, Mass.: Belknap Press, 1965, pp. 9–23.

"School Books in the United States." *American Annals of Education and Instruction,* 2 (1832): 371–84.

"Schools in Massachusetts." *American Annals of Education and Instruction,* 7 (1837): 97–103.

Scudder, Horace E. *Noah Webster*. Boston: American Men of Letters Series, 1881.

Scully, James A. "A Biography of William Holmes McGuffey." Ed.D. Diss., University of Cincinnati, 1967.

Shaw, Ralph R. and Shoemaker, Richard H. *American Bibliography, a Preliminary Checklist for 1801–1819*. 21 vols. New York: Scarecrow Press, 1958–1965.

Sheridan, Thomas. *A Course of Lectures on Elocution, together with two Dissertations on Language; and some other Tracts relative to those Subjects*. London: A. Millar, 1762.

———— *A Rhetorical Grammar of the English Language*. Philadelphia: Bell & Bailey, 1783.

Shoemaker, Ervin C. *Noah Webster, Pioneer of Learning*. New York: Columbia University Press, 1936.

Shoemaker, Richard H. *A Checklist of American Imprints for 1825, 1826, 1827, 1828*. Metuchen, N.J.: Scarecrow Press, 1969–1971.

Skeel, Emily Ellsworth Ford. *A Bibliography of the Writings of Noah Webster*. Ed. Edwin H. Carpenter, Jr. 1958; rpt. New York: New York Public Library & Arno Press, 1971.

Skeel, Jr. Mrs. Roswell. "Salesmanship of an Early American Best Seller." *Papers of the Bibliographical Society of America*, 32 (1938): 38–46.

Smith, Helen Evertson. *Colonial Days & Ways*. New York: Century, 1900.

Smith, Lydia A. H. "Three Spelling Books of American Schools, 1740–1800." *Harvard Library Bulletin*, 16 (1968): 72–93.

Smith, Nila Banton. *American Reading Instruction*. Newark, Del.: International Reading Association, 1965.

Smith, William E. *About the McGuffeys: William Holmes McGuffey and Alexander H. McGuffey*. Oxford, Ohio: Cullen Print Co., 1963.

Sullivan, Mark. *Our Times: The United States, 1900–1925*. Vol. 2. *America Finding Herself*. New York: Charles Scribner's Sons, 1927.

Sutton, Walter. *The Western Book Trade: Cincinnati as a Nineteenth Century Publishing and Trade-Book Center*. Columbus, Ohio: Ohio Historical Society, 1961.

Tarbox, Increase N. "Noah Webster." *The Congregational Quarterly*, 7 (1865): 1–16.

Tebbel, John. *A History of Book Publishing in the United States.* Vol. 1. *The Creation of an Industry, 1630–1865.* New York: R. R. Bowker, 1972.

Thomas, E[benezer] S. *Reminiscences of the Last Sixty-Five Years.* Vol. 2. Hartford: printed for the author, 1840.

[Thomas, Isaiah]. *New American Spelling Book.* Worcester: Isaiah Thomas, 1785.

Todd, Charles B. *Life and Letters of Joel Barlow, LL.D.* New York: G. P. Putnam's Sons, 1886.

"Todd, Henry John." *Dictionary of National Biography,* 19: 908–10.

Tuer, Andrew W. *History of the Horn Book.* London, 1896; rpt. New York: B. Blom, 1968.

Vail, Henry H. *A History of the McGuffey Readers.* Cleveland: Burrows Brothers, 1911.

Venezky, Richard L. *The Structure of English Orthography.* The Hague: Mouton, 1970.

"Walker, John." *Dictionary of National Biography,* 20: 531–32.

Walker, John. *A Pronouncing Dictionary and Expositor of the English Language.* 1803; New London: W. & J. Bolles, 1836.

Warfel, Harry R., ed. *Letters of Noah Webster.* New York: Library Publishers, 1953.

———— *Noah Webster: Schoolmaster to America.* 1936; rpt. New York: Octagon Books, 1966.

Webster, Noah. "An Address, delivered at the laying of the corner stone of the building erecting for the Charity Institution in Amherst, Massachusetts, August 9, 1820," in Amherst College, *A Plea for a Miserable World.* Boston: Ezra Lincoln, 1820.

———— *An American Dictionary of the English Language . . .* 2 vols. New York: S[herman] Converse, 1828.

———— *An American Dictionary of the English Language; first edition in octavo.* 2 vols. New Haven: published by the author, 1841.

———— *An American Dictionary of the English Language . . .* revised and enlarged. Springfield, Mass.: George & Charles Merriam, 1848.

———— *An American Selection of Lessons in Reading and Speaking. Calculated to Improve the Minds and Refine the Taste of Youth . . .* 3rd ed. Philadelphia: Young & M'Culloch, 1787.

———— *The American Spelling Book containing, an easy standard of Pronunciation. Being the First Part of a Grammatical Institute of the*

English Language. In three parts. 8th Connecticut ed. Hartford: Hudson & Goodwin, [1789].

—————— *The American Spelling Book* . . . the revised impression, with the latest corrections. Hartford: Hudson & Co., 1823.

—————— *American Spelling Book*, revised impression. Middletown, Conn.: William H. Niles, 1831.

Webster, N[oah]. *Biography, for the Use of Schools.* New Haven: Hezekiah Howe, 1830.

—————— *A Brief History of Epidemic and Pestilential Diseases* . . . 2 vols. Hartford: Hudson & Goodwin, 1799.

—————— *A Collection of Essays and Fugitiv* [sic] *Writings. On moral, historical, political and literary subjects.* Boston: for the author, I. Thomas & E. T. Andrews, 1790.

—————— *A Collection of Papers on Political, Literary and Moral Subjects.* 1843; rpt. New York: Burt Franklin, 1968.

—————— *A Compendious Dictionary of the English Language.* 1806; rpt. New York: Crown Publishers, 1970.

—————— *A Dictionary of the English Language; abridged from the American Dictionary, for the use of Primary Schools and the Counting House.* New York: White, Gallaher & White, 1830.

—————— *A Dictionary of the English Language; compiled for the Use of Common Schools in the United States.* Boston: John and David West, 1807.

—————— *A Dictionary of the English Language; compiled for the Use of Common Schools in the United States.* Hartford: George Goodwin & Sons, 1817.

—————— *Dissertations on the English Language with Notes, Historical and Critical. To which is added, by way of Appendix, an Essay on a Reformed Mode of Spelling, with Dr. Franklin's Arguments on that subject.* Boston: Isaiah Thomas & Co., for the author, 1789.

—————— *The Elementary Primer, or, First Lessons for Children: being an Introduction to the Elementary Spelling Book.* New York: M'Elrath & Bangs, 1831.

—————— *The Elementary Spelling Book; being an Improvement on the American Spelling Book.* Wells River, Vt.: White & Wilcox, 1831.

—————— *The Elementary Spelling Book; being an Improvement on the American Spelling Book.* Cincinnati: Corey & Fairbank, 1834.

—————— *The Elementary Spelling Book; being an Improvement on the American Spelling Book.* Lawrenceburgh, Ind.: James A. Morgan & Co., 1842.

—————— *Elements of Useful Knowledge. Volume I. Containing a Historical and Geographical Account of the United States.* Hartford: Hudson & Goodwin, 1802.

——— *Elements of Useful Knowledge. Volume II. Containing a Historical and Geographical Account of the United States.* New Haven: for the author, 1804.

——— *Elements of Useful Knowledge. Vol. III. Containing a Historical and Geographical Account of the Empires and States in Europe, Asia and Africa, with their Colonies . . .* New Haven: Bronson, Walter & Co., 1806.

[———] *An Examination into the Leading Principles of the Federal Constitution . . .* Philadelphia: Prichard & Hall, 1787.

——— *A Grammatical Institute, of the English Language, Comprising, An easy, concise, and systematic Method of Education, Designed for the Use of English Schools In America. In Three Parts. Part I. Containing, A new and accurate Standard of Pronunciation.* Hartford: Hudson & Goodwin, for the author, [1783].

——— *A Grammatical Institute of the English Language . . . Part I.* 6th ed. Hartford: Hudson & Goodwin, 1787.

——— *A Grammatical Institute of the English Language . . . Part II. Containing, a plain and comprehensive Grammar . . .* Hartford: Hudson & Goodwin, for the author, 1784.

——— *A Grammatical Institute of the English Language . . . Part III. Containing the necessary Rules of Reading and Speaking . . .* Hartford: Barlow & Babcock, for the author, 1785.

——— *History of Animals; being the Fourth Volume of Elements of Useful Knowledge.* New Haven: Howe & Deforest, 1812.

——— *History of the United States . . .* New Haven: Durrie & Peck, 1832.

——— *An Improved Grammar of the English Language.* New Haven: Hezekiah Howe, 1831.

——— *Instructive and Entertaining Lessons for Youth . . .* New Haven: S. Babcock and Durrie & Peck, 1835.

——— Letter. *The American Journal of Education,* 1 (1826): 315.

——— Letter. *Connecticut Journal* (New Haven), June 30, 1784.

——— Letter. *Connecticut Journal* (New Haven), February 9, 1785.

——— Letter. *Freeman's Chronicle* (Hartford), July 8, 1784.

——— Letter. *New York Journal,* September 23, 1784.

——— Letter. *Weekly Monitor and American Advertiser* (Litchfield, Conn.), February 1, 1785.

——— Letter. *Weekly Monitor and American Advertiser* (Litchfield, Conn.), February 15, 1785.

——— *A Letter to the Honorable John Pickering, on the subject of his*

Vocabulary; or, a Collection of words and phrases, supposed to be peculiar to the United States of America. Boston: West & Richardson, 1817.

——— *Letters to a young Gentleman commencing his education: to which is subjoined a brief history of the United States.* New Haven: Howe & Spalding, 1823.

——— *The Little Franklin: Teaching Children to Read what they daily speak and to learn what they ought to know.* New Haven: S. Babcock, 1836.

——— *The Little Reader's Assistant . . .* Hartford: Elisha Babcock, 1790.

——— *A Manual of Useful Studies: for the Instruction of Young Persons of Both Sexes, in Families and Schools.* New Haven: S. Babcock, 1839.

——— ed. *The New Testament in the Common Version. With amendments of the language by Noah Webster, LL.D.* New Haven: S. Babcock, 1839.

——— *Noah Webster, On Youth and Old Age: A Sophomore Latin Exercise given at Yale College, May 4, 1776.* New York: New York Public Library, 1954.

——— *Observations on Language and on the Errors of Class-Books; addressed to the members of the New York Lyceum . . .* New Haven: S. Babcock, 1839.

[———] "On Education." *American Magazine* (December 1787), pp. 22–26.

——— *A Philosophical and Practical Grammar of the English Language.* New York: Brisban & Brannan, 1807.

[———]. *The Prompter; or A Commentary on Common Sayings and Subjects . . .* Hartford: Hudson & Goodwin, 1791.

——— *Rudiments of English Grammar . . .* Hartford: Elisha Babcock, 1790.

——— *Series of Books for Systematic Instruction in the English Language.* [New Haven: n.p., 1830?].

——— *Sketches of American Policy . . .* Hartford: Hudson & Goodwin, 1785.

——— *The Teacher; A Supplement to the Elementary Spelling Book.* New Haven: S. Babcock, 1836.

——— *To Messrs. A. Picket and J. W. Picket.* New Haven: n.p., November 1836.

——— *To the Friends of American Literature.* N.p.: n.p., November 1831.

———— *To the Friends of Literature.* New Haven: n.p., October 1836.

———— *To the Public.* N.p.: n.p., November 1831.

———— *To the Public.* N.p.: n.p., November 15, 1831.

[————] "Webster's Dictionary." *New York Evening Post,* May 28, 1829.

Wishy, Bernard. *The Child and the Republic: the Dawn of Modern American Child Nurture.* Philadelphia: University of Pennsylvania Press, 1968.

Wroth, Lawrence C. *The Colonial Printer.* 1931; rpt. Charlottesville: University of Virginia Press, 1964.

Index

Lawsuits, 77-79, 157
Lectures on Elocution (Sheridan), 46
Ledyard, John, 29
Lee, General Charles, 21
Lee, Thomas J., 132, 152, 278
Lessons, in spellers, 33, 44-46, 52,
   53-54, 128, 129, 130
Lessons for Youth, 103, 163, 179
Licensing. *See* Publishers
The Little Franklin, 175, 177
The Little Reader's Assistant, 66, 101,
   102, 200
Lowth, Bishop Robert, 46, 47

Madison, James, 15, 29
A Manual of Useful Studies, 13, 177;
   promotion of, 179, 180-184
Marshall, Elihu H., 132, 152, 153
Martin & Ogden, 82-83
McGuffey, William Holmes, 11, 14,
   167, 169, 205
McGuffey Readers. See The Eclectic First
   and *Second Reader*
McMahon, Constantine, 180-182
Meigs, Wetmore, 20
Merriam, E. & L., 187
Merriam, G. & C., 192
Miller, Samuel, 149
Missionary Society of Connecticut,
   96
Morgan, Ephraim, 165, 171, 175,
   187, 190, 191, 267
Morgan & Co., 171
Morgan & Sanxay, 150, 159
Morse, Jedediah, and *Geography*, 15,
   64, 94, 102
Mount Sion Society, 58-59, 95
Moyes, Dr. Henry, 58
Murray, Lindley, and *The English Reader*,
   55, 100, 199-200; grammar, 55,
   178, 199

New American Spelling Book (Ruter),
   132
New American Spelling Book (Thomas),
   80, 98
The New England Primer, 11, 15, 32,
   63, 101, 102, 200
A New Guide to the English Tongue
   (Dilworth), 14, 32, 33, 38, 50, 55,
   97-98, 196, 197
New Testament. *See* Bible
New York Lyceum, 184
Newspapers, and Webster, 62, 118,
   153

Notices, in promoting speller, 94-95
"Observations on the Revolution of
   America," 25, 57
"Old Dilworth," 187-188
*The Only Sure Guide to the English
   Tongue* (Perry), 98
Orthography, 88-89; conflicting views
   on, 110-113; reform of, 59, 61,
   113-123, 185, 187; in spellers, 88-
   89, 120-122, 130; in textbooks,
   101-102

Palmer, Thomas, 54
Parker, Jerusha (niece), 183
Parker, Samuel, 179, 183
Patten, Nathaniel, 78, 79, 97
Perkins, Enoch, 29
Perkins, Rev. Nathan, 19
Perry, William, and *The Only Sure
   Guide to the English Tongue*, 36, 47,
   48, 50, 80, 98, 99, 124, 197
Philological Society, 64, 93
Pickering, Timothy, 38, 59, 60, 80,
   81, 93, 96, 100, 101, 115
Picket, Albert, and *Juvenile Spelling-
   book*, 100, 149, 152, 167, 168, 169,
   184, 210, 277, 278
Picket, John, 152, 167, 169, 210
Plagiarism, and "Dilworth's Ghost"
   controversy, 47-51
Price: of *American Dictionary*, 179, 182;
   of Dilworth, 26, 97; of school
   dictionary, 158; of spellers, 78, 85-
   86, 97, 141-142, 197, 238
Primers, 32, 96, 100-101, 132. *See also
   The New England Primer*
Printers. *See* Publishers
Promotion: of *American Dictionary*,
   139, 145-146; ethics of, 209-210;
   of *Institute*, 58-60; of last books,
   178, 180-184; of other books, 102-
   104; of spellers, 60, 90-100, 145-
   152, 185
Promotion, targeted: at children, 182;
   at clergymen, 148, 149, 180-181,
   184; at colleges and faculty, 59,
   91, 94, 95, 96, 146, 149, 178, 182;
   at educational organizations, 150,
   167, 169; at judges, 92, 149, 150,
   183; at lawyers, 150; at legislators,
   145-146, 182; at "literary men,"
   92, 139, 146, 147, 180, 184; at
   parents, 182; at students, 155; at
   teachers, 59, 92, 93, 95, 139, 148,

DATE DUE

OCT 25 '95'			

GAYLORD   PRINTED IN U.S.A.